William Henry Burbank

Photographic printing Methods

A practical Guide to the professional and amateur Worker. Third Edition

William Henry Burbank

Photographic printing Methods
A practical Guide to the professional and amateur Worker. Third Edition

ISBN/EAN: 9783337106133

Printed in Europe, USA, Canada, Australia, Japan

Cover: Foto ©ninafisch / pixelio.de

More available books at **www.hansebooks.com**

PHOTOGRAPHIC
Printing Methods:

A PRACTICAL GUIDE

TO THE

PROFESSIONAL AND AMATEUR WORKER,

BY THE

Rev. W. H. BURBANK.

THIRD EDITION.

NEW YORK:
THE SCOVILL & ADAMS COMPANY,
423 BROOME STREET.

1891.

Copyright, 1887,

BY SCOVILL MANUFACTURING COMPANY.

Preface to the Third Edition.

The appearance of a third edition of "Printing Methods" affords another opportunity of thanking the fraternity for the very cordial reception accorded to this effort to make better known our gentle craft of photography.

The author has the best of reasons for believing that this little book has proved useful and helpful to many, and that it has therefore given a sufficient excuse for its existence.

No material changes have been made in this new edition. Beyond the correction of the errors of the first editions nothing has been altered.

The portrait and the brief biographical sketch of the second edition have been retained; and the bromide print, by the Eastman Company, from an American film negative by Mr. W. J. Hickmott, of Hartford, Conn., and entitled "Brook on Conway Meadows," which appeared in the second edition, also reappears in this edition of the book.

PREFACE.

In the following pages the author has aimed to collect in easily accessible form, information and formulas connected with the production of photographic prints. His purpose has been to impart the information in the simplest and most practical way possible, and to avoid errors in the numerous formulas given, all of which he believes will stand the test of actual use. Sufficient material was collected to have filled double the number of pages of this little volume, but since to have done so would have been unduly to have increased the cost of the book without enhancing its usefulness, the writer has exercised his best judgment in the selection of the material at his command, giving only those methods which his own practice or that of others commended as useful and practical.

The work is rather one of compilation than of original research, and the author has not scrupled to make use of the work of others, giving due credit wherever the sources of information were known to him.

The opening chapters on the "Theory of Light" and its "Action on Sensitive Compounds" are merely condensed from "Abney's Handbook of Photography," and are given for the information of those who may care to know something of the chemical changes produced by the action of light upon the compounds most commonly used in photographic printing.

The author's best thanks are due to Mr. W. I. Lincoln Adams and Dr. Charles Ehrmann, of the *Photographic Times*, for the very valuable advice and assistance which they have freely given him, and for their careful reading of the proof; also to Mr. C. W. Canfield, for books furnished by him which were of great assistance in writing the chapters on "Carbon Prints" and "Photo-ceramics."

In conclusion, the author ventures to express the hope that the following pages may prove useful to his brother amateurs to whom the book is respectfully dedicated.

W. H. Burbank.

Newburgh, N. Y., July, 1887.

List of Photographic Works Consulted.

Abney, W. de W.—" A Treatise on Photography." New York, 1878. D. Appleton & Co.

Abney, W. de W., and Robinson, H. P.—" The Art and Practice of Silver Printing." New York, 1881. Scovill Manufacturing Company.

Geymet.—"Traité Pratique des Emaux-Photographiques." Paris, 1885. Gauthier-Villars.

Geymet—" Traité Pratique de Céramique Photographique." Paris, 1885. Gauthier-Villars.

Geymet.—" Traité Pratique de Photogravure sur Zinc et sur Cuivre." Paris, 1886. Gauthier-Villars.

Godard.—" Artiste, Peintre, Décorateur." Paris, 1885. Gauthier-Villars.

Hardwich, T. F.—" A Manual of Photographic Chemistry." New York, 1886. Scovill Manufacturing Co.

Husnik, J.—" Die Heliographie." Vienna, 1878. A. Hartleben.

Husnik, J.—" Das Gesammtgebiet des Lichtdrucks." Vienna, 1880. A. Hartleben.

Just, E. A.—" Der Positiv Process auf Gelatine-Emulsionpapier." Vienna, 1885. E. A. Just.

Liesegang, Paul E.—" Le Procédé au Charbon." Paris, 1886. Gauthier-Villars.

Mörch, J. O.—"Handbuch der Chemigraphie und Photochemigraphie." Düsseldorf, 1886. E. Liesegang.

Robinson, H. P.—" Pictorial Effect in Photography." Philadelphia, 1881. Edward L. Wilson.

Roux, V.—" " Traité Pratique de Photographie Décorative." Paris, 1887. Gauthier-Villars.

Roux, V.—"Traité Pratique de Gravure Heliographique." Paris, 1886. Gauthier-Villars.

Roux, V.—" Manuel de Photographie et de Calcographie." Paris, 1886. Gauthier-Villars.

VOGEL, H. W.—"Progress in Photography." Philadelphia, 1883. E. L. Wilson.

WILSON, E. L.—" Photographics." Philadelphia, 1883. E. L. Wilson.

Much valuable information has also been derived from volumes of the British Photographic Annuals, from Wilson's " Mosaics," from the " American Annual of Photography for 1887," and from the columns of the *Photographic Times* and the other American Photographic journals, to all of which the author gratefully acknowledges his indebtedness.

CONTENTS.

INTRODUCTION:
THEORY OF LIGHT—ACTION OF LIGHT UPON SENSITIVE COMPOUNDS—
RÉSUMÉ OF PRINTING PROCESSES.................................... 11

CHAPTER I.
PRINTING WITH IRON AND URANIUM COMPOUNDS..................... 17

CHAPTER II.
THE SILVER BATH.. 25

CHAPTER III.
FUMING AND PRINTING... 33

CHAPTER IV.
TONING, FIXING AND WASHING...................................... 41

CHAPTER V.
PRINTING ON OTHER THAN ALBUMEN PAPER........................... 51

CHAPTER VI.
THE PLATINOTYPE... 55

CHAPTER VII.
PRINTING WITH EMULSIONS... 65

CHAPTER VIII.
MOUNTING THE PRINTS... 90

CHAPTER IX.
CARBON PRINTING... 96

CHAPTER X.
PRINTING ON FABRICS... 105

CHAPTER XI.
ENLARGEMENTS.. 109

CHAPTER XII.
TRANSPARENCIES AND LANTERN SLIDES............................... 132

CHAPTER XIII.
OPAL AND PORCELAIN PRINTING.................................. 160

CHAPTER XIV.
PHOTO-CERAMICS—ENAMELLED INTAGLIOS.......................... 165

CHAPTER XV.
PHOTO-MECHANICAL PRINTING METHODS........................... 190

CHAPTER XVI.
VARIOUS METHODS FOR PUTTING PICTURES ON BLOCKS AND METAL PLATES FOR THE USE OF THE ENGRAVER........................ 205

CHAPTER XVII.
RECOVERY OF SILVER FROM PHOTOGRAPHIC WASTES—PREPARATION OF SILVER NITRATE, ETC.................................... 210

APPENDIX... 217

INDEX.. 221

INTRODUCTION.

THEORY OF LIGHT.

The almost universally accepted theory of light, and the one which explains the greatest number of observed phenomena, is that which is known as the wave theory. Light as such is merely a sensation. All space is assumed to be permeated with a fluid known as ether, capable of being acted upon by a light or heat source in such a way as to give rise to an unbroken and continuous series of waves. Of the original form of these waves we know nothing. In the case of unpolarized, or ordinary white light, they are supposed to be, and the supposition seems to be substantiated by experiments, compounded of an infinite number of different undulations, each series differing in length from crest to crest. According as the length of these undulations vary, so do their effects differ. Those of a certain length, for instance, are able to affect the waves of the retina; others affect nerves lying in the body, giving rise to the sensation of heat; while others still are known only by their power of producing chemical combinations or decomposition in certain compounds.

The perception of color is due to the varying lengths of the light waves, the shortest gives the sensation of a violet color, the longest that of a brilliant red, waves of intermediate lengths producing respectively the sensation of blue, green, yellow, or orange. The limits of the heat spectrum are at least as great as those of the color spectrum, while the limits of the chemically active rays are known to be much greater. The term *actinic* has been applied to all those rays capable of effecting decomposition in any compound, and their range varies for every photographic substance, thus producing greater or less sensitiveness. It may be laid down as a fundamental and unalterable law, that whenever light of any kind is absorbed by any body, work of some kind has been performed in that body. In the case of the compounds employed in photographic printing, that work is some chemical or physical change or decomposition.

ACTION OF LIGHT UPON SENSITIVE COMPOUNDS.

In order to understand something of the changes produced in various sensitive compounds, some knowledge of the ultimate structure of matter is necessary. We may consider every particle of matter to be made up of molecules, each molecule being further subdivived into atoms, the smallest divisible portions of matter. The arrangement of these atoms differs in various substances. When, for instance, the atoms of any compound are so arranged as to be incapable of forming molecules of a simpler type, a large amount of work would be required to separate them, and the atoms are said to occupy a position of stable equilibrium, such, for instance, as that of a pyramid standing on its base. Substances in which the atoms are in this state of exceedingly stable equilibrium, are, of course, useless for photographic printing purposes, and are said to be insensitive to light.

When, however, the atoms of a molecule are so arranged as to be capable of separating into more than one molecule, of less complex character it may be, it may happen that the atoms are in a condition of indifferent equilibrium, such, for instance, as that of the frustrum of a pyramid standing on a narrow section parallel to its base. Compounds in which the atoms are in this state of indifferent equilibrium are, as a rule, easily affected by light, separating under its action, and arranging themselves in a different order. The sensitiveness of the molecules of such compounds to light depends upon the fact that the molecules are in a state of constant vibration. The effect of the successive impact of the waves of light is to increase the force of these vibrations until sufficient force is generated to cause the atoms to overcome the attraction binding them together, when they arrange themselves in other groups, forming different compounds.

The final effect of the waves of light in breaking down the original arrangement of atoms, may be compared to the breaking down of a bridge under the increasing vibrations imparted to it by a body of troops marching over it in regular step, although the bridge might be capable of bearing double the weight. In both cases it is the regularity of the force communicating the vibrations which produces the result. That this theory is correct is shown by the observed fact that the bodies employed for photographic purposes are chiefly affected by the shorter waves of light, the quickly repeated blows increasing more rapidly the force and extent of the vibrations, and producing a more rapid breaking up of the atoms.

One more remark may serve to explain why in some printing processes the change in atomic composition is so great as to be visible to the eye, as in the case of prints on the ordinary silver paper; while in others, the change is so slight that the eye detects no alteration in physical appearance, as, for instance, in prints on bromide paper. This difference is due to the fact that the number of molecules affected in a brief interval of time is so small that the atomic change is invisible to the eye, or so like in physical appearance to the former condition as to escape detection until the application of the developer has rendered the change visible. The difference between the two images is not one of chemical composition, but merely of the number of molecules changed.

In the case of prints in silver the commonly accepted theory of the change produced by the action of light is that the molecule of silver chloride, Ag_2Cl_2, breaks up into one molecule of silver sub-chloride, Ag_2Cl, and one of chlorine, Cl. But if silver chloride is exposed in the presence of free silver nitrate, as is the case with sensitized paper, then fresh silver chloride is formed and hypochlorous acid is liberated, which is a compound of oxygen and chlorine. In practice it has been found that the darkening of the silver chloride takes place much more rapidly when some chlorine absorbing substance is present. Hence the common practice of fuming with ammonia, a chlorine absorber, although as vigorous prints may be produced by the addition of ammonium nitrate or potassium nitrate to the sensitizing bath.

It is to be remarked that the above theory of the action of light upon a sensitive silver surface, which is that of Captain Abney, of England, is disputed by many photographic chemists in this country. Professor Newberry, of Cornell University, a high authority, denies the existence of the sub-chloride, and claims that all the nitrate is converted into chloride. The subject is involved in great obscurity, and at present neither theory is to be implicitly accepted as the true one.

Many organic substances are capable of forming definite compounds with soluble silver salts, and the effect of the action of light is then made more complex. In the case of albumen paper sensitized on a solution of silver nitrate, an albuminate of silver is formed, and by the action of light the silver is reduced to a condition of organic oxide, unaffected by sodium hyposulphite, which dissolves the undarkened albuminate.

This is a brief statement of the action of light upon the compound of silver in common use by photographic printers, and it will serve to explain the changes produced in compounds of other metals occasionally employed for printing purposes, the ferric and uranic compounds being reduced to ferrous and uranous, which are amenable to the action of various developing agents. Salts of other metals are, as a rule, too insensitive to the action of light to be of value even for contact printing.

Résumé of Printing Processes.

The fundamental principle underlying all the various methods of photographic printing is that of molecular change produced in the sensitive compound by the action of light. In most of the processes this change is visible in all its stages, subsequent manipulations only serving to change the color of the image and to give it greater permanence. To this class belong all the well-known printing-out methods, the general characteristic of all being the greater or less degree of visibility of the impression when taken from the printing-frame; the main point of difference being the nature of the sensitive medium employed, usually, iron, uranium, silver, or platinum and iron together.

There is, however, an interesting class of printing methods in which the nature and extent of the molecular change produced by the action of light is visible only after developing or reducing agents have been employed; these bring out the latent image and affect its color tone.

Each of these two classes of printing methods has advantages peculiar to itself, advantages which will probably prevent either from supplanting the other. Of the first group, that of printing-out methods, the chief advantages are the ease and certainty with which an image of any desired strength and modification can be obtained; its adaptability to double or combination printing; and the wide range of tone which it is possible to give to the finished print. Among the advantages of the second group we may mention the following: rapidity of reproduction; artistic beauty of result; and, probably, greater permanence.

Historically speaking, the first family must claim precedence. It belongs to the antiquities of photography. It was the method first employed by the pioneers in photographic research; it is the one by which photography is generally known to the public of to-day, and it includes by far the greater number of printing methods commonly practised at the present time. It rightly, therefore, claims the first place in our consideration.

PHOTOGRAPHIC PRINTING METHODS

CHAPTER I.

PRINTING WITH IRON AND URANIUM COMPOUNDS.

ACCORDING to the investigations of Sir John Herschell, the double citrate of iron and ammonia is more readily acted upon by light than any of the other iron salts, the double oxalate of iron and potassium ranking next. As printing with the latter compound has none other than an experimental value, it will not be treated of in these pages.

The law upon which the process of printing with salts of iron is based, is that the ferric salts are by the action of light reduced to the ferrous salts, which are capable of being acted upon by various toning agents, such as potassium ferri-cyanide, gold chloride, platinic tetrachloride, mercuric chloride, potassic bichromate, cupric chloride, etc.

The developing solution most commonly employed is potassic ferri-cyanide, and for its use two methods are adopted, one being to coat well-sized paper with the solution of the iron salt, dry, print, and tone on a solution of potassic ferri-cyanide. The other and more convenient method is to coat the paper with a mixed solution of iron and ferri-cyanide and to fix the print in water.

If the first method be chosen, the following mode of procedure is to be adopted:

Citrate of iron and ammonia,	154 grains.
Water (distilled),	25 drams.

Apply this solution to the paper with a brush or sponge, or float the paper on it from one to three minutes. When dry, expose under the negative until a faint image is visible. For a blue print immerse in a solution of potassium ferri-cyanide, one to ten. When the image is fully developed or toned, wash thoroughly in water, adding a little citric or acetic acid to the first wash water. This will dissolve out all the soluble salts and leave the blue image unchanged.

If a purple image is desired, immerse the print in a neutral solution of gold chloride; gold, one grain, water, four ounces. The reduction of the gold takes place according to the law that the ferrous salts reduce salts of gold to the metallic state. To fix the pictures they are immersed in a bath of dilute hydrochloric acid and then well washed. This process gives the once noted chrysotype. Other tones may be produced by immersing the prints in a very dilute solution of platinic tetrachloride, mercuric chloride, cupric chloride, or potassic bichromate, of about the same strength as the gold solution mentioned above, always using the acid bath, followed by copious washing. These methods give very pleasing results and are worthy the attention of amateur printers. I cannot vouch for the permanency of prints so made, as I have not experimented with a view to test for permanency, but I have no doubt that the results are at least reasonably permanent if pure chemicals, water, and paper be used. Greater exposure will be found necessary with the salts of gold, platinum, etc., than when the ferricyanide is employed.

An interesting method of developing prints on paper prepared with the double salt of iron and ammonia is to float them on a 40 grain solution of silver nitrate to which a few drops of gallic acid and acetic acid have been added. The silver nitrate is reduced to the metallic state by the ferrous salt, and the metallic silver is deposited where the ferrous salt was present. The gallic acid causes a further reduction of silver, and an image in metallic silver is formed, which is presumably permanent.

I now come to the more usual method of using the citrate of iron in conjunction with the ferricyanide, thus uniting sensitizer and developer. This process has simplicity to recommend it, and when at its best it gives very charming results. But to insure the highest degree of excellence in blue prints, the following points must be most carefully attended to:

1. The chemicals should be pure.
2. The paper must be free from deleterious matter.
3. A few grains of bromide should be added to the mixed solutions; this confers greater keeping power to the paper, and adds to the density of the prints.
4. The first wash water should contain a little citric or hydrochloric acid, and the after washing should be most thorough.
5. The paper should be sensitized in a dim light, or pure whites will be unknown.
6. The paper should be sized. Albumen coagulated by heat is undoubtedly the best sizing, but the following arrow-root sizing will prove satisfactory: 154 grains of arrow-root, rubbed up with cold water, then poured into 25 ounces of boiling water, and 6 ounces of alcohol added. Float the paper on this solution for two or three minutes, and suspend to dry by the end which left the solution last, in order to equalize the coating.

Good blue prints can be made without attention to these points, but all the capabilities of the process will show themselves only when they are observed, and the good workman will always try to bring out the best there is in every process he experiments with.

Various formulæ for sensitizing.

```
1.—A—Red prussiate of potash,        -    -    -    1 ounce.
       Water,        -    -    -    -    -       8 ounces.
    B—Citrate of iron and ammonium,  -    -    1 ounce.
       Water,        -    -    -    -       2½ ounces.
            One part of B to two parts of A.
2.—A—Red prussiate of potash,        -    -    -    48 grains.
       Water,        -    -    -    -    -       1 ounce.
    B—Citrate of iron and ammonium,  -    -    64 grains.
       Water,        -    -    -    -    -       1 ounce.
       (For dense negatives use 108 grains of citrate.)
```

Keep solutions separate and in the dark, until wanted for use; then mix A and B in equal parts, or one part of A with two parts of B, as less or more intense prints are desired.

```
3.—A—Citrate of iron and ammonium,   -    -    1⅞ ounces.
       Water,        -    -    -    -       8 ounces.
    B—Red prussiate of potash,       -    -    -    1¼ ounces.
       Water,        -    -    -    -       8 ounces.
```

Mix equal parts when wanted.

4.—A—Citrate of iron and ammonium, - - $5\frac{1}{4}$ drams.
  Water, - - - - 5 ounces.
  B—Red prussiate of potash, - - - $6\frac{1}{4}$ drams.
  Water, - - - - 7 ounces.

Mix equal parts immediately before using.

Nos. 4 and 5 are recommended by the *Photographic Times*, and are thoroughly reliable.

5.—A—Citrate of iron and ammonium, - - 2 ounces.
  Water, - - - - - 8 ounces.
  B—Red prussiate of potash, - - - 2 ounces.
  Water, - - - - - 8 ounces.

Mix A and B in equal parts just before using. Keep solutions in the dark.

To sensitize paper for blue prints, lay the paper on a piece of clean glass, clipping it at the corners. Apply the solution with a piece of soft sponge, squeezed into the mouth of a short bottle. Dip the sponge in the solution, and squeeze moderately dry; than go over the paper in one direction; again dip the sponge and go over the paper once more at right angles to the first strokes, carefully avoiding streaks, which will occur if the sponge contains too much of the solution. When sensitized, the paper should present an even golden hue.

The paper should be dried in the dark and used at once. Print until the shadows are bronzed.

If, after the paper is washed, the sky and highest lights are perfectly white, the color can be deepened by immersing the prints for a few seconds in the following solution:

  Saturated solution sulphate of iron. - - 4 ounces.
  Sulphuric acid, - - - - - 4 drams.
  Water, - - - - - - 4 ounces.

Or the following:

  Acetate of lead, - - - - - 2 ounces.
  Water, - - - - - - 8 "

With the latter bath, the printing should be quite dark.

To give blue prints a green tone, print rather light, well wash, and immerse in the following bath:

  Water, - - - - - - 8 ounces.
  Sulphuric acid, - - - - - $\frac{1}{2}$ dram.

For brownish-black tones, immerse for five minutes, after washing, in a solution of:

Tannic acid,	1 dram.
Water,	4 ounces.

Then change to a solution of:

Carbonate of soda,	1 dram.
Water,	5 ounces.

Leave the prints in this solution for one minute; then change back to the tannin solution. Repeat this until the print has assumed a deep wine color; than wash and dry. When dry, the print will be almost black, but the whites will have a slightly reddish tinge.

The following process is recommended by the *Scientific American* for producing dark-brown tones:

Dissolve a small piece of caustic potash in five ounces of water. Immerse the blue prints in this solution until they assume a pale orange-yellow color. When all the blue tint has disappeared, wash in clean water. Now dissolve a partly heaped-up teaspoonful of tannic acid in eight or ten ounces of water. Place the yellow prints in this bath, and allow them to remain until they are as dark as you desire. Then take them out, wash well, and dry.

Sepia Tones.

Wash the prints thoroughly; place them in the tannin bath mentioned above, for a few minutes; then change to the soda solution, and repeat several times, but be very careful not to allow the soda bath to act too long.

Lilac Tones.

These may be obtained by immersing the washed prints in a dilute solution of ammonia, but the color is not permanent, and numerous experiments of my own have thus far failed to remedy this defect.

I have introduced some of the various ways which have been adopted to change the color of blue prints, more as a matter of interest to experiment-loving amateurs than because I believe them to have any practical value. In no case are the colors as brilliant as that of the original blue print, and the permanency of these metamorphized prints is more than doubtful. That there is a future in store for the iron process I do not doubt, but I do not think that it will come in any of these ways, but by some after treatment of prints made on paper sensitized with the iron solution alone, in some such way as platinum prints are produced, which are nothing more than a development of the iron process.

In my own experiments I have met with the best results by subjecting prints on iron sensitized paper to the action of various toning agents, notably the tetrachloride of platinum in the proportion of one grain to an ounce of water, followed by subsequent washing in dilute hydrochloric acid, and a thorough washing in clean water.

BLUE PRINTS.

Collanchi's Method.—Well-sized paper is coated twice with a solution made as follows:

Water,	90 parts.
Citric acid,	$\frac{3}{4}$ parts.
Chloride of iron,	$\frac{3}{4}$ parts.
Gum arabic,	$\frac{2}{10}$ parts.

The prints are developed by floating on a twenty-four per cent. solution of ferricyanide of potassium.

Pizzeghilli's Method.—The following three stock solutions are made up:

A—Water,		100 parts.
Gum arabic,		20 parts.
B—Water,		100 parts.
Chloride of iron,		50 parts.
C—Water,		100 parts.
Ammonio-citrate of iron,		50 parts.

The sensitizing solution is as follows:

Solution A,	20 parts.
Solution B,	6 parts.
Solution C,	8 parts.

The mixture immediately thickens, but after standing for some time it resumes its original tenuity. It is then ready for applying to the paper either with a brush or sponge, or preferably by floating from two to three minutes.

The paper prints very rapidly, and it is well to use slips of the sensitized paper to determine the proper exposure. The prints are developed with a twenty per cent. solution of ferricyanide of potassium, either by brushing the solution on the face of the print or by floating. Whichever method be adopted care must be taken not to allow any of the developer to touch the back of the print.

As soon as the print has gained sufficient vigor, it is rinsed in water, then immersed for a short time in dilute hydrochloric acid, and finally washed in clean water.

Poitevin's Process.

This process is based on the fact that ferric salts possess the property of making gelatine insoluble.

The paper is first floated on a warm solution of gelatine (1 to 15), to which some suitable pigment has been added.

When dry, it is sensitized by immersion in the following simple solution:

Ferric chloride,	480 grains.
Tartaric acid,	144 "
Water,	10 ounces.

The paper is dried in the dark. The effect of the action of light is to convert the ferric chloride to ferrous chloride in those parts on which the light has acted, thus rendering the gelatine coating soluble in hot water, where it is in contact with the ferrous salt.

It will be seen, therefore, that a reversed positive is necessary to yield a positive print. When sufficiently printed, the image is developed by simple immersion in hot water. The insoluble parts remain on the paper and form the image.

The great drawback to the process is the necessity of printing from reversed positives, but it is probable that this defect might be remedied.

Pellett's Process.

Black Lines on a White Ground.

Gum,	385 grains.
Sodium chloride,	46 grains.
Tartaric acid,	62 grains.
Perchloride of iron,	123 grains.
Water to make up to	$3\frac{1}{2}$ ounces.

Highly sized and smooth paper is to be evenly coated with this mixture, dried in the dark, and exposed under a negative.

Develop with a saturated solution of ferricyanide of potassium. Fix in a 1–10 solution of hydrochloric acid.

Printing with Uranium—Sensitizing Solution.

1.—Nitrate of uranium, - - - - 616 grains.
    Water, - - - - - 7⅞ ounces.

Developing Solutions.

For Brown Tones.

A.—Ferricyanide of potassium, - - 15 grains.
    Nitric acid, - - - - - 2 drops.
    Water, - - - - - 8⅜ ounces.

For Gray Tones.

B.—Nitrate of silver, - - - - 30 grains.
    Acetic acid, - - - - 4 drops.
    Water, - - - - - 11 drams.

The paper is floated eight minutes on the sensitizing bath. When dry, it is exposed under the negative, and then developed by floating on either of the baths A or B. After development, wash thoroughly in water slightly acidulated with hydrochloric acid.

If the print when floated on solution B lacks vigor, add a few drops of a saturated solution of gallic acid.

Uranium prints may be toned with gold, platinum, or other salts.

CHAPTER II.

THE SILVER BATH.

The usual method of rendering paper of any kind sensitive to light is to float it for a varying length of time on a solution of silver nitrate, having previously salted it, if it be plain paper, with some chloride, usually chloride of ammonium. The function of the chloride is to convert the nitrate of silver into the chloride of the same metal. In practice it has been found that the strength of the silver bath should not fall below thirty grains of silver to the ounce of water, lest the albumen be dissolved; and that, save in exceptional cases, there is no need of a greater strength than sixty to sixty-five grains to the ounce. The precise strength necessary to produce the best results with any given brand of albumen paper depends upon the amount of chloride used in salting; a paper weak in chloride requiring a weak bath, while one rich in chloride demands a strong one.

In the absence of any intimation from the dealer of the strength of the salting of any paper, it may be determined by the following method, for which I am indebted to another volume of this series ("The Art and Practice of Silver Printing"): "Cut up a quarter sheet of paper into small pieces, and place them in a couple of ounces of alcohol. This will dissolve out most of the chloride, and should be decanted off. Another two ounces of alcohol should be added to the paper, and, after thoroughly soaking, should be decanted off and added to the other spirit. The spirit containing the chloride, may then be placed in a glass vessel standing in hot water, when it will evaporate, and leave the chloride behind. It may be weighed, but since it is better to know how much silver chloride would be formed, the residue should be dissolved in a few drops of water, and a little silver nitrate added. The silver chloride will be precipitated, and should be carefully washed with water, and then be filtered, the paper being opened out and dried before a fire on filter paper. The chloride is then detached and weighed; three and a half grains of silver chloride would show that a weak bath should be used, whilst ten grains would show that a strong bath was required."

The strength of the negatives to be printed from has also to be considered in determining the strength of the sensitizing bath. A strong, hard negative will give better results on paper floated on a weak bath, say thirty-five grains to the ounce, and should be printed in the sun, for the reason that an intense light diminishes contrast. A weak negative on the other hand demands a strong bath, seventy-five or eighty grains to the ounce, and printing in diffused light to increase contrast. In cold weather the strength of the bath should be increased.

Preparation of the Bath.—First settle upon the strength of the bath and the number of ounces required; then weigh out the requisite number of grains, placing a piece of filter paper in each scale-pan, as a safeguard against accidental impurities. Place the silver in a clean bottle, and add to it the proper amount of water, which should be distilled, or boiled and filtered. If the water contains any chlorides, they will make their presence known by a milkiness in the solution, which should then be filtered. Your bath is now ready for immediate use, unless you wish to add some other soluble salts to it, as chlorine absorbers; in this case, sodium nitrate or ammonium nitrate will serve your purpose, adding as much of either as your silver weighed. In hot, dry weather the addition of one of these salts will be found advantageous, as tending to prevent that excessive dryness of the paper which is fatal to the best results. The best prints are obtained from paper which is not entirely free from water, for the reason that with very dry paper the chlorine liberated by the action of light is apt to attack the albuminate of silver, one of the compounds formed when albumen paper is sensitized with silver.

Many printers are in the habit of adding alum to the sensitizing bath, to prevent it from discoloring and to harden the albumen. The best way to add it, is to place a small piece of alum in the filter paper before filtering, or you may add one grain of alum to every ounce of solution, and then filter.

Never allow the bath to remain acid from the addition of nitric acid, as the acid attacks the albumen. Keep the bath neutral by the addition of a little carbonate of silver, which may be done by occasionally adding a few drops of sodium carbonate, which precipitates silver carbonate from a solution of silver nitrate.

FORMULÆ FOR SENSITIZING BATH.

FOR VERY STRONG NEGATIVES.

1.—Silver nitrate, - - - - - 35 grains.
    Water, - - - - - 1 ounce.
        Print in full sunlight.

FOR THIN NEGATIVES.

2.—Silver nitrate, - - - - - 80 grains.
    Water, - - - - - 1 ounce.
        Print in the shade.

3.—Silver nitrate, - - - - - 60 grains.
    Ammonium nitrate, - - - 60 grains.
    Ammonia, - - - - - 2 minums.
    Water, - - - - - 1 ounce.

This is the bath I commonly use, and the resulting prints have always satisfied me. To keep it in good order, it is only necessary to strengthen as required, and to add a few drops of ammonia occasionally.

The bath yields prints that tone with remarkable ease and richness with or without fuming; preferably without.

4.—Silver nitrate, - - - - 60 grains.
    Sodium nitrat, - - - - 60 grains.
    Alcohol, - - - - - ½ dram.
    Water, - - - - - 1 ounce.

For prints on plain, resinized, gelatinized paper and leatherized paper:

5.—Silver nitrate, - - - - 60 grains.
    Gelatine, - - - - - 5 grains.
    Water, - - - - - 1 ounce.

C. W. HEARN'S.

6.—Nitrate of silver, - - - - 40 grains.
    Distilled water, - - - - 1 ounce.

To every twenty ounces of solution add one dram of saturated solution of carbonate of soda. The bath will at once assume a creamy color; allow the solution to settle, then decant and filter. Carbonate of silver will deposit in the bottle, and this will take the organic matter from the bath and prevent it from discoloring. Allow the carbonate to remain in the bath, pouring the solution back upon after using. Then shake well and the bath will soon be ready for use again.

Keep the bath up to its full strength and occasionally add a few drops of the carbonate of soda solution.

The Ammonio-nitrate of Silver Bath.

Nitrate of silver,	2 ounces.
Water,	16 ounces.

When the silver is dissolved, take one-fifth of the solution, and add strong ammonia drop by drop until the brown oxide of silver first formed is redissolved, and then add it to the remaining four-fifths. Oxide of silver will again be formed, which is to be redissolved with pure nitric acid, care being taken to add only enough to redissolve the oxide. The solution will be slightly alkaline, and is not liable to turn red unless allowed to become impoverished of silver.

This bath gives pure rich tones of a bluish-black, without the use of the gold toning bath, but a small amount of chloride of gold should be added to the hypo bath.

This bath, although increasing sensitiveness and deepening the intensity of the prints, is now but little used, for the reasons that it does not coagulate albumen, that it is more liable to spontaneous change, and more easily discolored by organic matter, than the plain silver bath, and that free ammonia is liberated, which is a solvent of chloride of silver, which it attacks, giving rise to white lines and transparent markings.

On plain paper it gives a velvety appearance to the prints, which can hardly be obtained with simple nitrate of silver.

I have found that the method of applying it, recommended by Hardwich, is better than floating. The paper to be sensitized is laid down on blotting paper, and the solution evenly applied with a broad camel's-hair brush, used for that purpose only and kept scrupulously clean.

Floating the Paper.

It will be found a great saving of time to float at least a half sheet of paper, 11 inches by 18, and for this size a tray 12 inches by 19, and 3 inches deep will be required. A wooden tray coated with asphalt varnish is cleanly and cheap. There should be enough of the bath poured into to cover the bottom of the pan to a depth of at least half an inch, and it should have been most carefully freed from all impurities before the sensitizing is begun. Impurities and air-bubbles are the two great enemies of the sensitizing-room. Now grasp the paper by the two opposite corners, albumen side down, bring the hands together, and lower the convex side to the surface of the bath; separate the hands, and the paper will float on the surface. If it shows an obstinate tendency to curl up, gently breathe upon it. This difficulty may be overcome by placing the paper, the night before sensitizing, in a damp place. Now raise one corner and look for air-bubbles. If any are found, break them with the point of a glass rod, and again lower the paper. When it has floated the proper length of time, raise it by one corner very slowly, until another corner is free, which is then grasped by the other hand and the paper slowly withdrawn, allowed to drain a minute into a dish, and hung up by one corner to dry in the dark, or yellow light.

Some sensitizers draw the paper over a glass rod placed at one end of the dish, but there is some danger of streaks; others blot the paper when taken from the bath, but this practice is attended with danger, owing to the impurities present in most blotting-paper. If desired, the paper, when surface-dry, can be dried in a drying-box, which is easily made by constructing a box 30 inches long, 14 inches long, and 10 or 12 inches deep, with a hinged or sliding door. In one end, cut a hole six inches in diameter, and cover it on the inside with an inverted tin dish of the proper size. Fasten the box against the wall, with the end in which the hole was cut, high enough from the floor to allow a lamp to be placed underneath. About two inches from the top, string some wires two inches apart; on these suspend the paper by clips at two corners, close the door and light the lamp; the paper will soon be dry enough for printing or fuming.

Time of Floating.—This is largely determined by the strength of the bath; a strong bath requiring, as a rule, longer floating than a weak one, for the reason that the albumen is coagulated more slowly; from one to three minutes seems to be the common practice.

MANAGEMENT OF THE SILVER BATH.

To secure good results with any form of the silver bath, two points must be most carefully attended to, viz.: its strength and its freedom from impurities. Every sheet of paper sensitized, weakens the bath by depriving it of a portion of its silver. This loss must be made good, or the forgetful amateur will soon have the unpleasant surprise of seeing the albumen dissolve off the paper into the bath. Two methods are employed to keep the bath up to its original strength; one is to add a few drops of an 80-grain solution after every four sheets are sensitized. The other requires the possession of an argentometer, or hydrometer, an instrument for testing the specific gravity of liquids;.the argentometer being an hydrometer graduated to register grains of silver to the ounce of water. To use it, the glass jar which accompanies the instrument is partly filled with the solution, the hydrometer gently dropped into it, and allowed to come to rest. The number of grains of silver to the ounce is known by the number of degrees on the scale to which the instrument sinks. This being know, and the total number of ounces of the solution measured, it becomes an easy matter to determine how much silver must be added to bring the bath up to its original strength. If you have a total quantity of 12 ounces of solution, and the hydrometer registers 35, while your original solution was made up at 60 grains to the ounce, the bath have evidently lost 25 grains for each ounce of solution. This amount, then, must be restored to it in the shape of fresh crystals of silver nitrate; in this case 25×12, or 300 grains of silver.

METHODS OF REMOVING IMPURITIES.

The chief source of contamination to the bath is organic matter carried into it from the paper, in time causing a brownish or reddish discoloration of the solution, which must be removed, since paper floated on such a bath is darkened and unevenly sensitized. Several methods are in common use to get rid of this discoloration. The earliest, and perhaps one of the best, is to add a teaspoonful of kaolin to the solution, which is then well shaken up. The organic matter adheres to the kaolin and soon settles to the bottom of the bottle with it. When this has taken place, the solution is filtered, and it is again ready for use. Another method, which has the advantage of delaying sensitizing but a moment, is to add 1 dram of a 10 per cent. solution of permanganate of potash to the bath. The theory of this addition is that the oxygen liberated from the permanganate oxidizes the organic matter, which then falls to the bottom of the dish. This method, although good in emergency, does not leave the bath absolutely pure.

A favorite plan with many is to add a dram or two of a saturated solution of camphor, shake well, and filter; repeating the operation if the bath is not decolorized by the first treatment.

Still another method is to add a few drops of hydrochloric acid to the solution; this forms chloride of silver, which settles to the bottom, carrying the impurities with it. This is a very effective method, but leaves the bath acid from the formation of nitric acid; the solution must therefore be neutralized with ammonia or carbonate of soda.

My own method is to add a few grains of sodium carbonate and set the bottle in the sun. The organic matter soon becomes oxidized, and finally settles to the bottom; the solution may then be filtered or decanted.

To complete this part of the subject, I add a description of the boiling method which is sometimes necessary in the case of an old bath, which, in addition to organic impurities, contains an excess of the soluble salts with which the paper was salted. Evaporate the bath, by boiling or otherwise, to about half its bulk. Then add 10 drops of nitric acid for every 20 ounces of solution. Next add some granulated zinc; this causes the silver to precipitate in the metallic state; the precipitation is complete in two or three hours; pour off as much of the fluid as possible, and pick out all the zinc possible; then add hydrochloric acid to dissolve the remaining pieces of zinc. Filter the solution, and wash the deposit on the filter paper once or twice with water. Then dry the filter paper in the oven; remove the silver and place it in a crucible, which is to be brought to a red heat by any convenient means. Now cover the silver with nitric acid; place the mixture in an evaporating dish and slightly warm it. When red fumes cease to appear, add more acid until nearly all the silver is dissolved. Evaporate off all the fluid, and set aside to cool; then add water, but be sure to keep it over strength for the bath. Test with the argentometer, and add the amount of water necessary to give the proper strength for sensitizing.

Points in Sensitizing.

1. Have the paper damp before silvering.
2. Before floating ascertain the condition of the bath as to strength and alkalinity.
3. Do not allow the paper to become bone-dry before printing if you wish to have rich prints. Of course, it must be dry enough not to adhere to the negative; anything more than this is not only useless, but fatal to securing the best results.

CHAPTER III.

FUMING AND PRINTING.

Is FUMING necessary, or is it not? This is a question on which the authorities differ. It is claimed that fuming prevents measles, yields pluckier prints, and makes toning more easy. In America, it is the almost universal practice, while it is by no means common in England and on the Continent. But it must be borne in mind that paper in which a little moisture is present, yields better prints than one which is perfectly dry, and that the prevailing humidity in England and the Continent prevents the paper from becoming too dry. In the hot, dry summer weather of America, however, the paper quickly becomes over-dry, and fuming is resorted to to impart the necessary moisture. Paper sensitized on a bath containing nitrate of ammonia or sodium will require little or no fuming. My own practice is to use a strong sensitizing bath, float for two or three minutes, dry without heat, and omit the fuming. If you wish to fume, however, the drying-box mentioned on page 29 can be used by placing a saucer containing a dram or so of strong ammonia in the box, and, about an inch above this, a frame carrying a fine-wire screen, to equalize the distribution of the fumes.

Time of Fuming.—It is impossible to give any precise instructions on this point, so much depends on the quality of the negatives to be printed from, the strength of the bath, the quality of the paper, and the temperature. Hard negatives yield better prints on paper which has had very little fuming, as fuming promotes speedier bronzing in the shadows; a weak negative can be made to yield better prints by fuming. Some brands of paper require more fuming than others, and in cold weather fuming is to be carried on longer than is necessary in warm weather. From 15 minutes to one hour may be taken as the limits. The paper must be thoroughly dry before fuming is begun.

Printing.—It may be laid down as a rule, admitting no exceptions, that a good negative is essential to a good print on silver paper, which does not take kindly to thin, foggy negatives. The negative must be plucky, having points of opacity for the highest lights, and almost clear glass in the deepest shadows, with an almost infinite range of tones between, if prints of the highest order are desired. Given such a negative, no special instructions for printing are needed, except to caution the operator against printing in direct sunlight, save in the case of extremely hard negatives. Print in diffused light, and do not take the print from the frame until it is a shade or two darker than it is intended to remain, as it reduces somewhat in the toning and fixing bath. If some parts of the negative print more rapidly than is desirable, they should be masked by cotton wool arranged roughly to follow the outline of the subject to be masked.

The Printing Frame.—A frame that is at least one size larger than the negatives to be printed from is a great convenience. In the first place, in the larger frame the negative will be printed to the very margins; and in the second place, the larger frame will be a great help if it is desired to vignette clouds upon the print from another negative. A clear glass plate of the same size as the frame may be used to support the smaller negative.

Place the negative in the frame, film up, and upon it lay the paper with the sensitive surface down, that is, next to the negative. Put the back of the frame in its place and press it down with the springs. The frame is now ready to be exposed to the light.

Clouds may be printed in from a second negative by masking the sky of the original negative with a piece of card-board, cut in such a way as to follow the general outlines of the horizon; when the landscape is fully printed, the paper and the negative are removed from the frame, and the cloud negative substituted, care being taken to select one harmonizing with the general sweep of the lines of the landscape, and that the lighting of the clouds correspond with that of the view. The landscape is then masked with a piece of card-board, roughly cut to the horizon lines, disregarding isolated tree tops, etc., projecting into the sky; the mask is constantly moved up and down and sideways in order to secure a proper blending, but avoiding getting it above the horizon line. As the progress of the printing is easily seen by examination, the mask can be manipulated to favor slow printing places, and to retard the quicker ones.* Many landscapes are improved by vignetting, a process which often gives them a delightful air of vagueness and mystery. In the absence of a vignetting apparatus, a very fair makeshift can be made of a piece of card-board having an oval opening cut in it somewhat smaller than the negative. This is fastened about half an inch above the negative, the opening covered with a piece of ground glass or tissue, and the printing done as usual. I have found that very serviceable vignetters can be made of old paste-board boxes, large enough to cover the printing frame; the opening is cut in the bottom, the sides are cut down to about two inches in depth, and the printing frame is covered with it.

Odd-shaped prints, such as crescents, crosses, ovals, etc., are easily produced by cutting an opening of the size and shape desired in a piece of opaque paper, yellow post-office paper is good for the purpose, and placing this over that part of the negative which it is wished to print. Many very pleasing effects can be secured by this simple expedient.

PRINTING MAXIMS.

1. See that the paper is perfectly dry before placing it on the negative.

2. Place one or more pads of thick felt over the paper, to secure a firm and even pressure.

---

* A very simple and effective method of printing-in clouds is given in "The Art and Practice of Silver Printing." The sky in the landscape negative, if it be weak or have any defects as is commonly the case, must be blocked out with black varnish on the glass side, the edge of the varnish being softened off where required by dabbing it with a dabber made of wash leather. When the landscape is printed, the negative is removed and the cloud negative substituted for it; the paper is then properly adjusted and the whole frame is covered with a piece of zinc or cardboard curved at one end. The accompanying cut will explain the method. The straight line is the sky negative, and its junction with the landscape is partly covered with the curved shade. The printing must be done in diffused light.

3. Do not open the back of the frame to examine the print in a strong light.

4. Print in the shade, or direct sunshine, according to the density of the negative.

5. Print until the shadows just begin to bronze, if the highest lights do not show more than a faintly perceptible tinge of color. If they discolor badly, the negative will not yield the best results.

6. Sensitize the paper on a bath likely to give the best results with the negatives to be printed.

7. To avoid cockling of the paper in the frame allow it to remain a few moments at the same temperature and state of atmospheric moisture under which the printing is to be done; then place in the frame.

8. When using masks, keep them moving.

9. In vignetting, change the position of the frame occasionally to equalize the distribution of light.

10. Examine the print from the back as little as possible. Try to judge of the progress of the printing by the amount of discoloration in the shadows visible through the negative.

Printing on Ready-sensitized Paper.

With the advent of amateur photography, methods were sought for preparing sensitized paper with good keeping qualities and capable of yielding prints of as high a grade of excellence as those from freshly-prepared paper. No great difficulty was experienced in conferring good keeping qualities, but to secure the excellence of fresh paper proved a task of no little magnitude. While I do not believe that it is possible without much extra pains and labor to secure as good prints on the ready-sensitized paper as on the freshly-floated sheets, I acknowledge the great convenience of having paper always ready for instant use, to strike off a proof or to make finished prints. It is certainly possible to make very beautiful prints on the prepared article if one does not care for the darkest tones possible with the fresh paper.

The following method of working will, I believe, secure the best results with most of this paper. At least, it has never failed in my hands, and I, therefore, recommend it with great confidence.

The fact that it is the method recommended by Mr. A. D. Fisk for the paper he sends out, and that I have found it to work equally well on all other brands which I have tried, induces me to recommend it as a perfectly satisfactory method.

Two things must be most carefully attended to in using any brand of ready-sensitized paper: the free silver must be thoroughly washed away after printing, and the acidity of the paper must be reduced by an alkali bath before toning. Neglect of either of these points is to fail to secure the best possible results.

The following stock solutions are to be made up, each being carefully filtered before use:

1.—Gold chloride, - - - - 15 grains.
    Distilled or boiled water, - - - - 7½ ounces.
2.—Sodium bi-carbonate (best English), - - 480 grains.
    Distilled or boiled water, - - - - 8 ounces.
3.—Solution No. 2, - - - - ½ ounce.
    Water, - - - - - - 12 ounces.

No. 4.—Toning Bath.

Not to be made up until wanted for use.

Solution No. 1, - - - - 1 ounce.
Solution No. 2, - - - - - 1 ounce.
Distilled or boiled water, - - - 15 ounces.

No. 5.—Fixing-Bath.

Sodium hyposulphite, - - - - 1 ounce.
Sodium chloride, - - - - 24 grains.
Water, - - - - - - 5 ounces.

The printing should be one or two shades darker than the tone desired in the finished print. When the printing is finished, immerse the prints, faces down, one by one, in clean water, being careful that each print is thoroughly wetted before introducing another. Keep the prints in constant motion, turning them over now and then for five minutes. Pour off the water and add fresh; continue this until there is no further trace of milkiness in the wash water. Place the prints in solution No. 3, and allow them to soak while you prepare the toning bath No. 4. When the prints have soaked ten minutes in No. 3, transfer them to a dish of clean water to rinse them off. Then transfer, one by one, to the toning bath, in which they are allowed to remain until they assume the proper tone, being constantly turned to insure equal toning. Tone to a purple or lilac, wash in two or three changes of water, and then place them for twenty minutes in the fixing bath No. 5; a further immersal for ten minutes in a fresh fixing bath will do them no harm. While in the fixing bath the prints should be turned occasionally. The usual thorough washing for two or three hours must follow.

The toning bath, solution No. 4, contains two grains of gold, and will tone eight 5x8 prints; if you have more than that number of prints to tone, increase the proportions of No. 4 and No. 5 accordingly. Never use the fixing or toning baths but once.

The paper should be fumed 30 minutes.

The first condition for a good print is a good negative. The "Photographic Times" says that "the baths best adapted to ready-sensitized paper are those with borax, acetate, phosphate or tungstate of soda, and a compound solution of these substances known by the name of French azotate," and recommends the following bath:

Stock Solution.

Chloride of gold and sodium,	15 grains.
Water,	15 ounces.

Pour two ounces of this into the toning dish, and test with litmus paper, make alkaline with sodium bi-carbonate, and then add twenty grains of acetate of soda and eighteen ounces of water. Allow the bath to stand for half an hour before using. The bath should have a temperature of about 65 deg. Fahr.

I can vouch for the good results attainable with this bath, which is one eminently suited to cold weather, a time when success in toning is attended with some difficulty.

Willis' Permanent Silver Paper.

Float the paper as usual. When surface dry, blot off the edges and float the reverse side for about ten seconds on the following solution:

Citric acid,	462 grains.
Water,	14½ ounces.

Dry thoroughly, and store in a dark, dry place; paper thus prepared and kept will keep good for at least three months.

This same citric acid solution affords a simple means of preserving paper which it is desirable to keep for some time. It is only necessary to apply the acid with a sponge to the wrong side of the paper. This method is to be preferred to that in which the acid is added to the bath, since the acid does not come in contact with the silver, and being washed away before toning it does not injure the image, and toning is less tedious than when the acid is added to the bath.

Preserving Sensitized Paper.—A simple and effective method of preserving ordinary sensitized paper is to store the paper between sheets of blotting paper which have been previously soaked in a saturated solution of sodium carbonate and well dried. A deep printing frame forms a good press for the paper and pads. Paper thus protected, if it has been floated on a bath containing a little alum, will keep good for a long time, and will give as fine prints as those made on freshly-prepared paper, and vastly superior to those made on most of the ready-sensitized paper found in the market.

Defects in Silver Prints.

[From "Hardwich's Manual of Photographic Chemistry."]

1. *The Print is Marbled and Streaky.*—These defects are often seen before the print is toned; if so, reject the prints. But more often they are visible only after the toning. Causes: *a.* The paper has been badly albumenized, the albumen having been allowed to drain off in streaks. *b.* The sensitizing solution may have drained off in the same way when the paper was hung up to dry, consequently the paper prints deeper where the current of silver has been running. It is easy to distinguish between these two causes of failure. In the first, the image is red and faint; in the second, it is darker and deeper. Remedies: For the first case, reject the sample of paper; for the second, blot the paper after sensitizing and before drying.

2. *The Prints are Clean on the Surface, but Streaky when Examined by Transmitted Light.*—This is the measels and is sure to destroy the photograph within a very short time.

The appearance presented is that of a series of small, irregular yellow patches. These consist of sulphide of silver and lie in the texture of the paper. Causes: Too weak fixing solution; imperfect fixation, or a bad sample of paper. The remedies are obvious.

3. *The Print has a Cold and Faded Appearance when Finished.*—*a.* Too weak silver bath. *b.* Too short a time of floating. *c.* The negative has not sufficient contrast. *d.* The print has been over-toned. The remedies are self-evident.

4. *Spots on the Surface.*—Due, if white, to spots of dust either on the negative or the paper; if black, to pin-holes in the negative. Spots due to metallic particles in the paper can always be distinguished from all other spots, as they have a small black nucleus surrounded by a circle of white.

5. *The High Lights are Yellow.*—Either, *a.* The paper has become discolored through long keeping or excessive fuming; or *b.* The fixing bath has been acid, or the action of a neutral one continued too long.

6. *Intense Bronzing of the Shadows During Printing.*— Causes: *a.* Too strong a silver bath. *b.* Excessive fuming; or *c.* Long-continued printing from a strong negative.

7. *Yellow Spots on the Surface or Back of the Prints*— Caused by the contact with hyposulphite of soda. This salt should not be handled until the prints are toned.

Mealiness.—A name given to the small red or white spots which sometimes cover the surface of the prints. Dust on the negative or the paper is sometimes the cause, but more often the fault is due to the albumen. Paper which gives mealy prints should be returned to the dealer.

The Print Refuses to Tone.—Causes: *a.* Poor paper. *b.* Long keeping of the print before toning. *c.* The toning bath has been kept too long and lost its strength. In this case add more gold, or, better still, make up a new bath.

CHAPTER IV.

TONING, FIXING AND WASHING.

No. 1.—Stock Solution.

A.—Chloride of gold, - - - -	1 grain.
Water, - - - - -	20 ounces.
B.—Acetate of soda, - - - -	15 grains.
Water, - - - - - -	1 ounce.
C.—Saturated solution of sulphate of copper.	

When solution is complete, add B to A, and add 10-15 drops of C, allow to stand at least 24 hours before using. Tone only until the half tones are somewhat bluish by reflected light. This bath will keep.

No. 2.—For Brown Tones.

Chloride of gold, - - -	1 or 2 grains.
Acetate of soda, - - - -	60 grains.
Water, - - - - - -	36 ounces.

Allow the solution to stand one hour, then add enough of a saturated solution of sodium bicarbonate to make the bath alkaline. Tone till the lights assume a delicate lilac tint. This bath will not keep.

No. 3.—For Black, Velvety Tones.

Water, - - - - - -	8 ounces.
Acetate of soda, - - - -	15 grains.
Chloride of sodium - - - -	15 grains.
Nitrate of uranium, - - - -	1 grain.
Chloride of gold, - - - -	1 "

Dissolve the acetate and chloride first. Dissolve the uranium in one ounce of water, and neutralize with bicarbonate of soda solution; then add it to the acetate and chloride solution. Neutralize the gold with bicarbonate and add it to the bath. Test for alkalinity; if not alkaline, add enough bicarbonate solution to make it so. Allow it to stand some hours before using. Print deep and tone well. Will keep.

No. 4.—For Purple and Black Tones.

Water,	30 ounces.
Gold,	3 grains.

Add a few drops of a saturated solution of carbonate of soda. Print deeply, and tone to color desired. Ready for instant use, but does not keep.

No. 5.

Chloride of gold,	1 grain.
Tungstate of soda,	20 grains.
Boiling water,	8 ounces.

Ready for use, as soon as cold. Keeps well.

No. 6.—For Rich Purple Tones.

Phosphate of soda,	20 grains
Chloride of gold,	1 grain.
Water,	8 ounces.

Ready for instant use; but does not keep well.

No. 7.—Platinum Bath.

Bichloride of platinum solution,	30 drops.
Hypo,	3 grains.
Hydrochloric acid (C. P.),	5 drops.
Water,	5 ounces.

The platinum solution is made by dissolving enough of the salt in one ounce of water to give it a rich, sherry color, a few grains will suffice. This bath is slow, but good. It should be warmed to 70 deg. Fahr., and the free silver should be well washed out of the prints.

No. 8.—Borax Bath.

Chloride of gold,	1 grain.
Borax,	30 grains.
Boiling water,	8 ounces.

Ready for use when cooled down to 60 deg. Fahr. Gives rich brown tones, and keeps well. An excellent bath for ready-sensitized paper.

No. 9.—For Sepia and Black Tones.

Chloride of gold,	2 grains.
Sat. sol. chloride lime,	2 drops.
Chalk (precipitated)	3 grains.
Boiling water,	16 ounces.

The chloride of lime solution is made by shaking a teaspoonful of the chloride in a pint-bottle full of water. When the solids have settled, decant the clear portion, which should be kept in the dark.

Allow the bath to stand at least a day before using. It improves with age.

For sepia, tone but very little, just off the red; for a black, tone to a deep purple.

No. 10.—Equal volumes of No. 5 and No. 8.

No. 11.—CHARLES W. HEARN'S TONING BATHS.

WITH SAL SODA.

A.—Distilled or ice water,	64 ounces.
Acid sol. of chlo. of gold (4 grs. to 1 oz)	1 ounce.
Saturated solution of sal soda,	½ ounce.

Should be prepared one-half hour before use.

No. 12.—WITH CHLORIDE OF LIME.

B.—Water,	40 ounces.
Chloride of lime,	5 grains.
Chloride of gold,	4 grains.

If the chloride of gold is acid, it may be neutralized with carbonate of lime.

No. 13.—WITH CITRIC ACID.

A.—Citric acid,	1 ounce.
Water,	20 ounces.
B.—Chloride of gold,	15 grains.
Water,	15 ounces.

STOCK SOLUTION.

Take of A two and one-half ounces, and make slightly alkaline with saturated solution of bicarbonate of soda; of B one-half ounce and sixty-four ounces of water.

When ready to tone take sufficient of the stock solution, which should never be less than three or four days old, and add thereto one ounce of gold solution B; make alkaline with bicarbonate of soda.

No. 14.—THE PHOTOGRAPHIC TIMES TONING BATH.

Into seven and one-half ounces of water put seven and one-half grains chloride of gold and sodium. Label the bottle containing the mixture, *Chloride of Gold Solution*. Combine six ounces of water with one ounce of French azotate, to which add one and one-half ounce of the chloride of gold solution.

No. 15.—THE CHAUTAUQUA TONING BATH.

Dissolve fifteen grains of chloride of gold and sodium in fifteen ounces of water. Take of this solution three ounces, pour it in the toning dish, test for acidity with litmus paper, and neutralize with bicarbonate of soda, and add thirty grains of acetate of soda and thirty ounces of water. Prepare the solution an hour before using it.

If warm tones are wanted, add a little acetic acid to the first washing water.

For this bath the sensitizing silver should be neutral, for which purpose a small portion of carbonate of silver should be kept in the silver stock bottle.

No. 16.—SPAULDING'S TONING BATH.

STOCK SOLUTION.

Water,	15 ounces.
Gold chloride	15 grains.

To make up a toning bath for twenty cabinet size prints, take

Water	10 ounces.
Soda bicarbonate,	3 grains.
Common salt,	6 grains.
Stock solution of gold,	3 ounces.

No. 17.—THE PRICE FORMULA.

Into seven and one-half ounces of water dissolve fifteen grains chloride of gold and sodium, then add to it 300 grains of acetate of soda and seven drops of a saturated solution of chloride of lime.

This stock solution should be prepared at least twenty-four hours before being used. Take one-half ounce of it and mix with seven ounces of water.

No. 18.—FOR SEPIA TONES.

A.—Carbonate of potash,	1 ounce.
Water,	4 ounces.

B.—Gold chloride, - - , - - 15 grains.
Water, - - - - - . 7½ drams.

Solution A, after mixing and well stirring, is allowed to stand until clear, when it is filtered and bottled for stock. When wanted for use, add to ten ounces of water one dram of A and twenty drops of B. This will tone one sheet and gives a warm sepia. The bath will keep.

No. 19.—Equal parts of No. 6 and No. 18. This is a grand bath for rich warm tones, but it will not keep well.

No. 20.—For resinized, gelatinized, leatherized, and plain paper:

STOCK SOLUTION.

Gold chloride - - - - - 15 grains.
Water, - - - - - - 7¼ drams.

To make the bath, add two drams of the gold solution neutralized with a pinch of chalk, to ten ounces of hot water. Place two drams of acetate of soda in a quart bottle, and filter the above solution into it; make the bulk up to twenty ounces. This bath can be used in a few hours, but it improves by keeping.

When commencing to tone, place a few ounces of water in the dish, and add an equal quantity of the above solution. When the toning action begins to fail add more of the solution.

This is the bath recommended by Mr. Henry Cooper, the originator of the resin process, and it will be found a very good bath for fine work.

No. 21.—SULPHO-CYANIDE OF AMMONIUM.

Chloride of gold, - - - - - 1 grain.
Sulphocyanide of ammonium, - - - 20 grains.
Water, - - - - - , 2 ounces.

GENERAL DIRECTIONS.

No very definite instructions can be given in regard to the actual operation of toning the prints. It may be laid down as a general rule with most toning baths that the free nitrate of silver should be well washed out, and that the proper amount of gold solution needed to tone the prints in hand, must be neutralized with precipitated chalk. One grain of gold is considered sufficient to tone one sheet of paper, except in the case of ready-sensitized paper, which requires two grains at least to the sheet.

When ready to begin toning, place the prints one by one into the bath, face down; do not try to tone more than six prints at a time, unless you are using a large amount of toning solution. Keep the prints in constant motion, turning them over occasionally, and keeping careful watch over the progress of toning. If you wish the warm tones, sepia, brown and purple, remove the prints as soon as they show a lilac or purple tinge in the half tones. For black, tone till the prints appear somewhat bluish, then remove, and wash in two or three changes of water before fixing.

Remarks on the General Composition of Toning Baths.

It will be noticed that in all the formulæ for toning solutions an alkali of one kind or another is added to the gold.

This was not the practice of the early practitioners. Sulphur was the agent first used for imparting a pleasing color to silver prints, but the fugitiveness of the tones imparted by sulphur led to a search for other toning agents, and sulphur was soon discarded in favor of gold. Chloride of gold was added to the usual hyposulphite of soda fixing bath. This process was simplicity itself. The prints were immersed in the combined toning and fixing bath immediately after leaving the printing frame, no preliminary washing being necessary. The first action of the bath was to dissolve the unchanged silver salts, and to leave the image of the red color seen in a well-washed print. The red color soon passed into a blue or black and the toning was complete.

It was soon found, however, that the tone thus produced was due partly to a deposit of gold and partly to the communication of sulphur. The older the bath, the more fugitive the tints, for the reason that a freshly mixed bath toned the prints by a deposit of gold, while an old bath toned by sulphuration. Hence, the Sel d'Or bath, as the mixed bath was termed, was soon discarded in favor of alkaline solutions of chloride of gold, first introduced under the name of Sutton's alkaline toning bath. The philosophy of the addition of an alkali to the gold solution is that an aqueous solution of gold deposits the metal on the surface of the print too rapidly to give a pleasing tone.

Hardwich's theory is that the addition of an alkali to a solution of chloride of gold forms an oxide of gold which possesses no toning power, but which being decomposed by the excess of chloride of gold, enables a larger quantity of the metal to be thrown down without injury to the print from communication of chlorine.

But the whole subject is involved in too much difficulty to allow any theory to gain universal acceptance. One thing, however, is certain, viz., that it is not a matter of indifference what alkali is added since the more the action is retarded, the more ruby color becomes the deposit of gold. This is the reason why some alkalis give purple tones, while others give black.

Much more might be written on this interesting subject, but enough has been said to give the operator an intelligent idea of the action of the toning bath, and of the reasons for the additions commonly made to it.

A bath weak in gold, because slower in its action, is to be preferred to the more concentrated one usually employed. The slowness of the action produces a more even and firm deposit of gold and gives tones which will suffer little if any change during fixing.

In this subject so good an authority as Mr. Andrew Pringle writes: " All processes of deposition of one substance upon another are more completely performed slowly than quickly. * * * * So in toning, I take it that we shall have a more complete deposit of metallic gold if we tone slowly by using a solution not too strong in gold chloride." And Prof. W. K. Burton states that the more gold the image can be made to take, the better and more permanent the result. A rich deposit of gold is more surely given by slow toning than by the quicker method commonly used.

The Fixing Bath.

Its Purpose.—The fixing bath is used to dissolve out all the unchanged silver, which, even after toning, would darken on exposure to light.

Its Composition.—The following is the best formula known to me:

Hyposulphite of soda,	4 ounces.
Water,	20 ounces.
Ammonia,	½ dram.

The ammonia serves a three-fold purpose: it prevents the possibility of an acid reaction, softens the albumen film, thus shortening the operation of fixing, and it has a tendency to prevent blistering. One ounce of solid hyposulphite will fix three sheets of paper.

How long to Fix.—The length of time required for complete fixation varies somewhat with different brands of paper; from 15 to 20 minutes is about right; and in order to be on the safe side, it is well to place the prints for ten minutes in a fresh bath to dissolve out the hyposulphite of silver formed in the first.

MAXIMS FOR TONING AND FIXING.

1. Have your toning solution slightly alkaline, and at a temperature of about 60 deg. Fahr.
2. Tone to sepia, purple, or blue, according as warm, brown, or black prints are desired.
3. Keep the prints in constant motion in both toning and fixing baths, avoiding air bubbles.
4. Make the fixing bath alkaline with ammonia.
5. Use a fresh fixing bath for each batch of prints, and pass the prints through two fixing baths.
6. Wash thoroughly after toning.
7. Do not try to fix more than three sheets of paper with one ounce of hypo crystals.

WASHING.

The final washing must be most thorough. Whatever may be the true explanation of the fading of silver prints, it is certain that permanency is promoted by a liberal deposit of gold, complete fixation, and thorough washing.

I know of no better method of washing the prints than that of allowing them to soak in a pan of clean water for two or three hours, taking them out one at a time every fifteen minutes, allowing them to drain a moment or two from one corner, and then place them in another pan of clean water. It is a good plan also to lay the prints face uppermost on pieces of glass and then to give them a good sponging, using plenty of clean water. If this is done two or three times, and the prints changed every fifteen minutes, two or three hours' washing will eliminate nearly all traces of hypo. They should then be tested for hypo, using the following test solution :

> Permanganate of potash - - - - 2 grains.
> Carbonate of potash - - - - 20 grains.
> Water - - - - - - 40 ounces.

A few drops of this solution should be added to a pint of the last wash water; if any hypo is present the rose color of the original solution will change to a greenish hue. If this test detects hyposulphite, the prints may be immersed for a few moments in the following hypochlorite solution.

STOCK SOLUTION.

EAU DE JAVELLE.

> Dry chl. of lime (hypo chl. of lime), - - 2 ounces.
> Carbonate of potash, - - - - 4 ounces.
> Water, - - - - - - 40 ounces.

Mix the chloride of lime with 30 ounces of the water. dissolve the carbonate of potash in the remainder. Mix, boil and filter.

To use: to one ounce of the stock solution add twenty ounces of water. Soak the prints for ten minutes in this dilute solution, and then wash for fifteen minutes. The prints are now reasonably certain to be free from hypo, and will have as high a degree of permanence as can be given to silver prints.

A limited number may be washed well enough in a tray. Rock the tray occasionally or move them by continually slipping out the bottom one and placing it upon the top. The water should be changed seven or eight times, and during the earlier part of the process the changes should be more frequent than during the latter part. A thorough elimination of the fixing solution is essential to the permanence of the photograph. There is little danger, therefore, of continuing the washing too long. Some even allow water to run over the prints all night. It is supposed by many, however, that an excessively prolonged soaking in water weakens the print.

THE HYPOCHLORITE OF ZINC HYPO ELIMINATOR.

This eliminator, a favorite one with German and Austrian photographers, is now an article of trade under the name of Flandreau's S. P. C. Hypo Eliminator. Accompanying the package as purchased of the stockdealer, is a packet of iodide of starch, of dark purple color, which, when brought into contact with prints, or the water dripping from them, will bleach immediately if only a trace of hyposulphite be present.

To remove these last traces of the obnoxious salt, a tablespoonful of Flandreau's S. P. C. Hypo Eliminator, added to one quart of the last washing water, and allowing the prints to remain therein for a few moments, and then rinsing them off again with pure water, will effect a thorough elimination, without which albumenized paper prints will always be liable to turn yellow or to fade.

The eliminator should not be used in large proportions, as by too strong solutions the whole silver deposit might suffer.

RULES FOR PRINTING AND TONING IN COLD WEATHER.

1. Sensitize on a silver bath sixty-five grains strong.
2. Keep the silver and toning baths at a temperature of 70 deg. Fahr.
3. Before silvering, bring the paper to about the same temperature as the bath.
4. Dry the paper thoroughly before and after fuming.
5. Fume thirty to sixty minutes.
7. Warm the negative and pads before printing.
8 Do not print in the cold outer air.
9. Have the wash water and fixing solution at the same temperature as the silver and'toning baths.

Observance of these rules will insure plucky and well-toned prints in the coldest weather.

CHAPTER V.

PRINTING ON OTHER THAN ALBUMEN PAPER.

As there are many who dislike the gloss of albumen prints, a brief description of other papers is given.

PRINTING ON PLAIN PAPER.

Prints on plain paper form a good basis on which to color. The two most common formulæ are the following:

1.—Chloride of ammonium,	60 to 80 grains.
Citrate of soda,	100 grains.
Chloride of sodium,	20 to 30 grains.
Gelatine,	10 grains.
Distilled water,	10 ounces.
2.—Chloride of ammonium,	100 grains.
Gelatine,	10 grains.
Water,	10 ounces.

First swell the gelatine in cold water, then dissolve by heat in the ten ounces of water, adding the salts. The solution is then filtered and the paper floated on it for three minutes. Sensitize on a sixty-grain bath of silver nitrate. Print deep, and wash, tone and fix as for albumen paper. Toning bath No. 20 is especially adapted for plain paper. Avoid over-toning.

Excellent prints may be made on drawing paper by this method.

PRINTING ON RESINIZED PAPER.

The term resinized has been given to paper coated with resins in place of albumen. Such paper gives prints of wonderful softness and delicacy, and tones easily. The process deserves more attention than it has yet received. Three formulæ are given, of which I would especially recommend No. 3 for the soft and delicately graded tints it gives.

No. 1.—BERTRAND'S.

Immerse plain paper for three minutes in the following solution:

Alcohol,	20 ounces.
Benzoin,	2 ounces.
Chloride of cadmium,	1 ounce.

When dry, sensitize on a sixty-grain bath. Print deep, well wash, and tone in bath No. 21. Fix and wash as for albumen.

No. 2.—Mr. Henry Cooper's.

Frankincense,	10 grains,
Mastic,	8 grains.
Chloride of calcium,	5 to 10 grains.
Alcohol,	1 ounce.

The paper is immersed in this solution and hung up to dry. When dry it is smoothed with a hot iron and sensitized as usual; sensitizing bath No. 5 is the one recommended by Mr. Cooper. The prints which should be deep are best toned on bath No. 20.

No. 3.—Mr. Henry Cooper's.

Coat the paper with an emulsion prepared as follows:

Dissolve three ounces of fresh white lac in twenty ounces of strong alcohol; filter or decant, and add as much water as possible without precipitating the lac; dissolve one ounce of the best white gelatine in twenty ounces of boiling water, first swelling the gelatine in cold water. When the gelatine is dissolved, add the lac solution, stirring vigorously. In case the gelatine is precipitated by the alcohol, add more hot water.

The paper is to be immersed in this emulsion for three minutes, or it may be floated on it for the same length of time. When dry, smooth with a hot iron, and float for two minutes on the following solution:

Chloride of ammonium,	10 grains.
Lactate of magnesium,	10 grains.
Water,	1 ounce.

When again dry, sensitize on a sixty grain bath, and print deep. If the prints are not vigorous enough, immerse them in the following bath:

Citric acid,	5 grains.
White sugar,	5 grains.
Water,	1 ounce.

This bath improves with use. Toning bath No. 20 works well with this paper.

Either of these processes give fine results on drawing paper.

Resinized paper should be fumed until the paper prints blue, fifteen to twenty minutes is sufficient. Over-toning must be avoided.

Printing on Leatherized and Gelatinized Papers.

Very fine mat surface prints can be made on a salted paper known as leatherized paper. It is a strong, fine-surfaced paper and comes ready salted. It should be floated thirty seconds on a bath forty-five to sixty grains in strength, and fumed until it prints blue. Print rather deeply, thoroughly wash away the free nitrate, and tone on bath No. 20. The toning should not be carried too far, or weak prints will be the result.

Gelatinized Paper.—This is the name which I have given to paper floated two to three minutes on a gelatine solution, then dried, and floated two minutes on the lactate of magnesium and chloride of ammonium bath given above. When the paper is again dry it is floated two to three minutes on a silver bath, forty-five to sixty grains strong, and fumed for fifteen to twenty minutes.

The printing should be deep, the free nitrate well washed out, and the prints toned on bath No. 20. The resulting prints are remarkable for softness, delicacy of gradation, and beauty of tone.

As I have never seen the process described, I venture to recommend it only after a thorough trial.

The gelatine bath is compounded as follows:

Gelatine, - - - - -	10 grains.
Chrome alum solution (1 to 50), - - -	10 drops.
Water, - - - - - -	1 ounce.

When solution is complete, filter and float plain paper on the bath for two minutes, avoiding air bubbles. Prints made on paper thus prepared cannot be distinguished from those made on resinized paper, and it has the advantage of requiring a smaller number of chemicals.

With it the prints can be given a tone closely resembling the best work on bromide of silver paper, and by using drawing-paper very artistic results may be obtained.

I have recommended toning bath No. 20 for these rarely used processes for the reason that they all need but little toning, and this bath is so weak in gold that there is little danger of over-toning. Any other bath, however, can be used with good success if it is made weak in gold.

CHAPTER VI.

THE PLATINOTYPE.

THIS is the most recent advance in printing with iron salts. The process was worked out by Mr. W. Willis, Jr., and has been made the subject of a patent. The Willis process can be worked only by licensees, although I believe that the ready-sensitized paper is supplied by the agents in this country to all who order it. But it is possible to work the platinum process without taking out a license, and I therefore give details which will enable any one to prepare his own paper. The directions are condensed from a pamphlet published, in Vienna, in 1882, by Pizzeghilli and Hubl. Plain paper, of an even, firm texture, is sized by floating for two or three minutes on one of the following solutions:

SIZING FOR PLATINUM PRINTS.

Water,	20 ounces.
Gelatine,	60 grains.
Chrome alum,	6 grains.
Aniline blue (powdered),	10 to 20 grains.

The gelatine is soaked in the water for one hour, and then dissolved with gentle heat. When nearly cool the chrome alum and the aniline blue are added and the solution filtered. The prints to be sized are floated or immersed a short time in this solution;

No. 1.—FOR BLUISH-BLACK TONES.

Gelatine,	154 grains.
Alum,	46 grains.
Alcohol,	7 ounces.
Water,	28 ounces.

The gelatine is first soaked in the water until soft, and then dissolved at a temperature of 140 deg. Fahr. When solution is complete the alum and alcohol are added, and the liquid filtered.

No. 2.—For Brownish-black Tones.

Arrow-root,	154 grains.
Boiling water,	28 ounces.
Alcohol,	7 ounces.

The arrow root is first rubbed up in cold water, and added to the boiling water; then the alcohol is poured in and the solution filtered.

In order to secure an even coating, it is best to refloat the paper when dry, and suspend the reverse way.

No. 1.—Stock Solutions.

Chloro-platinite of potassium,	80 grains.
Water,	1 ounce.

No. 2.—Ferric oxalate solution as found in the trade.

If the solution gives a precipitate with red prussiate of potash, or becomes turbid when boiled with ten times its bulk of water, it should be rejected.

[Note.—The author has never experienced any difficulty in procuring ferric oxalate of Eimer & Amend, 205 to 211 Third Avenue, New York, but for the convenience of those who may wish to prepare it for themselves, methods for making both the potassic ferric oxalate and the ferric oxalate are given.

Potassic Ferric Oxalate.—Add neutral oxalate of potassium to chloride of iron solution and evaporate to crystallization. The resulting crystals are the salt required.

Ferric Oxalate.—This salt may be obtained by dissolving hydrated peroxide of iron in a strong solution of oxalic acid.

Pizzeghilli recommends the following method:

"Five hundred parts of ferric chloride are dissolved in water and precipitated by an excess of caustic soda; after which the precipitate is well washed, and collected on a cloth. When the bulk of the water has run through, the material is poured from the filter, and 200 parts of pure crystallized oxalic acid added; but this addition should be made in the dark, and the whole is allowed to remain at a temperature of 30 deg. C. for some days, in order that solution may be complete.

The liquid being now made up, if required, to the volume of 2,800 parts of water, a liquor is obtained which contains about one-fifth of its weight of ferric oxalate."]

No. 3.—Chlorate of Iron Solution.

Solution No. 2,	31 ounces.
Chlorate of potash,	6 grains.

A.—Sensitizing Solutions.

No. 1,	408 drops.
No. 2,	374 drops.
Water,	68 drops.

B; gives more vigorous prints than A; good for thin negatives:

No. 1,	408 drops.
No. 2,	306 drops.
No. 3,	68 drops.
Water,	68 drops.

The paper to be sensitized should be fastened to a board by drawing tacks, and one of Solutions A or B evenly spread over it with a squeegee muffled in flannel, or a large brush, carefully avoiding streaks. The sensitizing should be done by yellow or feeble white light. As soon as the surface is dry, the sensitized sheets must be dried thoroughly at a temperature of 86 to 100 deg. Fahr.

The mixed sensitizer must be used up within 15 or 20 minutes.

The sensitized sheets and the prints must be preserved from the effects of moisture in a box containing a little dry chloride of calcium. All the subsequent operations are the same as recommended for the Willis process, of which the following very complete directions are taken from an article by Mr. H. Edwards Ficken, published in "The American Annual of Photography" for 1887.

"The Platinotype Process.

"One has but to see a fair platinotype print to be struck by the charm of its softness and delicacy, and, if compared with a silver print from the same negative, by its superiority in every way. In platinotype prints the whites have a higher artistic effect, the shadows a deeper richness, and the grays more value in the half-tones than can ever be obtained from the best silver print, the velvety feeling of the picture and the absence of glaze conducting largely to this. I have written before of the beauty of this process, comparatively little known here, but exceedingly popular on the other side, and it is significant that a recent number of the English *Building News*, one of the highest and most conservative professional papers, containing a notice of the Photographic Society's recent Exhibition in London, calls especial attention in high commendation to the platinotype prints shown, and adds: 'The delicate gray tint is decidedly preferable to the purply tones which photographs usually have. It has been left to the platinotype process to show that artistic shades of black and gray can be produced.' There also appeared in our own *Photographic Times* (No. 259), an article on the process by Mr. G. Watmough Webster, whose opinion every one must respect, which so fully covers the ground that it leaves but the little I have said above to complement it. I can only say, almost in Mr. Webster's words, that to any one who has not tried the process, the simplicity and ease of its working and the beauty of the results will be simply a revelation.

"I will endeavor now to describe it as clearly and exactly as possible that failure may be precluded; and there should not be any failure if the following directions and hints are faithfully followed.

"I may premise that all the material, chemicals and paper, can be purchased ready for use, a great convenience for amateurs with their limited time, and simplifying greatly their labors.

"*Keeping Apparatus Dry.*—At the beginning it must be impressed upon the attention that unless all the material used in making prints—the printing frame, negative, etc.—are perfectly dry, the resultant print will have a slaty color, instead of the warm, rich black it should possess.

"*Sensitizing the Paper.*—The first operation is the sensitizing of the paper for contact printing, for I would advise everyone to sensitize their own paper just before using it. It is very little trouble, and the freshly prepared paper gives richer prints. This should be done in a room lighted by a yellow light, or not too strong gaslight. The sensitizing solution is made by dissolving fifteen grains of platinum salt in a quarter ounce of iron solution (the exact quantity for a sheet 18 by 22 inches), shaking the solution until the platinum salts are dissolved. It must be used almost as soon as made, as it will not keep over half an hour. Place the paper to be sensitized, face upwards, on a sheet of plate glass having a wooden frame, so that it can be secured at the corners by thumb tacks; pour the solution on the middle of the sheet and spread evenly over the entire surface with a wad of clean flannel. Allow no streakings to remain; swab the solution first one way, then the other, across the paper with a light touch till it looks perfectly smooth. Now hang up by the corners till dry. This should take not under ten minutes, nor over twelve. If it dries too quickly, some of the image will float off in the developing bath and cause a loss of half-tone, and if it dries too slowly, the subsequent print will appear flat.

"*Drying the Sensitized Paper.*—If the air be very dry in the room where the paper is dried, it will be necessary to create a moister atmosphere, otherwise the sensitizing fluid sinks too deeply in the paper and gives a flat print. I obtain this moistness by pinning the paper above the bath tub, when the paper seems drying too rapidly on the surface, and turning on the hot water, the steam arising from it dampening the air very rapidly. After the paper seems dry, when it will have a lemon-yellow color, it is well to hold it for a few minutes in front of a stove to ensure its thorough dryness, protecting it, of course, from any strong white light. It can now be measured off and cut up for the size prints to be made, and put away till wanted.

"Before describing how to preserve the sensitized paper, it may be well to give the caution always to put the iron solution in a dark closet to keep it from the light, and always to use fresh flannel on the squeegee.

"*Preserving the Paper.*—In preserving the paper I use two tin tubes about four inches diameter, each having a receptacle at the bottom containing dry chloride of calcium, to extract all moisture from the tubes and paper. One I label 'paper' and the other 'prints.' In the first I store the cut-up sensitized sheets, and in the other the prints as fast as made. Care must be taken to avoid all contact between the paper and the chloride, which would stain the print, producing white spots.

"*Printing.*—Printing is done as usual, the sensitized paper put over the negative in the ordinary printing frame and exposed to direct or diffused light, according to the character of the negative. The printing frame should be held for a few minutes before the stove, and a sheet of thin rubber put between the negative and the cover of the printing frame. The correct exposure is ascertained by inspecting the paper in the usual way, but it is much more difficult at first to decide upon the proper exposure, as much of the detail and the most delicate tones are invisible till the after development. This must be remembered. Practice, however, soon decides, and by carefully noting the following hints, little difficulty will be experienced even at the first. As a general rule the exposure is complete when the detail in the high lights becomes faintly visible. With very dense negatives, and rather dense negatives are best for this process, the printing should be continued until all the details in the lights are visible. During exposure the parts affected by light become of a pale grayish-brown color, and finally, perhaps, of a dingy orange tint under those parts of the negative which is clear glass or nearly so. Beware of over-exposure for thin negatives, and note that prints look slightly darker when dried after development, and prints in half-tone only, if printed too dark, have usually a flat appearance.

"The material for development is a flat-bottomed dish of agate iron ware, about 12 by 14 inches in size, to contain the developing solution, and a small gas stove, with ring burner, to place under it to heat the solution to the proper developing temperature, and a couple of porcelain-lined trays, 16 by 19 inches in size, to wash the developed prints in.

"The development should be effected in a feeble white light, or by gaslight, and may be done at the end of the day's printing.

"*Developing Solution.*—The developing solution is made by dissolving 12 ounces of oxalate of potash in 44 ounces of water, and made acid by the addition of 2½ drams of oxalic acid, or enough to turn blue litmus paper pink. This will give a depth of about half an inch in the tray for 8 by 10 prints. The potash is most readily prepared in hot water, adding the salts by degrees, and stirring till all is dissolved. The solution must now be heated to a temperature varying between 170 and 180 deg. Fahr., and this is the standard, though higher and lower temperature may be used, for which, reasons will be given later.

"*Development.*—The development of the prints is effected by floating them, face down, upon this hot solution of oxalate of potash for a *few seconds*, and is best performed by laying one end of the print upon the bath at the right hand of the tray, and sliding it evenly towards the left, lowering the print with an even movement and without stoppage, until it is entirely in contact with the liquid, where it must remain not less than five seconds. It may remain longer, as a prolonged floating does no great harm beyond unnecessarily softening the paper and its sizing; and, in fact, it is my practice, after the first floating and appearance of the image, to float the print once or twice more in the deepest shadows only, to get all the possible depth out of them.

"Just as in the appearance of the latent image when developing the negative, which gives a never-ending pleasure, so will the same delight be felt in the appearance of the print after this floating for a few seconds on the hot solution. It is like magic; the whole view flashes up, it seems instantaneously, in all its beauty, and is the most full repayment for what little trouble has gone before.

"As the heat of the developing solution is greater than the hands are accustomed to, take care not to injure the first prints by starting at the sudden shock of the touch on the fingers of the hot liquid. A little practice will soon enable one to almost avoid touching the bath at all.

"Again a caution. Look out for crystals on the surface of the developing bath, and do not develop till these are dissolved or removed. Air bubbles must also be carefully avoided in floating the prints, as they form white spots; but if they should make their appearance, by any little inadvertence, immediately touch them once or twice to the bath, when they will be removed.

"Prints having deep shadows, especially when over-printed, require a development of at least ten seconds. Subjects entirely in half-tone require only five seconds. Over-exposed prints must be developed at a temperature between 10 and 20 degrees lower than the standard, and under-exposed ones higher, although this will not always save the print, for with either extreme a little flatness may appear.

"It is best to try and give such exposures in the printing frame, as a uniform temperature at about 170 to 180 deg. Fahr., as already stated, will insure perfect results.

"The developing solution may be used almost indefinitely, although in this, as in all my other photographic work, I prefer fresh solutions; but it must be kept in a dark closet, and, before using again, should be decanted from the crystals, which may have formed, and enough fresh solution of oxalate of potash added to bring the bath up again to the required quantity.

"*Washing the Prints.*—The developed prints must now be washed in at least three baths of a weak solution of hydrochloric acid to thoroughly clean them. Citric acid may also be used, but I find the other more convenient. For the size of trays given above, one ounce of the hydrochloric acid to sixty-four ounces of water will be sufficient. Immerse the prints, face down, in the first acid bath, and let them remain there about ten minutes; then remove to the second bath and treat in the same way. If they do not communicate to the last acid bath the slightest tinge of color, they may now be well washed in clear water, otherwise a third acid bath, perhaps slightly weaker, must be given them. While in the baths, move the prints about so that the solution washes them freely, but take care not to abrade them.

"They are now finished, and need only drying to render them ready for mounting.

"If, after drying, the prints are more or less yellow, it may come from the sensitizing fluid not having been acid enough.

Again, prints may appear strong, yet more or less fogged; this may come from over-exposure in printing. The cure for this has already been given: reduce the temperature of the developing solution.

"It is really all simpler than it reads; the chemicals are few and easily used, the sensitizing of the paper is easily and quickly done, the printing is soon picked up, the development is almost purely mechanical, and the cleaning and washing entirely so. The ease of the whole thing, however, should not be the only temptation to try it; its beauty is unapproachable and lends itself with equally good results to strong effects in portraiture and all atmospheric tones of landscape and marine views.

"I would say, in conclusion, that there can be obtained from the Platinotype Company, London, Eng., specially prepared paper in the sizing for the making of sepia-colored prints, which, for some subjects, is particularly beautiful, and a solution for mixing with the ordinary oxalate of potash developer, which combines to give the finished sepia color. I have tried it with great success. Willis & Clements, of Philadelphia, supply all the other material."

Platinum prints may, I believe, be regarded as permanent, platinum black being one of the most stable colors, unaffected by atmospheric changes. The process is simplicity itself, and this, together with the exceeding beauty and artistic effect, would undoubtedly commend the process to art-loving amateurs, were they not deterred by the necessity of taking out a license. But I have found that the ready-sensitized paper will keep in good condition if placed in a box with a tight-fitting cover, with chloride of calcium sprinkled over the bottom, care must be taken to prevent the paper from coming in contact with the chloride, or white spots will show themselves in the prints when developed.

Pizzeghilli's process, described above, gives prints of the highest degree of excellence, and the process is free to all.

The chemical explanation of the formation of the image in platinum black is probably that the action of light converts the ferric oxalate to the ferrous state and that immersion in the hot solution of potassic oxalate immediately reduces the platinum to the metallic state wherever it is in contact with the ferrous salt. The portion not so reduced remains in solution with the potassic oxalate. Directions for recovering this will be found in the chapter on "Wastes."

Warm or sepia tones may be given to platinum prints by the following method, which is that of Signor Borlinetto:

Dissolve nine and three-quarter ounces of neutral oxalate of potash in thirty-two and one-eight ounces of boiling water, and then add 154 grains of oxalic acid. When solution is complete, add three and a quarter ounces of a saturated solution of chloride of copper; shake well to insure complete mixture. The printed proofs are immersed in this solution at a temperature varying from 170 to 200 degs. Fahr., and they soon tone to a rich sepia. The tint can be changed by raising or lowering the temperature. As soon as the prints have assumed the desired tint they are washed in the usual way in the acid bath, and then immersed for a short time in a one to twenty solution of sulphate of iron. They are then washed once in water made slightly acid with sulphuric acid, and after the usual half hour's washing in running water, they are hung up to dry.

As these prints resist nitric, sulphuric, and even fluorhydric acid, they are presumably permanent.

AMERICAN FILM NEGATIVE. BY W. J. HICKMOTT, HARTFORD, CONN.

PRINTED ON
EASTMAN'S PERMANENT BROMIDE PAPER—GRADE B.

CHAPTER VII.

PRINTING WITH EMULSIONS.

Gelatino-Bromide.—The chief point of difference between printing on paper prepared with emulsions and printing on paper sensitized in the bath, is, that in the former case we have the sensitive compound of silver suspended in an exceedingly fine state of division, in a vehicle of gelatine or collodion; whereas, in the latter we have a thin coating of an aqueous solution of the sensitive salt. Organic substances such as gelatine or collodion are sensitizers of silver, and, in consequence, emulsion papers are more sensitive than papers floated on the bath, for the reason that the atoms of the molecules are in a state of less stable equilibrium in the former case than in the latter, and therefore are more easily separated by the action of light.

The most common form in which emulsion paper presents itself to the amateur is the well-known bromide of silver paper, which is now a standard trade article. But since good results can be obtained on paper coated with a chloride of silver emulsion, which, to the best of my knowledge cannot be purchased, full directions are given of the apparatus and chemicals needed to prepare different emulsions, together with directions for making the emulsions and coating the paper.

Apparatus.—This need not be of a very complicated or expensive nature. First of all, some sort of a vessel is required as a water-bath, to hold the solutions, which have to be kept at a certain temperature. I have always used a common tin pail having a tightly-fitting cover. Two or three earthenware, porcelain, or glass vessels, of a pint or more capacity, a thermometer of the pattern used for taking the temperature of hot solutions, a supply of glass stirring-rods, a filter of some kind, and a Bunsen burner, spirit lamp, or kerosene lamp, complete the modest plant required for making the various kinds of emulsion.

A very compact and convenient digesting apparatus is found in the infants' food-warmer kept by most druggists. This consists of a covered porcelain-dish, which fits into a metal water-bath, the source of heat being a candle.

A simple and efficient filter is easily made by tying two thicknesses of an old pocket-handerchief around the top of a fluted-top lamp chimney.

The coating-room must contain the indispensable glass or stone slab, accurately levelled, and a supply of clean glass plates of a size corresponding to that of the paper to be coated.

Bromide of Silver Emulsion.

1.—Gelatine (soft),   42½ grains.
    Bromide of potassium,   26 grains.
    Water (distilled),   1 ounce.
2.—Nitrate of silver,   32½ grains.
    Water (distilled),   1 ounce.

Dissolve the bromide first, then add the gelatine, and dissolve by gentle heat (95 deg. to 100 deg. Fahr.); bring the silver solution to the same temperature, and add in a small stream to the gelatine solution, stirring vigorously, of course, in non-actinic light. Keep the mixed emulsion at a temperature of 105 deg. Fahr., for half an hour or an hour, according to the degree of sensitiveness required, previously adding one drop of nitric acid to every five ounces of emulsion. Allow it to set, squeeze through working canvas, and wash two hours in running water. In my own practice, I manage the washing easily enough by breaking the emulsion up into an earthen jar filled with cold water, and placed in my dark room sink. A tall lamp chimney, standing in the jar immediately under the tap, conducts the fresh water to the bottom of the jar, and keeps the finely divided emulsion in constant motion; a piece of muslin, laid over the top of the jar to prevent any of the emulsion running out, completes this simple, inexpensive, but efficient washing apparatus.

The washing completed, you are ready to melt and filter the emulsion preparatory to coating the paper. When melted, and before filtering, it is well to add of glycerine and alcohol each about one-tenth of the whole bulk of the emulsion, the glycerine preventing troublesome cockling of the paper as it dries, and the alcohol preventing air-bubbles, and hastening the drying. This addition made and the emulsion filtered, you are ready to coat your paper, which may be coated just as it comes from the stock dealer, plain Saxe or Rives, or better still, given a substratum of insoluble gelatine, made as follows:

Gelatine, - - - - -	1⅜ grains.
Water, - - - - -	1 ounce.

Dissolve and filter; then add 11 drops of a 1:50 filtered chrome alum solution. The paper is to be floated for half a minute on this solution, avoiding air bubbles, and then hung up to dry in a room free from dust. The purpose of this substratum is to secure additional brilliancy in the finished prints by keeping the emulsion isolated from the surface of the paper. If you are floating the whole sheet, now is the proper time to cut it to the size you wish to coat, but for anything less than 6½x8½, I would recommend cutting in double or quadruple sizes, 8x10 for 5x8 and 4x5 prints, as the paper is easily cut down after the emulsion is dry.

COATING.

Apparatus.—A stone, marble or glass slab large enough to hold at least half a dozen glasses of the size paper you are coating, and most accurately levelled; a dozen or more pieces of glass of the same size as your paper; a porcelain or agate ware tray of the same size; a ruby lamp; a deep tray of a size to hold your jug of emulsion and the smaller tray; a spirit or kerosene lamp enclosed in a box suitably ventilated and protected against the egress of white light from the lamp inside, (this is easily secured by punching holes around the top and bottom of a tin box of suitable size, and covering it with another somewhat larger in every way, but without a top), and a goodly supply of spring clothespins, to be had of any hardware merchant for 20 cents a dozen. The above is a complete inventory of my own outfit. Having then provided yourself with these articles, with the addition of a squeegee muffled with a piece of soft flannel, an article which you can easily make by procuring a piece of small black rubber tubing of the proper length, and placing it in the centre of a strip of flannel of equal length, and about two inches wide; you then fold the flannel over on itself, thus enclosing the rubber tube, and fasten the whole between two narrow, thin strips of wood, drawing the rubber up close to the wood, you are ready for coating. For this purpose you must secure the temporary use of some small room in which the paper can be coated, hung up and left to dry. This room must meet three requirements: it must be dry, free from dust, and capable of being made absolutely light-tight during the drying of the paper. I am fortunate enough to have undisputed control of a small attic which serves admirably.

Into this room, provided with a table large enough to hold your marble slab, on which the slab is carefully levelled, you carry all the articles mentioned above. The spirit or oil lamp is placed in its box, on which stands the large tray previously filled with water at 100 deg. Fahr., and containing the jar of emulsion and the small tray filled with warm distilled water. The ruby lamp stands on a table in front of you; the glasses well cleaned and warmed to blood heat, and the paper with the side to be coated uppermost are placed on the table at your right; within convenient reach of your right hand stands the tray of warm water, and the levelled slab is within easy reach on your left. Turn the ruby lamp down as low as is consistent with the power of vision. Now immerse a sheet of the paper in the water in the small tray, leaving it there for a minute or two; then place it accurately on one of the glass plates, and sweep off all superfluous water with the squeegee, at the same time removing all wrinkles and air bells, and place in an upright position to dry slightly, while you prepare a second plate in the same manner. Now balance the first plate on the tips of the fingers and thumb of the left hand, and pour on a sufficient quantity of the emulsion, about 1 dram for every 10 square inches of paper. I use a silver soup ladle holding just enough to cover a whole plate. Gently tilt the plate from you until the further end is completely covered; then as gently tilt it towards you until the emulsion completely covers the paper; then carefully place it on the levelled slab to set. Continue this operation until the slab is covered, when the paper first coated will probably have become sufficiently set to be stripped from the glass and hung up by clothespins to dry, which in my room requires from six to ten hours.

Other Methods of Coating Paper with Emulsion.

While the method of coating described above is the one preferred by the author for coating a small quantity of paper, other means of securing the same result are available. A very good method of coating is to place the melted emulsion in a clean porcelain tray of the requisite dimensions, and to place this in a second larger tray containing water heated to about 95 or 100 deg. Fahr. Some means must be devised of suspending a levelled glass slab above the smaller tray in such a way as to leave about two inches of one end of the tray uncovered. This may be done by having the larger tray somewhat deeper than that containing the emulsion, and using glass plates large enough to reach across the larger tray.

The water may be kept at the proper temperature by any convenient means.

The paper to be coated is previously dampened, and then floated, sheet by sheet, on the emulsion, carefully avoiding air bubbles. As soon as the paper has been laid down on the emulsion, the glass plate is put in position, one end of the paper is grasped with a pair of broad horn or glass pincers and drawn slowly over the end of the glass plate, upon which it is smoothly laid down and allowed to set, when it is stripped off and hung up to dry.

A better way, perhaps, is to remove the glass plate bearing the paper to the usual levelled slab. By adopting this method no delay in coating is necessitated, and the glass covering the tray need not be so accurately levelled as it must be if the emulsion is allowed to set over the tray. The author has devised a little machine for coating long rolls of paper which he has found to work admirably and greatly to facilitate the operation of coating.

It differs from other machines for this purpose accessible to the ordinary experimenter in the fact that the paper is drawn from the machine, coated side up, directly to a long-levelled slab, while all other forms of machine known to the writer require the suspension of the paper after coating, a mode of working which allows the emulsion to run down the paper before setting, giving rise to ridges and uneven coating.

The accompanying figures and description will, it is hoped, make the construction and practical working of the machine sufficiently intelligible.

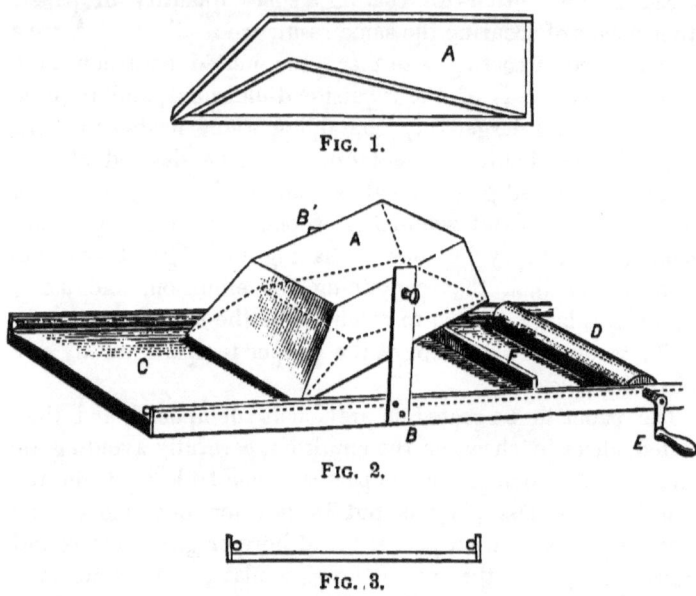

Fig. 1.

Fig. 2.

Fig. 3.

Fig. 1 shows a side plan of the emulsion-holder. Fig. 2 the apparatus complete, and Fig. 3 an end-view of the base board, showing the wires under which the paper is drawn.

The box A is constructed as shown of any close-grained thin wood, and well shellacked. The narrow slit is covered with a piece of fine linen, well glued on. It is impossible to give any definite dimensions for the box, as they vary according to the width of the paper to be coated. Its width must be the same as the width of the film desired ; its length need not exceed 3 to 4 inches, and its height must be sufficient to allow enough emulsion to be poured in to coat the longest strip of paper likely to be coated.

The base board C, Fig. 2, is made of a piece of pine one inch thick, twelve inches long, and as wide as the emulsion-holder. At each side, strips one-half inch thick, two inches high and eighteen inches long are screwed, to which two brass wires, one-half inch in diameter, are fastened at the ends in such a way as to allow the turned-up edges of the paper to pass freely under them. Two uprights, B, B, are firmly screwed to the base board. Between these uprights the emulsion-holder is suspended by means of thumb-screws. The box must be suspended at such a height as to allow all the emulsion to flow out when the box is in position for coating. A roller, D, Fig. 2, is placed at the end of the side strips. The base board, C, should be covered with a piece of glass.

To Use the Apparatus.—The desired length of paper is wound on the roller, the apparatus is placed on a level with the end of a levelled slab or board from six to fifteen feet in length, the free end of the paper drawn under the box and clamped between two strips of thin wood, having strips of sheet rubber fastened on the inside. A screw-eye is inserted about half an inch from each end of one of these strips, through which a short piece of string is passed; this string is provided with a small brass ring, left free to travel back or forth on the string. To this ring is fastened a long piece of twine which passes through a screw-eye underneath the further end of the levelling slab, thence through a screw-eye fastened in the ceiling of the room, and through other screw-eyes is brought back within convenient reach of the operator's hand.

The box is filled with emulsion, and the paper is drawn slowly along until the end of the slab is reached. The box is then raised to a horizontal position to stop the flow of emulsion, the clamps removed and fastened to the end of the uncoated paper. The apparatus is then moved sideways until a clear portion of the slab lies in front of it, and another strip of paper coated as before.

To insure success with this apparatus, it is necessary that it work smoothly and evenly, and that perfect accuracy be secured in its construction.

To prevent any of the emulsion running under the edges of the paper, the roller must be about half an inch wider than the box, and the paper cut the same width as the roller, and turned up one quarter of an inch on each side. This is effected by means of the side wires which are fastened close to the glass top of the base, beneath and behind which the paper is drawn. These wires should not extend beyond the end of the base board at the back, being fastened to the thin strip, F, between which and the base board the paper passes. The ends of this strip are cut away to allow the turned-up edge of the paper to pass between them and the side strip. Fig. 4 shows the arrangement.

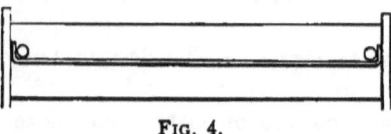

FIG. 4.

As it is usually necessary to dampen the paper before coating, the paper, as it is wound on the roller, is drawn under water placed in a tray. This should be done rather slowly in order that the paper may be thoroughly dampened.

The author has found this apparatus thoroughly practical, and gives these details of its construction and working with the hope that it may prove serviceable to the fraternity at large.

No. 2.—For Brown Tones.

A.—Gelatine,	231 grains.
Bromide of potassium,	115 grains.
Iodide of potassium,	25 grains.
Water,	5 ounces.
Nitric acid,	2 drops.
B.—Nitrate of silver,	172 grains.
Water,	5 ounces.

The directions given above are to be followed in making this emulsion.

If prints having a more mat surface are desired, decrease the amount of gelatine, but its bulk should not be less than that of the bromide of potassium.

For enlargements, the best effects are produced by coating drawing-paper, omitting the gelatine sizing.

Exposure.

For contact printing artificial light is best. The time of exposure varies with the intensity of the light, the density of the negative, and the distance at which the latter is held from the source of light while making the expsosure, the time increasing as the square of the distance. Thin negatives are best printed from at a distance from the lamp; thick ones should be held quite near.

The tone of the print may be varied by giving a prolonged exposure and using a very diluted developer with 8 to 10 drops of a 1 to 10 solution of common salt added.

Development.

The most common developer for bromide prints is the usual ferrous oxalate developer, both solutions being kept acid. Other developers, however, can be employed. If the pyro developer is used for the purpose of getting brown tones, the developer should be weak in the alkali, and the prints should be immersed in a 1 to 10 sulphite of soda solution before fixing, to prevent staining.

Pleasing brown tones may be given to prints on bromide paper by immersion for a minute or two in a bath composed of equal parts of the following solutions:

1.—Water,	100 parts.
Nitrate of uranium,	1 part.
2.—Water,	100 parts.
Ferricyanide of potash,	1 part.

The prints must be well washed before toning, and the washing, after toning, should not be prolonged beyond half an hour, as prolonged washing will destroy the color, owing to the solubility of the ferricyanide of uranium formed when the above solutions are mixed. The tone of the prints may be greatly modified by varying the proportions of the ferricyanide.

Eastman's Developer.

A.—Oxalate of potash	1 pound.
Hot water,	3 pints.

Acidify with oxalic acid. Test with litmus paper.

B.—Proto-sulphate of iron, - - - 1 pound.
Hot water, - - - - 1 quart.
Sulphuric acid (or citric acid, ¼ oz) - - ½ dram.
C.—Bromide potassium, - - - 1 ounce.
Water, - - - - - 1 quart.

These solutions keep separately, but must be mixed only for immediate use.

To Develop.

Take, in a suitable tray, A, 6 ounces; B, 1 ounce; C, ½ dram.

Mix in the order given; use cold. After exposure, soak the paper in water until limp; then immerse in the developer.

The image should appear slowly, and should develop up strong, clear and brilliant. When the shadows are sufficiently black, pour off the developer and flood the print with the

Clearing Solution.

Acetic acid, - - - - - - 1 dram.
Water, - - - - - - 1 quart.

Do not wash the print after pouring off the developer and before applying the clearing solution.

Use a sufficient quantity to flow over the print, say 2 ounces for an 8 x 10. Allow it to act for one minute, and then pour it off and apply a fresh portion; repeat the operation a third time, then rinse in pure water and immerse for ten minutes in the

Fixing Bath.

Hyposulphite soda, - - - - 3 ounces.
Water, - - - - - 1 pint.

On the Use of Bromide as a Restrainer.—Although all the above formulas for developers contain a certain percentage of bromide, I would recommend that it be not used. Too much bromide tends to produce an unpleasant yellowish or olive-green tone, while a careless use of it will utterly spoil the print. The best method of controlling development is to begin with an old developer, substituting the freshly-mixed one when the shadows and general outlines are well out, changing back to the old developer if necessary.

Dr. Charles Ehrmann, to whom I am indebted for many valuable suggestions, kindly furnishes the following method of restraining the action of the developer: In case the print proves to be over-exposed, and no old developer is at hand, quickly pour the developer off the print, and flood it with the plain oxalate solution. Allow this to remain on the print for a moment, then pour off the greater portion of it, and continue the development by adding gradually as required small quantities of the original developer.

Enamelling.

Prints on smooth paper ("A" or "B" Eastman's) may be given a beautiful, polished surface, superior to that obtained by burnishing, in the following manner: Sprinkle the surface of a glass plate with powdered French chalk, rub it evenly over the surface with a tuft of cotton wool, continuing to rub it lightly until the chalk is all removed; then coat the glass with the following collodion:

Soluble gun cotton,	48 grains.
Alcohol,	4 ounces.
Sulphuric ether,	4 ounces.

As soon as the collodion is well set, slide it face up, into a tray of water, in which is floating, face down, the permanent bromide print, which has just been fixed and washed, grasp the plate and print by one end and lift them together from the water, avoiding bubbles, and draining the water from the opposite end; squeegee the print into contact with the plate and set away to dry. Before the print is quite dry apply a coat of starch paste to the back. After drying, the print can be peeled off from the glass, and the face will present a polish almost as high as the surface of the glass from which it has been removed. The print is then ready to mount, as follows: Moisten the face of the mount with a damp sponge and lay it upon the print; rub down with a soft cloth and put under pressure to dry.

Another Method.

Squeegee the wet print, face down, on a polished piece of hard rubber or ebonite; when dry the print will peel off with a fine polished surface. The print should be slipped on to the rubber plate under water to avoid air bells.

FLEXIBLE PRINTS.

Permanent bromide prints soaked in a mixture of glycerine, 5 ounces, and water, 25 ounces, and dried, will not curl, and may be used for book illustrations unmounted. The heavier papers "B" and "C" are especially adapted for this purpose.

STRAIGHTENING UNMOUNTED PRINTS.

After drying, prints may be straightened by the scraping action of a sharp-edged ruler applied to the back; the corner behind the ruler being lifted as the ruler is passed along.

BLACK TONES LIKE PLATINUM PRINTS.

A.—Boiling water, - - - - 500 parts.
     Neutral oxalate of potassium, - 125 parts.

Acidulate with oxalic acid.

B.—Boiling water, - - - - 500 parts.
     Sulphate of iron, - - - 185 parts.
     Sulphuric acid, - - - - 1 part.
C.—Water, - - - - - 300 parts.
     Bromide of potassium, - - 10 parts.

Mix immediately before use in the following proportions: 60 parts of A; 10 parts of B; 1 part of C.

FOR SEPIA TONES.

Double the time of exposure, and reduce the strength of the developer one-half.

FOR BROWN TONES.

A.—Boiling water, - - - - 160 parts.
     Sulphite of sodium, - - - 60 parts.
     Carbonate of sodium, - - - 30 parts.
     Pyro, - - - - - 10 parts.

Dissolve the sodium salts in the water, and when cold add the pyro.

B.—Water, - - - - - 60 parts.
     Bromide of potassium, - - 10 parts.

PHOTOGRAPHIC PRINTING METHODS.

Mix 1 part of A with 5 to 6 parts of water, and add a few drops of B. Before fixing, immerse each print for five minutes in the following solution:

Sulphite of sodium,	1 ounce.
Alum,	1½ ounces.
Water,	10 ounces

FERROUS-CITRO OXALATE DEVELOPER.

A.—Citrate of potassium,	700 grains.
Oxalate of potassium,	200 grains.
Water,	3½ ounces.
B.—Ferrous sulphate,	300 ounces.
Water,	3½ ounces.

Mix equal parts.

Preserving the Ferrous Oxalate Developer.—It is claimed by La Grange and Obernetter that tartaric acid keeps ferrous sulphate from oxidation better than any other acid, and I have long been in the habit of renovating old developer by pouring it into a *white* glass bottle, adding a few drops of a solution of tartaric acid in water (1 to 40), and placing the bottle in full sunlight for a few hours. With a developer renovated in this way, I have successfully developed many dozens of bromide prints.

HINTS.

Mealy Mottled Prints—Over-exposure and short development.

Greenish Tones—Over-exposure and too much bromide.

Fixing—Use fresh hypo solution for each batch of prints. The operator can tell when a print is fixed by looking through or upon it in a good light; unfixed portions will be a greenish yellow.

Do not dry the prints between blotters.

Rock the tray well while developing.

Keep the prints in motion while in the fixing bath.

Be very sparing in the use of bromide.

Turn the prints over while in the clearing solution.

Start development with old developer; finish with freshly mixed.

A jet of water playing in the surface of the prints will be apt to cause blisters.

To avoid yellow prints four things are absolutely necessary:
First—The developer must be acid.
Second—The clearing solution must be used as directed.
Third—Fresh hypo solution is required for fixing each batch of prints.
Fourth—The washing must be thorough after fixing.

If blisters make their appearance use a little common salt in the first washing water after fixing.

Treating Bromide Prints with Platinum.

M. Leon Vidal, of Paris, has lately introduced a method of treating bromide prints with platinum. The tone thus produced is a rich bluish-black, and the results are, presumably, permanent.

The following is the method recommended by M. Vidal:
Make up the following solutions:

1.—Platinum tetrachloride,	15 grains.
Hydrochloric acid (C. P.),	1 ounce.
Water,	70 ounces.
2.—Copper chloride,	2 grains.
Water,	24 ounces.

The prints should be over-developed and washed in the usual acid bath; then immerse twenty or thirty minutes in Solution No. 1. This converts the silver image into one in platinum.

If the image seems in danger of growing too intense, the print is removed from No. 1 before the process of conversion is completed, and placed in a tray containing a sufficient quantity of Solution No. 2. The effect of this bath is to convert any unconverted silver into the white chloride of silver, thus enabling one to judge of the extent of the change from silver into platinum. If the image now appears too weak, the print may be restored by development in the usual way with ferrous oxalate, and the restored image again treated with Solution No. 1. In this way no difficulty will be experienced in obtaining any desired degree of intensity in the platinum bath.

The prints after treatment and washing must be fixed as

usual. The process is interesting from a chemical point of view, and the results obtained by it are very pleasing.

From the *Photographischen Mittheilungen*, for April, 1887, I take the following description of C. Vogel, Jr.'s, modification of Vidal's treatment with platinum: "The advantages of this modification are that the treatment with platinum is made after fixing, in full daylight, and that the tone is warmer.

"After development, fixing, and a twenty minutes' washing, the print is immersed, face down, for fifteen or twenty minutes, in the following bath :

Potassio-platinic chloride, - - -	15 grains.
Distilled water, - - - - -	32 ounces.
Hydrochloric acid (C. P.) - - -	2 drams.

"It is then washed for a short time in a 15 per cent. solution of chloride of copper, which converts the silver in the print into chloride of silver and imparts a warmer tone.

"If the print is too weak after treatment with the chloride of copper, it is redeveloped with ferrous oxalate, and, after a thorough washing, the tone is strengthened by immersion in the cupric chloride bath until the desired strength is secured.

" The print is then fixed in hypo for five minutes to dissolve out the remaining chloride of silver, passed through a five per cent. alum solution acidulated with hydrochloric acid, and washed for twenty minutes.

" Over-exposure is not necessary with this process, and the platinum bath can be used repeatedly by occasionally adding fresh potassio-platinic chloride."

In order to bring the subject of bromide prints down to date, I append the following description of their availability for photo-engraving purposes, taken from the *Photographic Times and American Photographer*, of April 29th, 1887 :

"BROMIDE PRINTS FOR PHOTO-MECHANICAL ENGRAVING."

" There seems to be no end of the practical applications to which bromide paper is suited. While its popularity for contact-printing is steadily increasing, and its use for making portrait-enlargements is growing more universal every day among both professional and amateur photographers, new fields of usefulness are constantly presenting themselves; as the making of quick proofs from wet negatives, and now, by the bleaching process, we shall describe its advantages for the photo-engraver's use. Heretofore red silver prints have alone been at the disposal of the draughtsman. Now, instead of these prints upon which the artist made his outline sketch and from which the photographic half-tones were removed by bleaching preparatory to its reduction to a "black-and-white" negative for photo-relief work, the permanent bromide paper of Eastman is proposed, and it promises to work more satisfactorily than either of its predecessors.

"With it there are many advantages. Ordinary photographs, rendered into lines, are generally enlarged to three or four times the original negative, in order to present in the reproduced cut the drawing of the artist much finer and more delicate than it was on the original. With bromide prints, considerable time is saved by making the magnified positive in one operation. This does away with the making of a glass positive and, from it, the enlarged negative with the repeated focusing, exposing, developing, fixing and consequent printing, which consumes so much time.

"If an ordinary cabinet-size portrait is to be printed in the columns of a newspaper in its original dimensions, the negative or positive must be first considerably magnified before the print can be made in the ordinary way. With bromide paper, under any conditions, it requires but a short time to make an enlarged print, and thus the reduction in time and labor is accomplished.

"The 'A' paper is eminently adapted for work with pen and ink, no technical difficulties having been encountered by those who have tried it. Deep blacks can be piled up with ease, and the finest lines or stipple are at the command of the artist. With permanent bromide paper, although it has to undergo all the manipulations of developing, fixing and washing, the gelatine surface is not removed, and serves, when dry, as a strong sizing. This solidity or hardness is exactly what the arrow-root paper has never been able to give satisfactorily, such prints having been refused repeatedly, as being too soft and spongy for the making of ink lines of excessive sharpness and exactitude. The ordinary printing paper, especially when sensitized with ammonio-nitrate of silver, has always been a source of annoyance to artist, as well as to photographic printer.

"The process of bleaching out bromide prints with a strong alcoholic solution of bi-chloride of mercury is the same as that with other papers, and, provided all hyposulphite of soda has been thoroughly removed, shows as clear whites as are required, from which to copy a black and white negative.

"As regards the positive black tone of a bromide print, objections might be raised as to the difficulty of seeing distinctly enough the black lines or dots made with Indian ink. But to do away with this difficulty is easy enough. In exposure and development, the paper allows so much latitude that a perfectly ashy-grey tone, even in the deepest shadows of the negatives, is at the command of the photographer. If, however, accustomed taste should demand the inevitable red one, this color can also be given to a bromide print, sufficiently bright and intense. The well-known uranium intensifier answers well for this purpose. The well-washed print need only to be soaked for two or three minutes in a one per cent. solution of nitrate of uranium, and, after having been removed from it, a few drops of a two per cent. solution of red prussiate of potash be added, and the print be again submerged in the compound, to at once assume that peculiar reddish-brown tint which results upon negatives from the uranium intensifier. The process is under complete control, a deeper color merely depending upon an increased amount of the red prussiate.

"Uranium-toned prints cannot, however, be well bleached with bi-chloride of mercury, as a yellow tinge, not favorable to the subsequent photographic reproduction, will remain.

"Better results are obtainable with cyanide of potassium. Preparatory to its application the drawing should be immersed in a weak solution of iodine in alcohol for several minutes, and then floated with an alcoholic solution of cyanide, which almost immediately whitens the print.

"This solution may be made by adding as much alcohol to a saturated solution of cyanide in water, as it will take. There is but little taken up by pure alcohol, but in its mixed state with water, strong enough of alcohol not to attack the Indian ink work, there is sufficient strength to reduce color and silver deposit."

GELATINO-CHLORIDE PAPER FOR DEVELOPMENT.

The following method, recommended by Mr. B. J. Edwards, will be found simple, practical, and capable of yielding the finest results:

The Emulsion.

1.—Gelatine,	300 grains.
Cold water,	4 ounces.
2.—Nitrate of silver,	240 grains.
Distilled water,	2 ounces.
3.—Chloride of ammonium,	100 grains.
Water,	4 ounces.

Mix separately. Soak the gelatine for fifteen minutes; then warm all the solutions to about 120 deg. Fahr. Now by yellow light add the silver solution to the gelatine, and then the chloride, adding gradually, with constant stirring. Keep the emulsion at a temperature of 120 deg. Fahr. for an hour, then allow it to set. When set, wash as described above for bromide of silver emulsion. Then melt, add one ounce of alcohol and one-half an ounce of glycerine, and filter. The emulsion is now ready for coating the paper, which is done precisely as in the case of the bromide emulsion, except that ordinary gas or kerosene light may be used.

Development.

Make a stock solution, as follows:

Citric acid,	5 ounces.
Distilled water,	20 ounces.
Strong ammonia,	2 ounces.

Three parts of this, mixed with one part of the ordinary ferrous oxalate developer, form the developer.

With medium exposure this developer will give a rich purple tone. For black tones, give a shorter exposure, and develop with equal parts of the above solution and the ferrous oxalate developer. By decreasing the strength of the developer, any shade of color from black to ruby-red may be obtained. The warmer tones are produced by adding six or eight parts of the citrate of ammonia solution to one part of the ferrous oxalate.

It is well to begin development with a solution weak in ferrous oxalate, adding more if needed.

The fixing is done in the usual hyposulphite of soda bath, 1 to 6.

This method is strongly recommended to amateurs, on account of the great range of beautiful tones which may be given to the prints.

Wellington's Method With Citric Acid.

The Emulsion.

1.—Chloride of sodium,	20 grains.
Bromide of potassium,	40 grains.
Citric acid,	100 grains.
Soft gelatine,	40 grains.
Water,	8 ounces.
2.—Nitrate of silver,	100 grains,
Citric acid,	100 grains.
Water,	8 ounces.

No. 2 is to be added to No. 1 in a fine stream with constant stirring, both solutions having been previously raised to a temperature of 150 deg. Fahr. To the emulsion thus formed, add 200 grains of hard gelatine which has been well swelled in cold water. Stir until the gelatine is dissolved. Then allow the emulsion to set, after which it is to be broken up and washed as usual. The emulsion is now melted, one-half ounce of alcohol and two drams of glycerine added, and the emulsion filtered. Coat the paper as described above.

This emulsion will be found very slow. Twelve to fifteen minutes' exposure to the light of a kerosene lamp will not be excessive with negatives of ordinary density.

The Development.

The following solutions are made up:

1.—Oxalate of potassium,	2 ounces.
Chloride of ammonium.	40 grains.
Water,	20 ounces.

2.—Ferrous sulphate, - - - - 4 drams.
  Citric acid, - - - - 2 drams.
  Water, - - - - - - 20 drams.
3.—Bromide of potassium, - - - 1 ounce.
  Water, - - - - - - 3 ounces.

Mix equal parts of Nos. 1 and 2 and add one dram of No. 3 to each ounce of developer.

The image should appear in about one minute, and with correct exposure, development will be complete in about five minutes.

After development, rinse the prints in three or four changes of water and place in a strong solution of alum for ten minutes. They are again well washed, and toned in the following bath :

Acetate of soda, - - - - 80 grains.
Chloride of gold, - - - - - 1 grain.
Chloride of lime, - - - - 8 grains.
Boiling water, - - - - - 6 ounces.

The bath is ready for use as soon as cold. Leave the prints in this bath until they assume a strong purple tint. Fix for ten minutes in a 1 to 10 solution of hyposulphite. The finished prints will have a beautiful pink tone.

EDER'S METHOD.

The Emulsion..

1.—Gelatine, - - - - 360 grains.
  Chloride of sodium, - - - 108 grains.
  Water, - - - - - 6½ ounces.
2.—Nitrate of silver, - - - - 231 grains.
  Water, - - - - - 3½ ounces.

The gelatine is first swelled and then dissolved in the six and one-half ounces of water, and the chloride of sodium is then added. The nitrate solution is then added gradually to the gelatine solution at a temperature of 104 deg. Fahr. The emulsion is allowed to set, divided up, and washed in the same manner as other emulsions.

It is then melted, ten per cent. of alcohol and glycerine added and then filtered, and the paper coated in the usual manner.

Development is best effected with the citrate of ammonia

and ferrous sulphate solution given below, although the ordinary ferrous oxalate developer will answer.

FERROUS CITRATE DEVELOPER.

A.—*Stock Solution.*

Pour 700 parts of water upon 150 parts of citric acid, and add 160 parts of strong ammonia. Test the solution with litmus paper, and, if not alkaline, add ammonia until it is so. Then add 100 parts additional of citric acid.

B.—*The Developer.*

Sulphate of iron (sat. sol.),	30 parts.
Stock solution,	90 parts.
Chloride of sodium solution (1 to 30)	2 or 3 parts.

The image at first assumes a light yellow tint, which changes to a reddish brown and finally to a deep black. By diluting the developer with 2 or 3 volumes of water, a bright red tone can be obtained.

Fix in a 1-16 hypo solution.

The tone of the prints will be greatly improved if they are toned after fixing in the following bath:

1.—Sulpho-cyanide of ammonium,	308 grains.
Hyposulphite of soda,	30 "
Water,	17¼ ounces.
2.—Chloride of gold,	8 grains.
Water,	17½ ounces.

These solutions are to be mixed before using, adding No. 1 to No. 2. This bath will keep good for a week or more, and may be strengthened by adding fresh gold. The toning must be stopped as soon as the right shade is seen.

As a rule, any of the toning baths given in the chapter on Toning may be used for toning chloride of silver prints, notably the "Chautauqua" bath. It is advisable to harden the film previous to toning by immersing the plate in a solution of alum.

GELATINO-CHLORIDE PRINTING-OUT PAPER.

Paper coated with these emulsions is to be printed in diffused sunlight just as albumen paper is printed. The printing should be deep.

Mr. J. Barker's Method.

Gelatine (hard and soft, equal parts),	175 grains.
Chloride of ammonium,	18 "
Rochelle salts,	50 "
Nitrate of silver,	75 "
Alcohol,	2 drams.
Water,	5 ounces.

By using an orange-yellow bottle, all the following operations can be performed in daylight. Pour the water into the bottle, add the salts and then the gelatine; allow the mixture to stand about fifteen minutes to swell the gelatine, then dissolve at a temperature of 100 deg. Fahr. When the gelatine is dissolved, add the silver, in crystals, all at once, put in the cork, and gently shake the bottle for several minutes. Emulsify at 100 deg. Fahr. for ten minutes, then add the alcohol. The emulsion is now allowed to set, then broken up and washed slightly in two or three changes of water. It is then melted, two drams of glycerine added, the emulsion filtered, and the paper coated by yellow light.

Printing, Toning, and Fixing.

Print slightly darker than required. Chloride prints should not be examined in white light. Yellow light, however, will not injure them. When finished, wash for five minutes in two changes of water, and immerse a few minutes in the following solution:

Sulpho-cyanide of ammonium,	1 ounce.
Water,	20 ounces.

The prints are taken from this bath directly to the toning bath, which may be any of those given in the chapter on Toning. Fix for twenty minutes in a 1 to 16 solution of hyposulphite of soda.

The Collodio-Chloride Process.

Place $123\frac{1}{2}$ grains of nitrate of silver in a glass beaker, pour over it 92 drops of distilled water and dissolve by heat. Drop this solution into a bottle containing 10 drams of alcohol.

Then add 123½ grains of soluble gun cotton, and after thorough shaking, 5⅜ ounces of ether; shake well until a grayish-white collodion forms.

In another bottle dissolve 15½ grains of chloride of lithium, and 15½ grains of tartaric acid, in 10 drams of alcohol. This solution is to be added to the first, drop by drop, with constant stirring. The collodion thus formed will keep indefinitely in a tightly-corked bottle stored in a dark place.

COATING THE PAPER.

Fasten a knob to a piece of thin wood of the same size as the paper to be coated. Enamelled paper is then pinned to this at three of the corners, allowing the paper to project about a quarter of an inch beyond the wood at the right hand and lower edges, which may be turned up a little if desired. Hold the wooden support by the knob in the left hand, and pour the collodio-chloride upon it in sufficient quantity to cover well. After gently rocking for a minute or two, return the surplus collodion to the bottle and hang the paper up to dry. The paper will keep good for some weeks.

If good enamel paper cannot be had, paper coated with the following emulsion will give good results:

1.—Nitrate of barium,	1½ ounces.
Hot water,	10 ounces.
2.—Sulphate of soda,	2 ounces.
Hot water,	10 ounces.

Filter each solution through closely-woven muslin, and then mix them. Allow the white deposit formed to settle; then draw off the water as closely as possible. Add sufficient hot water to fill the vessel, allow the precipitate to settle again, and pour off the clear liquid. Repeat this five or six times, and then make up to 15 fluid ounces with water. Add two ounces of white gelatine and dissolve by gentle heat. Then add one ounce of water in which 15 grains of chrome alum have been dissolved, and lastly, two drams of glacial acetic acid, which must be well stirred in.

The enamel substratum is now ready for applying to the paper, either by floating the paper upon it, or, preferably, by coating the paper with it, as described in the section on bromide paper. The paper must be thoroughly dried before applying the collodion.

Collodio-chloride paper should not be printed as deeply as albumen paper, as the prints lose very little vigor during the subsequent operations. As soon as the deepest shadows just begin to bronze, the prints are removed from the frames and stored in a dry place, protected from air and light. When thus protected, they may be kept for weeks before toning.

Toning.

First wash the prints in three changes of water, face downwards, to avoid spotting of the whites. When the washing is complete they are toned in the following bath:

1.—Sulpho-cyanide of ammonium,	- -	10 drams.
Distilled water,	- - - -	60 ounces.
Hyposulphite of soda,	- - -	9 grains.
2.—Chloride of gold,	- - - -	22 grains.
Water,	- - - - -	60 ounces.

These are stock solutions and will keep.

To make the toning bath, mix No. 1 and No. 2 in equal parts, pouring No. 2 into No. 1, and add a teaspoonful of chalk. The bath should be made up some hours before wanted for use.

The prints are immersed in the bath one at a time. The color will change into yellow, then into brown and purplish-brown. As soon as this color is seen, the prints are placed in the fixing bath: hypo, 1 ounce; water, 12 ounces; 10 minutes' immersion is sufficient to secure perfect fixation. Wash for one or two hours.

The following method will be found the best for trimming the prints preparatory to mounting. The prints are, if dry, soaked in clean cold water until perfectly flat; the trimming glass is laid upon the face of the prints, and both removed from the water. The print is then adjusted on the glass, and its edges cut with a pair of long-bladed shears. By this method of trimming, the delicate surface of the prints will not be injured. The prints should be dried before mounting, which is best done with the following mountant:

Dissolve 2 ounces of gelatine in 10 ounces of water, and pour in one ounce of alcohol, stirring all the time.

In the finished print there is a greater range of gradation than in an albumen print, therefore it is that good collodio-chloride may be printed from even weak negatives.

A very high gloss and neat surface can be given to the prints by drying them on glass. A clean glass plate, quite dry, is powdered over with talc and rubbed off with a pad of cotton wool; then it is dusted. A sufficient quantity of the talc remains to facilitate the separation of the print when dry. The wet print is laid on the glass, face down; it is then rubbed under a few sheets of blotting paper, and lastly with an india rubber squeegee. After the print has become quite dry, it is removed from the glass. From a mat glass it comes off with a mat surface.

Varnish for Collodio-Chloride Prints.

Benzine,	2 pounds.
Para gum,	¼ ounce.
Mastic,	1 ounce.
Canada balsam,	1 ounce.

CHAPTER VIII.

MOUNTING THE PRINTS.

In mounting prints, several important points must be considered. The mount itself is, of course, the most important consideration, as it may contain chemical substances injurious to the permanency of the print, and its color may detract from the beauty of an otherwise charming picture. For both these reasons I would strongly advise the rejection of the plain white mounts so much used. They are very apt to contain injurious chemicals, and they certainly destroy in great degree the pictorial effect of the picture. A white border adds very little to the light and shade of the photograph and diminishes its brilliancy.

Nothing can be better both as a safeguard to permanency and an aid to pictorial effect than a mount of a pale, neutral gray. The color is soft, pleasing, and harmonizes well with the tones of the picture. The tint is alike suitable for exhibition purposes, for framing, or for the formation of albums.

A second consideration is the size of the mount. For most purposes it will be found best to select a mount about half the size of the print larger each way, thus giving a margin of a quarter of an inch on each side. If the photographer's name and the title of the picture are to be written or printed below, it is well to allow one-eighth of an inch more margin at the bottom than at the top.

I know of no better way of placing the print in its proper position on the mount than to rule lines one-quarter of an inch apart on the four sides of a stiff card somewhat larger than the largest mount likely to be used. These lines should be numbered, beginning with the line nearest the centre, and each side of the rectangle formed by any four of these lines must have the same number.

To use this mounting board, the mount is first of all laid down on it in order to determine the number on the lines nearest its edges when the mount is accurately centered. This done, the mount is removed, and the print, which should have previously received a coating of the mounting medium, is placed face down on the mounting-board and centered, using the ruled lines as guides. The mount is now carefully placed over the print with its edges at the lines previously noted as the proper ones, and pressed firmly down upon the print. Now remove the mount, and the print will be found adhering to it in the proper position. All that now remains to be done is to lay a clean piece of blotting paper over the print, and with a roller or the palm of the hand gently remove all air bells or wrinkles. A very effective way of doing this is to polish a piece of very thin brass, of a size corresponding to the size of the mount, with French chalk, and to lay it, polished side down, over the print; inclose the whole in a piece of folded card-board large enough to cover both sides of the mount, and pass the whole through the rollers of a wringing machine tightly screwed down. This will cement the print firmly and smoothly to the mount. Of course, the possession of a burnisher makes this method useless.

Treatment of the Prints.

Before mounting, the prints previously trimmed, should be soaked in clean water until they lie flat; the surface water is then drained away, the prints blotted and laid face down, one upon another on a clean piece of glass. The mounting medium is then evenly and thoroughly applied by means of a stiff, flat brush, or a sponge thrust into the mouth of a wide-mouthed bottle. The prints are now ready to be placed on the mounts.

The Mounting Medium.

Many formulas have been given for making mounting mediums; some of the best of these are here given:

Starch Paste.—Place a large teaspoonful of pure white starch in a cup, with sufficient cold water to cover it. After two or three minutes' soaking, the cup is filled with boiling water and the starch well stirred.

Glue Paste.—Take clean, light glue, and shred it. Soak for five or six hours in enough water to cover it. Then pour off the water, and add fresh. Dissolve by heat. After thinning down to the proper consistency with warm water, it is ready for use.

Gelatine Paste—will not cockle the prints.

Eighty grains of soft gelatine are soaked in 3 drams of water and dissolved by gentle heat; when solution is complete, 2 ounces of alcohol are added. When cool, this sets into a jelly, and can be used by melting it in a water bath.

W. J. STILLMAN'S MOUNTANT.

One ounce of gelatine is soaked for several hours in cold water. The water is then drained off as completely as possible, and the swelled gelatine is placed in a wide-mouthed bottle and the bulk made up to 10 ounces with alcohol; half an ounce of glycerine is then added, and the bottle placed in hot water until solution is effected, the contents of the bottle being occasionally stirred. This mountant will keep indefinitely, and only needs to be heated when wanted for use.

MOUNTING IN OPTICAL CONTACT WITH GLASS.

A method of mounting is now to be described which is remarkable for the softness and brilliancy which it imparts to the prints and for the amount of detail in the shadows which it brings out.

Optical contact is an expression used to denote the close union which takes place between a print and a piece of glass, when the former is squeegeed to the latter.

In the case of bromide or chloride prints nothing further is necessary than to immerse both print and glass in a dish of clean water, the print above the glass. When the former lies perfectly limp and flat, the glass is gently raised by one end and lifted from the dish, carrying the print with its face in contact with the glass. The back of the print is covered with a piece of rubber cloth and the squeegee used to remove possible air bells and wrinkles. Then set aside to dry. The beauty and brilliancy of prints so mounted will be a surprise and delight to those who have never seen them.

When albumen prints are to be mounted in optical contact,

it is necessary to give both the prints and the mounting glass a preliminary treatment with a warm solution of gelatine.

Two ounces of soft gelatine are soaked in cold water until soft; boiling water is then poured on the softened gelatine in sufficient quantity to make a rather thick solution. When the gelatine is all dissolved the solution is filtered through muslin into a clean porcelain or glass tray standing in a hot water bath.

The prints should previously have been trimmed slightly smaller than the glasses on which they are to be mounted, and soaked in cold water. The glasses must be perfectly clean and free from scratches and other markings. Plate or patent plate glass is the best to use.

Take one of the glasses and place it in the warm gelatine solution, leaving it there until it assumes the temperature of the bath.

One of the prints is then taken from the water in which it has been soaking, and placed face down in the gelatine above the glass, allow it to remain in the solution half a minute or so, care being taken that every part of it is saturated with the solution.

The glass is now raised from the bath, carrying the print with it. With a squeegee remove all excess of gelatine, allowing it to run back into the dish. In the same way remove all excess of gelatine from the face of the glass. Lay it aside to set, then with a clean sponge dipped in hot water clean the glass, but do not touch the back of the print. When thoroughly dry, clean the face of the glass, and the mount is finished, unless you wish to protect your print still further from all chances of deterioration by covering the back of the print with a second glass, binding the edge with the material sold for binding lantern slides.

Well-washed prints mounted in this way are as safe from all chances of change as it is possible to make them, I believe, and they are far more beautiful than prints mounted on card-board.

If it is desired to frame prints mounted in this way, take card board of the size and color desired, cut a rectangular opening in the center half an inch smaller than the glass on which the print is mounted. This will allow the glass to overlap the opening a quarter of an inch all around. Lay the glass in position on the back of the card-board and draw a line completely around it. Using this line as a guide, glue strips of cardboard on the back of the mat, thus making a well in which the glass mount will be securely held when the backboard is tacked in.

Mounting on Plate Paper.

The most artistic method of mounting on card or paper is to mount on plain white plate paper, with the plate-mark sunk in, as in the case of engravings.

This style of mounting is especially adapted to bromide or platinotype prints, as it adds very much to their engraving-like appearance.

The directions which follow will enable the operator to mount prints in this way without any great difficulty.

The only novelty about the method is the production of the plate-mark which in large printing establishments is done by means of metal plates and expensive machinery. The amateur, however, can produce as good results with card-board and an ordinary copying press.

To make the plate-mark, procure a piece of thick *hard* card-board, and cut it one inch longer and one and one-half inches wider than the prints to be mounted. Do this neatly and accurately, using a square to get the corners true and square. Round off the corners with a sharp knife. This is the plate used for making the plate-mark.

Mount the print on the paper with one of the gelatine mountants given above. Then lay over the print a piece of glass cut to the size of the card-board plate. Carefully adjust it over the print to leave a margin of one-half an inch on each side of the print, five-eighths of an inch at the top, and seven-eighths at the bottom. Draw a light pencil line around the two upper corners to insure the plate-board being placed in the exact position occupied by the glass. Remove the glass, substitute for it the plate-board, and place under a copying-press with two or three felt pads laid over the mount, and screw down as tightly as possible. Leave the mount under pressure for some time to get a good impression.

PHOTOGRAPHIC PRINTING METHODS. 95

The size and shape of the plate-board may be varied to suit the taste of the operator, giving more or less margin than the one described above. Heavy drawing paper can be used instead of plate paper, and it will be found to give good results.

CHAPTER IX.

CARBON PRINTING.

The name of carbon prints is applied to images produced on a paper coated with a gelatine solution containing a pigment of the desired color, which, after drying, is sensitized in a bath of bichromate of potassium.

Prints in carbon are undoubtedly as permanent as the substratum on which they are made, if refined lamp-black be used; if other pigments are employed, the permanency of the resulting prints depends upon the nature of the pigment.

The possibility of working the process depends upon the fact that the effect of light upon a gelatinous mixture containing bichromate of potassium, is to make those parts affected by it insoluble in water.

If, therefore, paper prepared as above be exposed to light, beneath a negative, and then immersed in hot water, those parts upon which the light has not acted will be dissolved, while the rest will remain attached to the paper.

The prints are produced by single or double transfer; the former, when reversed negatives are used; the latter when ordinary negatives are employed. In both cases the same carbon tissue is used.

The Negatives.

Negatives capable of giving good prints on silver paper will yield satisfactory results on carbon tissues. Thin negatives should be coated on the back with the following mat varnish, which is to be preferred to tissue paper since it allows those parts of the negative which must remain transparent to be cleaned by the local application of mastic varnish with a brush, and also because it gives a good surface for retouching. The formula for the mat varnish is as follows:

Dissolve one dram of powdered sandarac in fourteen drams of ether; add fifteen grains of Canada balsam, and five or six drams of pure benzine, and filter. The varnish is to be flowed over the back of the negative, which is not to be warmed. It will dry within two hours.

The varnish may be tested by spreading a few drops on a piece of cold glass and allowing it to dry. When dry, it should have the appearance of ground glass. If the grain is too fine, add one or two drams of benzine.

If more density is desired, flow the varnish over the negative a second time.

Retouching may be done on this varnish with the stump and plumbago, with a crayon or with a pencil.

REVERSED NEGATIVES.

A method of stripping films from glass for reversed negatives will be found in the Chapter on Photo-Ceramics. Reversed negatives may be easily obtained in the camera by exposing the plate with the glass side towards the lens, making the necessary correction in focusing for the thickness of the glass.

DRYING THE SENSITIZED TISSUE.

The paper may be suspended by means of spring clips at the two upper corners. This method will answer for the smaller sizes, but when large sheets are to be dried it is safer to adopt the following method: A thin piece of wood, one inch wide, is placed across one end of the sensitizing tray, one end of the tissue is raised from the bath, and placed upon the wood; a second strip of the same size is laid upon the paper, and the two strips of wood are fastened together with clips. The paper may now be hung up to dry, without fear of its tearing. To prevent curling of the tissue as it dries, a thin strip of wood to which two clips have been attached, should be clipped to the lower edge of the paper.

The cut will make the description clear.

The drying may be hastened by immersing the sensitized tissue in an alcohol bath, or it may be placed, face down, upon a piece of well-cleaned glass, then covered with rubber cloth and lightly squeegeed; it is then removed from the glass and hung up to dry.

Developing Trays.

When only a few pieces of the tissue are to be developed, the arrangement figured below will be found very convenient. It consists of a table large enough to hold two trays of suitable size, one for hot water and the other for cold. The water is warmed by a small oil stove, not shown in the cut.

For work on a large scale, vertical baths are used, in which many pieces of tissue can be developed together, the pieces of tissue being suspended in the water.

Formulæ.

No. 1.—For Single Transfer.

Hard gelatine,	4 ounces.
Water,	25 ounces.

When dissolved, add seventy-five grains of chrome alum dissolved in five ounces of water, and enough acetic acid to restore fluidity.

No. 2.—For Double Transfer.

Hard gelatine,	4 ounces.
Fine sulphate of baryta,	2 ounces.
Water,	20 ounces.

Mix thoroughly and stir in a solution of twelve and one-half grains of chrome alum in one ounce of water.

To coat the paper, roll it up tightly, face outwards; lay the roll upon the surface of the liquid, seize the loose end, and gradually unroll the paper; then hang up to dry.

PHOTOGRAPHIC PRINTING METHODS. 99

PIGMENT SOLUTIONS.

No. 1.—*The Preliminary Jelly.*

Transparent sheet gelatine,	10 parts.
White sugar,	4 parts.
Water,	25 parts.

Soak the gelatine in water until soft, then gradually raise the temperature until the gelatine is dissolved. Add the sugar, and stir well. When the jelly has set, turn it out of the bowl and cut off the bottom to remove all sediment.

2.—*For Purple Brown Tones.*

Refined lamp-black,	72 grains.
Alizarine lake,	60 grains.
Indigo,	13 grains.

Grind these fine with four ounces of the jelly given in No. 1, and add to six pounds of the same jelly, and mix well.

3.—*Black Tones.*

Jelly,	2 pounds.
Lamp-black,	50 grains.

4.—*Red Tones.*

Jelly,	2 pounds.
Venetian red,	3 ounces.
Indian ink,	8 grains.

5.—*Transparency Tissue.*

Jelly,	2 pounds.
Indian ink,	200 grains.

The tissue compound is to be strained through cambric into a tray standing in hot water. The paper is coated as recommended for the single and double transfers, and then dried.

When dry, the tissue is sensitized by immersion for a brief period in the following solution:

Bichromate of potash,	1¼ ounces.
Ammonia,	1 dram.
Alcohol,	4 ounces.
Water,	30 ounces.

Then suspend to dry in a dark room supplied with a constant current of pure cold air. The drying should take place within 5 or 6 hours, or failure will occur.

PRINTING.

The negative must first receive a "safe edge" in the shape of a quarter-inch edging of black varnish, in order to protect the outside edges of the tissue from the action of light.

Exposure is about twice as rapid as with silver paper, and as the progress of the printing is not visible, a photometer must be employed to determine the proper time of exposure.

The photometer is simply a small box of wood, or other material, having a double cover in which is cut a rectangular opening covered with a piece of glass, painted a dark chocolate color, corresponding to the tint assumed by silver paper after 90 seconds' exposure to sunlight, a narrow slit being left unpainted across the center of the glass.

Between the first and second covers a slip of sensitized silver paper is pressed, one end projecting from a narrow slit cut in one end of the box. The box is placed in a position to receive the same quality of light as that which falls upon the negative.

As soon as the paper, visible through the unpainted portion of the glass, darkens to the color of the painted portion, one tint has been obtained, and the paper is pulled forward until a fresh portion is exposed to the light.

This operation is continued until the print is judged to be sufficiently exposed. A little practice soon enables the printer to determine how many tints each negative requires. Negatives of medium density require an exposure of two or more tints; those covered with tissue paper or mat varnish will need longer exposure.

The number of tints, once found for each negative, should be marked on its back.

DEVELOPMENT.

Carbon prints must be developed from the back of the tissue in order to secure good half-tones. For this purpose the prints are cemented, face down, upon the single or double transfer paper, according as reversed or unreversed negatives were used in printing.

SINGLE TRANSFERS.

For single transfers, the exposed tissue and a piece of single transfer paper, a trifle larger than the plate, are soaked in clean cold water until the tissue lies perfectly flat. The two pieces are now placed face to face, lifted out of the water, placed upon a piece of clean glass, and perfect contact secured by using a squeegee on the back of the tissue previously covered with rubber cloth. The two pieces are then placed for a few minutes between blotters, and then placed in water at 100 deg. Fahr.; in a short time the backing paper of the tissue can be easily removed; gentle washing with hot water will soon dissolve those portions of the print unaltered by the action of light, leaving an image in carbon on the transfer paper, which, after rinsing in cold water, immersion in an alum solution, followed by another rinsing, is ready to be hung up to dry, after which it is ready for mounting.

DOUBLE TRANSFERS.

The double transfer support must be used when the prints have been made from ordinary negatives. For this purpose a piece of double transfer paper, somewhat larger than the print, is coated with a solution of beeswax in turpentine, the wax solution being applied with a piece of flannel and polished with another. It is then immersed in clean cold water with the print, and treated as described for single transfer.

When the development is completed, the tissue is ready to be transferred to its final support, be it card, glass, ivory or porcelain This is done by soaking a piece of double transfer paper, when the prints are to be mounted on cards, in water at about 100 deg. Fahr. Allow it to soak until the surface feels soft and slimy, meanwhile soaking the print on its temporary support in cold water. The two are then brought into contact as before, laid down upon a piece of glass, transfer paper uppermost, and the squeegee applied lightly. The cemented pieces are now hung up to dry, and when quite dry the two papers are separated, the image remaining on the transfer paper. After rinsing, going through the alum bath, again rinsing and drying, the prints are ready for mounting on cards.

If the final support is to be ivory, glass, porcelain, or any other similar substance, both the developed print and the ivory or other substance, are immersed in a warm five-grain solution of gelatine, and squeegeed into contact, excess of gelatine being removed with a damp sponge. The two are then placed to dry between blotters under pressure. When quite dry, the paper is stripped off, leaving the carbon image upon its final support.

Instead of using a piece of waxed transfer paper for the first transfer, some operators prefer to employ a finely mulled zinc plate, waxed and polished as before. The subsequent operations are the same as described above.

The author feels that a word of caution is necessary to those who may try this process. Cases of bichromate poisoning are by no means rare, and the operator should exercise the utmost care in all his manipulations, particularly if he have any cuts or scratches on his hands, in which case it would be better to defer washing the tissue until the cuts are entirely healed. The safest plan is to wear rubber gloves when working with the tissue.

A method for making transparencies in carbon will be described in the chapter devoted to that subject.

Prints made as described above will be either mat or slightly polished. If a high gloss is desired, the print is developed on a piece of glass polished with French chalk and coated with thin, plain collodion, and washed until all traces of greasiness are removed. The exposed tissue is now mounted upon the collodionized glass, a piece of rubber cloth placed over the tissue, and the squeegee applied gently. The subsequent operations are the same as described above.

Carbon Prints from Ordinary Negatives Without Transfer.

The method about to be described gives unreversed positive, from ordinary negatives without single or double transfer. If a piece of exposed carbon tissue be developed on glass it only needs a backing of white paper to bring out the detail, and as the positive is seen through the glass it will be non-reversed although taken from an unreversed negative.

The glass plates on which the tissue is developed are prepared by giving them a thin coating of the following solution:

a.—Gelatine,	· · · · ·	80 grains.
Water,	· · · · ·	5 ounces.
b.—Chrome Alum,	· · · ·	3 grains.
Water,	· · · · ·	1 ounce.

Add *b* to *a* when the gelatine is dissolved.

The piece of exposed tissue is put upon the prepared plate as in the usual transfer method. The tissue is then covered with a piece of rubber cloth and squeegeed into perfect contact; a weight is next placed on the rubber cloth and allowed to act for a few minutes. Development is the same as described above.

FAILURES IN THE CARBON PROCESS.

[From Liesegang's "Le Procédé au Charbon."]

1. The pigmented gelatine dissolves in the bichromate solution. The solution is too warm; it must be cooled by adding ice.

2. The gelatine runs while drying. The drying room or box is too warm.

3. The paper, when dry, is too stiff and refuses to lay smoothly upon the negative. The paper was dried too quickly at too high a temperature.

4. The paper sticks to the negative. Either the paper, the negative, or the padding is moist. If the paper is at fault it must be given a coating of very dilute collodion, and allowed to dry thoroughly.

5. The gelatine refuses to adhere to the glass. Either the paper was allowed to remain too long in the bath of cold water or the bichromate bath has become decomposed through age.

6. The sensitized gelatine becomes insoluble even in darkness. This most commonly happens in hot moist weather. Add one per cent. of carbonate of soda to the bichromate bath and dry the tissue in a current of air.

7. The tissue is not easily detached, or the proof develops poorly, remaining too black. The exposure was too long, or too much time has elapsed between exposure and development.

8. The tissue leaves the support too quickly and the print is weak. Too short exposure; lower the temperature of the developing bath.

9. The edges of the proof adhere to the support. Either the safe edge was neglected, or the gelatine has become decomposed.

10. Dark spots appear on the prints. If they do not disappear in the developing bath, they are caused by insufficient washing of the collodion in cold water.

11. The proofs lack half-tones. Either the paper was dried too quickly, the bichromate bath is too old or weak, or the tissue has been kept too long.

12. The print after being placed on the transfer paper will not leave the glass. The glass was not well waxed, or too much of it was removed in polishing.

13. The print when stripped from the glass is covered with bright spots in the high-lights. The water in which the transfer paper was soaked was too warm or too cold; the gelatine was either dissolved or not sufficiently softened.

14. The print has a coarse-grained appearance. Either the print when on the glass was soaked too long in cold water before transferring to the transfer paper, or the water was too warm, or the print was dried too quickly.

CHAPTER X.

PRINTING ON FABRICS—PRINTING ON LINEN.

SIZING SOLUTION.

Water, - - - - - -	1 ounce.
White glue, - - - - -	2 grains.

SALTING SOLUTION.

Chloride of ammonium, - - - -	2 grains.
Water, - - - - -	1 ounce.

Immerse the linen in the salting solution for one or two minutes. When dry apply the sizing solution to the part to be printed. When again dry, the silver solution, forty-five grains to the ounce, is put on with a tuft of cotton. The linen is then dried and fumed. Printing is done in the usual way, first attaching the cloth to a piece of pasteboard. Toning is done in any good bath, the print is fixed in hypo and well washed, using boiling water for the final washing.

PRINTING ON SILK.

Chloride of ammonium, - - -	100 grains.
Iceland moss, - - - -	60 grains.
Boiling water, - - - - -	20 ounces.

When nearly cold filter and immerse the silk for fifteen minutes. The silk is sensitized by a sixteen minutes' immersion in a twenty-grain silver bath made slightly acid.

When dry, the silk is attached to a piece of card-board, and slightly over-printed. After printing, wash in two or three changes of water, and tone in any good bath. Fix for twenty minutes in a 1 to 4 fixing bath. The after-washing must be thorough.

PLATINUM PROCESS.

The platinum process of Willis can be confidently recommended for obtaining positive prints on various fabrics, using the materials prepared specially for this purpose, not those for contact or solar work. The following description of the process is taken from the Platinotype Company's Manual, and may be implicitly relied on:

The sensitizer consists of a mixture of the platinum and iron solutions.

Two solutions of iron marked A and B are employed. By varying the proportions in which these solutions are mixed different effects may be obtained from the same negative. But it will be found advisable in printing from negatives having the same general characteristics to adhere nearly to one fixed proportion.

The following mixtures are good:

1.—Iron solution A,	- - - - -	1 part.
" " B,	- - - -	3 parts.
2.—Iron solution A,	- - - -	1 part.
" " B,	- - - -	1 part.

1. Gives good half tone and is suitable for brilliant negatives with strong contrasts.

2. Gives less half tone; with negatives thin or weak it gives more brilliant prints than 1.

By increasing the proportions of iron solution A, half tones will be destroyed.

By increasing the proportion of B, half tones will be increased.

It is not advisable to reduce the proportion of A lower than given in formula 1, otherwise there will be a tendency to produce prints with stained or fogged whites.

The mixture of solutions A and B may be preserved in the dark, for future use, in a corked bottle.

The sensitizer is made by mixing—

Solution 1 or 2,	- - - - -	1 part.
Platinum solution,	- - - -	1 part.

This sensitizer should be used within ten minutes of its preparation.

The sensitizing solution is applied to the fabric by means of a small piece of fine sponge until the material is saturated. It is then removed from the glass plate and dried until it is *absolutely* dry.

When dry, the color of the surface should be a pure yellow, sometimes almost orange. If a faint tint of gray should appear, it will usually indicate that too much heat has been used in drying.

The precautions used in the protection of sensitized paper from damp apply equally to fabrics.

Sensitizing should be conducted in a clear yellow light, or by gas or lamp light.

The glass plate and sponge used for sensitizing are readily cleaned by a weak solution of hydrochloric acid. They should be kept free from any trace of old or decomposed sensitizer, otherwise stains will be formed in the print. When sensitizing a large number of pieces of fabric, it is necessary to clean the glass and sponge at intervals during the operation, say between every tenth piece.

When a portion only of a piece of fabric is sensitized, all excess of moisture must be removed from the *edges* of the spot so sensitized; this may be effected by sponging these edges with a drier sponge. If, notwithstanding this treatment, the edges of the spot show stains on development, a larger proportion of the iron solution A should be used in the sensitizer.

It is difficult to estimate the quantity of mixed sensitizer requisite to coat a piece of fabric. With a rather fine kind of linen it is found that each square foot requires a little more than $1\frac{1}{2}$ drams of the sensitizer. Smaller areas of this fabric require a slightly increased proportion of the sensitizer. Thicker fabrics require more sensitizer in proportion to their thickness. Oatmeal-cloth and thick sateen require three or four times as much as linen.

The printing and development of sensitized fabrics are conducted similarly to paper. The developing bath should be very hot; the nearer it is to the boiling point the better. The exposed fabric is first of all floated with its printed surface downwards upon the developer, and it is then immersed in it for at least five seconds. The acid clearing bath is made by mixing 1 part hydrochloric acid with 45 parts water.

With linen and the finer sorts of cotton fabric (Nainsook, for example) no difficulty in working should be experienced, but thicker fabrics, such as jean, sateen, oatmeal-cloth, require very careful management. In drying these thicker materials very great care is requisite to secure perfect desiccation without decomposition. A more gentle heat should be used in these cases. Silks and satins do not, as a rule, answer well, but some of the purer kinds of silk, which have very little "dressing," give good results. The denser kinds of Sarsanet and the soft silks are the best.

The Carbon Process.

Prints may be obtained on fabrics by means of carbon tissue, the fabric forming the final transfer. The method of obtaining the print does not differ from those described in the Chapter on Carbon Prints.

The fabric is coated with the usual solution of insoluble gelatine, and the final transfer made upon it as usual.

CHAPTER XI.

ENLARGEMENTS.

GENERAL DIRECTIONS.

The Negatives.—Negatives for enlargements should not be as intense as those intended for contact printing. Very thin negatives can be employed for enlarging from by flowing over the bath a coating of thin collodion, to which has been added sufficient of a yellow aniline dye to impart a decided tinge.

In all cases the negative should be placed face downwards with the film side towards the paper or glass on which the enlargement is to be made.

The Light.—For enlargements in the solar camera on paper sensitized in the bath, daylight or the electric light must be used. For enlargements not exceeding two or three diameters on bromide paper, opals, or other substances coated with a sensitive emulsion, gas or lamplight may be employed in an enlarging lantern; also the oxy-hydrogen or the lime-light.

Enlargements of greater dimensions are best made by daylight.

THE APPARATUS.

The Solar Camera.—This instrument is so well known that no description of it is needed. The form in general use in America is Woodward's.

Enlarging Camera for Emulsions.—As paper coated with emulsion prints much more rapidly than paper sensitized in the bath, a simpler form of camera can be employed. That given below is the best known to the author. It can also be used for reducing and copying in the same scale as the original.

If the enlargement is to be made on glass or other similar substances coated with emulsion, the plate is placed in the usual plate-holder and the exposure made as in ordinary view work. If, however, paper coated with emulsion be the medium adopted, a film carrier of the usual pattern may be employed or the paper may be smoothly pasted by the edges on a glass plate.

The form of construction of this camera is made apparent by the illustration here shown. The experienced copyist will not need any such simple directions for use as we append.

DIRECTIONS FOR USE.

To copy a negative in the natural size, place it in the kit on the front of camera and button it in. Attached to the center frame of the camera is a division upon which, on the side toward the camera front, a lens is mounted. Suppose this to be a quarter-plate portrait lens, the focal length of which we will suppose to be four inches—draw back the center frame and the lens twice the focal length of the lens (eight inches); slide the back frame with ground glass the same distance from the center frame. To enlarge with the same lens to eight times the size of the original, the center of the lens must be four and a half inches from the negative, and the ground glass be thirty-six inches from the center of the lens. To reduce in the same proportion, reverse and have 36 inches from the center of the lens to the negative, and from the center of lens to ground glass, four and a half inches.

Enlargements with an Ordinary Camera.—If the operator possesses a view or portrait camera of sufficient size and of great focal length, he can, by using a short focus lens, make enlargements in the camera direct from the negative. In this case it is only necessary to place the negative in a window with a piece of ground glass behind it. The camera is supported on a table in such a way as to allow the center of the lens to be opposite the center of the negative. By looking through the ground glass of the camera all the necessary adjustments are easily made.

An Improvised Apparatus.

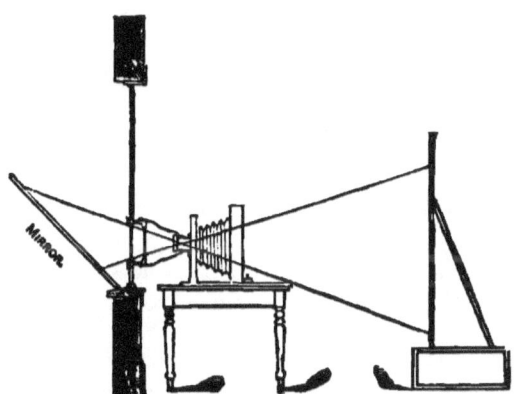

This cut represents an enlarging apparatus that any photographer can improvise from ordinary apparatus and material, with the expenditure of a few hours' time. To construct it proceed as follows:

Cut a hole in the dark-room shutter two sizes larger than the largest negative to be enlarged from; fit into the opening a frame about two or three inches deep, glazed on the outside with a sheet of ground glass. On the inside edges of the frame, top and bottom, arrange grooves in which to slide the negative; when the negative is in position it will be brilliantly illuminated against the ground glass. Now, on a table or shelf, adjusted in front of the negative-box, place an ordinary camera having the ground glass removed, point the lens toward the negative, and connect the lens and negative-box by means of a bag of opaque cloth, open at both ends and provided with elastic bands to close it tight around the lens and negative-box. This will prevent any light coming into the dark-room, except through the lens.

In this apparatus the camera body serves no useful purpose; all that is required is to support the lens. In case a portrait lens is used it should be put in position so that the back lens will be next the negative instead of as shown in the cut.

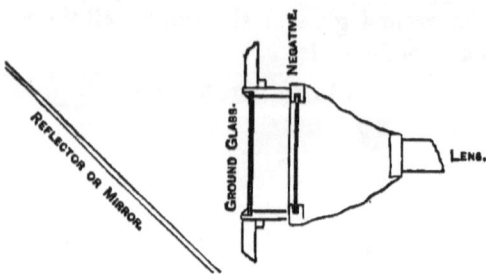

The easel to hold the sensitive paper is the next requisite, and this may be constructed by fastening a large, flat board in an upright position, upon a box of suitable size to serve as a base, so that the whole may be moved to and fro to regulate

THE EASTMAN ENLARGING APPARATUS.

the size of the enlargement. The face of the easel should be covered with white paper. Now, if the easel is put in position, facing the camera, the image can be focused on the screen by sliding the camera backward or forward on the shelf.

While the foregoing directions will enable anyone to construct a practical apparatus for enlarging, many will prefer a

more convenient and finished outfit, and for such the following apparatus has been devised. See the accompanying figures.

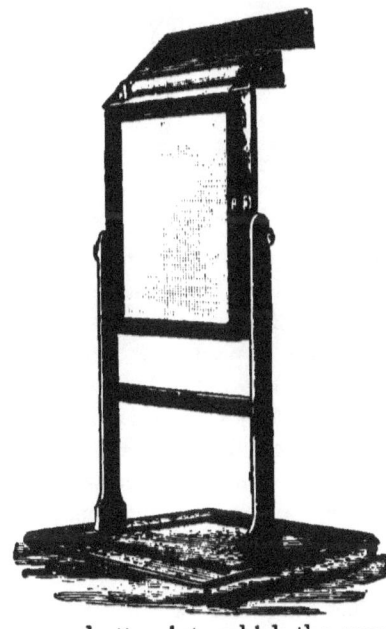

The Camera.—This camera is similar to an ordinary "front focus" view camera, except in the back, which has a fixed ground glass and a carrier for the negative which slides into the camera, inside the ground glass. This carrier is adjustable so that it will take any negative from $3\frac{1}{4} \times 4\frac{1}{4}$ inches, or smaller, up to and including 8 x 10 inches. The camera is built with especial reference to steadiness and is well finished. Provision is made in the back for making a light-tight joint around the opening of the darkroom shutter, into which the camera fits.

The Easel consists of a base, supporting two uprights, in

which slides the exposing screen. On the face of the screen
swings a hinged frame which clamps the sensitive paper flat in
position. The swinging frame is arranged to receive smaller
frames or kits, adapted to clamping any size of paper. On
the top of the screen is a light-tight box, provided with bear-
ings, in which revolves the spool carrying the roll of sensitive
paper. Each box is supplied with a wooden spool, and the
paper is wound for the market upon a strong paper tube, which
slides onto the wooden spool. Thus, a tube carrying any width
of paper, not above the capacity of the easel, can be used with
the same box.

The easel is arranged to slide back and forth on a track laid
on the floor of the dark-room.

The advantages of the specially constructed apparatus, above
described, over anything devised as a makeshift, are almost too

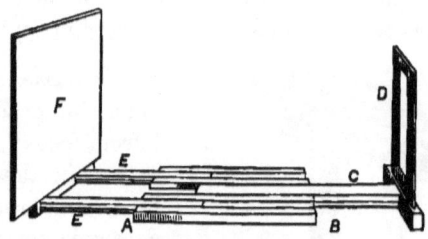

obvious to require enumeration. Although by means of an ex-
temporized apparatus, just as good *quality* of work may be
done, when the operator proposes to adopt the process regularly
in his business, he will find, in using the better apparatus, that
the time saved in adjustment, and the paper saved by using it
in the roll, in which form it is much less liable to accidental
injury, will soon pay for a complete outfit such as described.

I am indebted to the "British Journal Photographic Almanac" for the description of the following easily constructed
and thoroughly efficient enlarging apparatus which may be
used in an ordinary room, and which will answer for daylight
or artificial light:

The baseboard, A B, is two feet long and two inches thick.
Its width will be determined by the width of the easel-board F.
A wide groove is cut in A B, in which slides the thinner three-

inch slab C, which carries the lens-board D. On each side of the center groove two narrower grooves are cut, in which run the two square rods E E, carrying the easel-board F. The size of F will depend on the size of the largest enlargement to be made. The lens-board D is grooved to take the ordinary sliding front used on the camera, and allows the lens to be raised or lowered as required.

All the parts should be accurately and strongly put together. The actual process of enlarging with this apparatus does not differ from that adopted when the regular enlarging camera is used. The room in which the enlargement is to be made must be thoroughly darkened, one window having a wooden shutter

ENLARGING APPARATUS FOR ELECTRIC LIGHT. IN USE IN THE EASTMAN FACTORY.

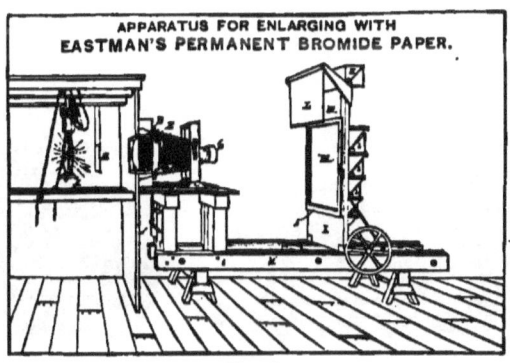

Fig. 6.

in which a hole is cut and a frame made to receive the negative. One end of a hood of black cloth is nailed to this frame, and the other end being fastened to the lens-mount by means of a rubber band. The necessary adjustments are made by drawing out the lens-carrier D, and the easel-board F, to which the paper is fastened with drawing pins.

For enlargements with artificial light it is only necessary to enclose the source of light in a light-tight box provided with suitably protected ventilation holes at the top and bottom, and having an opening provided with a piece of ground glass, in which to place the negative.

Electric Light.—When a large quantity of work is to be

116 PHOTOGRAPHIC PRINTING METHODS.

provided for, the arc electric light is most convenient as it is powerful and (practically) uniform. Any artificial light requires a pair of double condensers, and they should be arranged as in figure 6.

Large condensers, if made of fine glass, are very expensive, but an inferior grade that costs only a moderate sum may be used if a sheet of very fine ground glass be mounted between the convex surfaces of the two lenses.

Enlarging with the Oil Lantern.—For small enlargements a magic lantern burning oil may be used to advantage. One of the most compact and convenient forms of lantern known to the writer is that known as the New York Magic and Enlarging Lantern, figured below.

READY FOR USE.   IN PACKING CASE.

The lantern is very light and compact; no oppressive heat is generated; the condensing lenses are four and five-eighth inches in diameter. There is no loss of light, and altogether it is a very desirable piece of apparatus.

The Lens.—Any lens that will make a negative can be used, and the proper size for the lens depends wholly upon the size of the negatives to be enlarged from. Rapid rectilinear lenses of short focus and large enough to cover the negative will answer every purpose.

Vignetting Enlargements on Opals and Emulsion Papers.—If an apparatus similar to the Eastman is used, the enlargement may be vignetted by constantly moving to and from the lens a piece of pasteboard about 18x22 inches, having a hole of the proper shape cut in the center. The lens should be stopped down to secure long exposure in order to allow the vignetter time to act.

Mounting Enlargements on Cloth.

Cover a canvas stretcher with a piece of common white muslin by stretching it tightly while dry, and tacking it on the outside edges. Give the cloth a coating of starch paste, rubbing it well in and avoiding streaks and lumps. Place a piece of rubber cloth on a smooth table, and on it lay the wet print, face down. Wipe off all excess of water with a squeegee, and then give the back of the print a coat of paste. Now lay the stretcher, face down, upon the print, and rub it into contact, using a thin paper knife under the edges of the frame. Turn the stretcher over, and remove the rubber cloth. When dry, the print will be stretched tightly.

TABLE FOR ENLARGEMENTS.

Copied from the "British Journal Almanac for 1882."

Focus of Lens.	Times of Enlargement and Reduction.							
In.	1 In.	2 In.	3 In.	4 In.	5 In.	6 In.	7 In.	8 In.
2	4 4	6 3	8 2 3/4	10 2 1/2	12 2 2/5	14 2 1/3	16 2 2/7	18 2 1/4
2 1/2	5 5	7 1/2 3 3/4	10 3 1/3	12 1/2 3 1/8	15 3	17 1/2 2 11/12	20 2 6/7	22 1/2 2 13/16
3	6 6	9 4 1/2	12 4	15 3 3/4	18 3 3/5	21 3 1/2	24 3 3/7	27 3 3/8
3 1/2	7 7	10 1/2 5 1/4	14 4 2/3	17 1/2 4 3/4	21 4 1/5	24 1/2 4 1/12	28 4	31 1/2 3 15/16
4	8 8	12 6	16 5 1/4	20 5	24 4 4/5	28 4 2/3	32 4 4/7	36 4 1/2
4 1/2	9 9	13 1/2 6 3/4	18 6	22 1/2 5 5/8	27 5 2/5	31 1/2 5 1/4	36 5 1/7	40 1/2 5 1/16
5	10 10	15 7 1/2	20 6 2/3	25 6 1/4	30 6	35 5 5/6	40 5 5/7	45 5 5/8
5 1/2	11 11	16 1/2 8 1/4	22 7 1/3	27 1/2 6 7/8	33 6 3/5	38 1/2 6 5/12	44 6 2/7	49 1/2 6 3/16
6	12 12	18 9	24 8	30 7 1/2	36 7 1/5	42 7	48 6 6/7	54 6 3/4
7	14 14	21 10 1/2	28 9 1/3	35 8 3/4	42 8 2/5	49 8 1/6	56 8	63 7 7/8
8	16 16	24 12	32 10 2/3	40 10	48 9 3/5	56 9 1/3	64 9 1/7	72 9
9	18 18	27 13 1/2	36 12	45 11 1/4	54 10 4/5	63 10 1/2	72 10 2/7	81 10 1/8

Lento
" "

It is assumed that the photographer knows exactly what the focus of his lens is, and that he is able to measure accurately from its optical center. The use of the table will be seen from the following illustration: A photographer has a *carte* to enlarge to four times its size, and the lens he intends employing is one of six inches equivalent focus. He must, therefore, look for 4 on the upper horizontal line, and for 6 in the first vertical column, and carry his eye to where these two join, which will be at 30—7½. The greater of these is the distance the sensitive plate must be from the center of the lens, and the lesser, the distance of the picture to be copied. To *reduce* a picture any given number of times the same method must be followed, but in this case the greater number will represent the distance between the lens and the picture to be copied; the latter, that between the lens and the sensitive plate. This explanation will be sufficient for every case of enlargement or reduction.

If the focus of the lens be twelve inches, as this number is not in the column of focal lengths, look out for 6 in this column and multiply by 2; and so on with any other numbers.

COPYING CAMERAS.

These cameras are made of hard wood shellacked, not varnished. Naturally, they are without swing, but in every requisite they are complete; and for this particular service, as well as others, the American Optical Company's make is sought for before all others. They are made to order of any length of bed desired, either rigid or detachable, and with either single or double bellows.

FINISHING PERMANENT BROMIDE ENLARGEMENTS.

BY G. HANMER CROUGHTON.

In working upon drawing paper, from life or from photographs, the paper chosen is one that is strongly sized, because a higher degree of finish can be obtained upon such a surface. In the necessary manipulations of preparing the paper for solar prints—the developing and fixing and subsequent washing—the sizing of the paper is entirely washed out; it is so with the platinum print, the hot developer taking the size out of the paper and making it as soft and absorbent as blotting paper. With a permanent bromide print, although it has to undergo all the manipulations of development, fixing and washing, the gelatine surface is not removed, and when dry serves as a strong sizing to the paper. This necessitates a somewhat different method of treatment than upon the softer paper, but all the manipulations for producing an artistic effect upon solar or platinum prints can be followed upon permanent bromide and from my years of experience I can say confidently, that the best results can be obtained quicker and better.

Crayon Finishing.—The only difference is in the material used. Instead of using a stumping sauce alone, I find a mixture of No. 1 Conti Crayon, finely crushed with an equal quantity of crayon sauce, the best for all stumping purposes. Most crayon artists put in their background with a chamois leather. You cannot use a chamois skin upon permanent bromide paper, but a soft tuft of cotton is just as effective and can be manipulated in exactly the same manner; then the fingers can be used as a stump, and the background graded with the above mixture, worked with the fingers quicker and better than with the stump. If you should get your background too dark or uneven, lay the picture flat, sprinkle a little pumice powder over it and rub lightly with the fingers all over, using more powder where you wish your background to be lighter.

The stumping of hair, shadows in drapery, etc., can be done with a paper stump with the mixture above, in exactly the same manner as upon any other paper, with the difference that the print being so much more perfect in gradation and more brilliant than a solar, there is not near so much stumping needed. In fact, a good permanent bromide enlargement needs very little stumping, the principal work being sharpening and deepening with the point, and flat tints with the mixture, over drapery, etc. The shadows of drapery can be deepened with Nos. 2 and 3 Conti, in the usual manner, softening and grading with the finger or stump.

The use of rubber and ink eraser for taking out lights is well known to crayon artists. The same method of taking out the lights can be used on permanent bromide paper and with greater effect, for the lights can be taken out cleaner and with greater facility than upon absorbent paper where the crayon is rubbed right into the fiber of the paper. Another advantage is that you can use the scraper upon these prints for taking out lights and even lightening dark places. With a sharp scraper lights can be taken out in lace, white draperies, etc., giving great brilliancy without abrading the paper, for the picture being entirely upon the surface, you can scrape quite through the deepest tint before reaching the paper itself.

The finishing of the face must be done with a harder crayon

PHOTOGRAPHIC PRINTING METHODS. 121

than usual, as the harder surface of the paper requires a harder crayon to work upon it. The best for the purpose is No. 0 Conti superfine in wood. A No. 1 of the same kind will also be required for the darker touches. This work upon the face is more in the manner of mending and joining gradations than the usual work upon the solar, and it is in this respect that a permanent bromide print is so much superior to any other, and requires so much less work, while the result is much finer.

Pastel.—With the pastel there is no difference in the manipulations, the gelatino-bromide taking pastel with the greatest facility.

Water Color and India Ink.—For water color or ink it will be necessary to wash the surface of the print with a weak solution of ammonia till all the greasiness disappears, and to be careful not to wash one color over another till the first is thoroughly dry, not alone surface-dry, but be careful that the gelatine is dry before washing over the same place, or blisters may result.

Note.—In case any paste has been allowed to get on the face of the print, in mounting, it should be washed off with tepid water and a soft sponge, and the print allowed to dry thoroughly before any crayon work is done on it.

It has been found by experience that prints take the crayon better if they have been dried and afterwards soaked in water before mounting. The preliminary drying hardens the film.

ENLARGEMENTS ON OPAL GLASS.

Very fine results can be obtained by Mr. W. T. Wilkinson's method, the details of which are as follows:

Water,	10 ounces.
Ammonium bromide,	150 grains
Ammonium iodide,	20 grains.
Ammonium chloride,	50 grains.

When the salts are dissolved add sufficient hydrochloric acid to render the solution just acid. Add 100 grains of soft gelatine, and place in a pan of cold water; gradually raise the water in the pan to the boiling point, and when the gelatine is all dissolved, add 450 grains of silver nitrate in crystals, and shake vigorously until all the silver is dissolved. This last addition should of course be made in red or yellow light. Replace the bottle containing the emulsion in the water bath and boil for half an hour. Then add 450 grains of hard gelatine, previously soaked in 5 ounces of cold water, pouring in all the water. As soon as this last addition is dissolved pour the emulsion into a flat porcelain dish or plate, and place in the dark to set.

All the after operations, breaking up, washing, melting, filtering and coating, are the same as described in Chapter VII.

The plate being intended for enlargements can be exposed as soon as set firmly without waiting for them to dry. After exposure, develop with ferrous oxalate, and fix as usual.

For retouching these enlargements, if on ordinary opal glass, a coating of retouching varnish must be applied to give the necessary tooth for working up.

If preferred, the plates may be coated with any of the emulsions given in Chapter VII.

Enlargements on Canvas.

Thoroughly free the canvas from grease by washing it in a dilute solution of carbonate of soda, then rinse and mount on a stretcher. When dry coat with any of the emulsions given in Chapter VII. diluted one-third with water. The emulsion given above for enlargements on opal glass gives exceedingly fine results, but it must be diluted one-third.

To coat the canvas, flow the emulsion over it till it is completely covered, then drain the emulsion away as closely as possible, and hasten the setting by rocking the canvas.

The exposure may be made as soon as the film has set, or the canvas may be left to dry.

After the exposure is made, the canvas is removed from the stretcher, and formed into a tray by turning up the edges and clipping the corners with spring clothes-pins. Develop with ferrous oxalate. Washing and fixing are done by pouring the solutions carefully in and out of the tray, in order not to wet the back of the canvas, which must of course rest upon a board of the proper size.

When fixed, the canvas must be floated face downward for half an hour on frequent changes of water, then floated for thirty minutes upon a saturated solution of alum, again floated upon clean water, fastened to a stretcher and dried. The picture may then be touched up or painted to suit the taste of the operator.

ENLARGEMENTS BY THE POWDER PROCESS.

An enlarged transparency is made, varnished, and retouched with the pencil wherever necessary. A clean glass plate of the same size is polished with French chalk, and coated with plain collodion. When dry, the collodion side is coated with the following:

Dextrine,	1 dram.
White sugar,	1¼ drams.
Bichromate of ammonia,	½ dram.
Water,	3 ounces.
Glycerine,	3 drops.

The plate is now dried in the dark room with gentle heat and exposed, while still warm, under the transparency, about three to ten minutes, according to the light.

After exposure a faint image will be visible; this is developed by dusting on with a fine camel's-hair brush any impalpable powder of the desired color. Ivory-black for black tones; ivory-black, to which a little Indian red has been added, for warm tones.

When fully developed, the image is covered with plain collodion and placed in a dish filled with water, slightly acidulated with sulphuric acid. As soon as the water ceases to be tinged with yellow, the plate is dried, and, when dried, transferred as in the case of carbon prints, to double transfer paper, which forms the final support of the print.

ENLARGEMENTS ON CANVAS IN THE SOLAR CAMERA.

Preparation of the Canvas—Mr. Vidal's Method.—Painter's canvas is rubbed with fine emery and alcohol until perfectly smooth; then rubbed with alcohol until only a thin coating of paint remains on the canvas. This rubbing is to be done in circles beginning at the center, and care must be taken not to lay the canvas bare. The canvas is then well washed in water and then coated evenly with a paste, made of kaolin and alcohol. This coating is allowed to dry hard, and the stretcher well shaken to remove all superfluous kaolin. The canvas is then salted and sensitized with any of the baths in common use. After the operations of toning, fixing, washing, and drying, the canvas is given a coating of megilp, and is then ready for the painter.

ENLARGEMENTS IN THE SOLAR CAMERA BY DEVELOPMENT.

Fully printed enlargements can be obtained in the solar camera, but with intense negatives the printing is very much prolonged. In this case the development method may be adopted. In this method the partially printed paper is developed to obtain detail and density. Mr. A. Hesler's method, as given in "Wilson's Photographics," is a good one to follow.

Salting Solution for Plain Paper.

Skim milk,	½ gallon.
Acetic acid, No. 8,	3 ounces.

Stir the mixture well, and place it in a porcelain dish; gradually bring it to the boiling point, constantly stirring. The curd is then strained through muslin, and the resulting serum, when cold, is filtered until clear. To each ounce of this is then added—

Iodide of potassium,	16 grains.
Bromide of potassium,	4 grains.

The paper is floated on this salting solution until it lays smooth, avoiding air bubbles. The paper is then dried with moderate heat, and sensitized by floating two minutes on the following

Sensitizing Bath.

Nitrate of silver,	640 grains.
Water,	16 ounces.
Acetic acid,	2 ounces.

The paper is exposed while damp in the solar camera, and printed to a depth corresponding to the intensity of the negative. An intense negative requires printing until the detail is well out, and the resulting print is developed with a weak developer. Thin negatives do not need to show any details in the print which must be developed with a strong developer.

The following solution gives a developer of medium strength:

Development.

Pyrogallic acid,	- - - -	90 grains.
Water,	- - - - -	32 ounces.
Acetic acid,	- - - - -	2½ ounces.
Citric acid (saturated solution), -	-	10 drops.

For prints from hard negatives use less pyro; more for prints from weak negatives. To develop, lay the print face up on a piece of board or glass covered with a piece of white blottingpaper. With one sweep of the hand pour on enough of the developer to cover the print completely. If stains or fog occur, either the print is overtimed or light struck. If it develops slowly and stains from this cause, add more citric acid. When the development is complete, wash the print in clean water and fix in the usual hypo bath. Retouching and finishing in colors are done to suit the taste of the artist.

PLATINUM ENLARGEMENT IN THE SOLAR CAMERA.

The following details of the platinum enlargement process are taken from the Platinotype Company's Manual.

The sensitizer is made by dissolving forty grains of the solar platinum (black label), and one ounce of the solar iron solution (black label). The platinum salt will dissolve quickly by shaking it in a bottle containing the iron. The solution should be used within fifteen minutes.

Three and one-half drams of the sensitizer will cover a 25 x 30 sheet. Other sizes require a proportionate amount of sensitizer.

The paper should be placed on a plate of glass and held in its position by clips.

The sensitizer should then be applied to the sheet by a tuft of cotton, in as even a manner as possible. This operation requires care. It is better to begin at one end of the sheet, putting a little of the sensitizer on at a time, and gradually work down to to the end. It is well to perform the operation rather quickly to prevent the uneven soaking in . of the sensitizer.

When the sheet of paper has been sensitized it should be allowed to become surface dry and then be perfectly dried before a fire or stove, or in a hot cupboard. Great care must be taken to dry the paper thoroughly, but without scorching it.

Five minutes will be sufficient time to allow the paper to become surface dry before the final drying takes place.

For solar work the endless roll rough paper is generally used, it being the best for crayons and pastels; but for water colors and ink pictures a thinner kind is preferred. Thin papers are not larger than 18x22. In using the thin paper for copies, unsized paper will answer, and solar materials can be used with it, but for very delicate work the specially sized paper and *contact materials* should be used.

PRINTING.

Negatives to be printed in the solar camera should be of the density of *thin contact negatives*. Gelatine negatives give grayish prints. Very thin negatives give flat prints, and dense ones hard prints without detail. Sometimes it is better when printing from dense negatives, to use less platinum in the sensitizer—25 grains to the ounce of iron instead of 40 grains—so also is the opposite correct when printing from thin negatives—50 grains will be better than 40 grains.

DEVELOPMENT.

To develop large solar prints, a V-shaped trough should be used. A sufficient quantity of developer is heated in this trough by a row of small gas jets placed underneath, or by any other convenient device. The temperature of the solution must not be less than 170 deg. Fahr.

The print is developed by being slowly and steadily drawn through the liquid at the bottom of the trough. It is held under the surface of the liquid by a heavy glass rod. This glass rod revolves as the print is drawn under it. To perform this operation with ease it is better for two persons to be engaged about it. One should hold the lower edge of the print, dip it into the trough, then place the glass rod over it and begin to pull through slowly and steadily, the other person holding the upper edge, lowers the sheet easily in a corresponding manner.

The developer is made by dissolving 5 ounces neutral oxalate potash in 16 ounces water.

It frequently happens that the oxalate potash, such as is usually sold as "Neutral" will, on testing, show a strong alkaline reaction. In such cases the addition of a few drops of saturated solution of oxalic acid will bring it all right. But care must be taken to avoid making the developer too acid, as it will have a tendency to make the prints appear very black and white, and much of the fine detail in the high-lights will be destroyed. A slightly acid solution will be found the best.

Clearing and Washing

After the print is pulled through the developer it should go *at once* to the acid solution. This solution is made by mixing 4 ounces C. P. muriatic acid in a two-gallon pail full of water.

Always use three acid baths, but the third need not be more than half the strength. Clearing takes five minutes for each bath.

Washing takes three or four rinsings of about five minutes each. The prints can then be hung up to dry.

It is of the utmost importance to clear the prints well, using plenty of acid solution and turning the prints constantly.

Yellowing of the prints comes principally from imperfect clearing and washing, and also from an excessively alkaline developing solution. For further instruction on Clearing and Washing see the Chapter on Platinotype.

Precautions Against Damp.

To secure the most brilliant results the sensitized paper *before*, *during* and *after* its exposure to light, should be kept as dry as possible.

It is of the first importance that the printing frames and pads be quite dry. Between the sensitized paper and the pads a thin sheet of vulcanized india-rubber may be placed with great advantage.

The effect of damp is seen in a want of vigor, a general muddiness of tone, and where the sensitized paper has been exposed to its influence for some days, in the impaired purity of the whites. Paper in a damp state takes much longer to print than dry paper.

During the making of solar prints the paper can be kept dry by oil lamps, or by a row of gas jets placed at the bottom of the plan board, but this is only necessary during damp, or hot-damp weather. Remember that keeping the paper dry during printing will effect great saving of time in the exposure.

ENLARGEMENTS FROM ENLARGED NEGATIVES.

An enlarged positive is first made in the copying camera, and developed, fixed, and washed as usual. The positive is then retouched if necessary, and a negative taken from it either by contact or in the copying camera. After being touched up, prints are taken from the negative in the usual way. The advantage of this process is that a double touching up of weak places is possible, and that the printing from the enlarged negative is more rapid than printing in the solar camera.

CARBON ENLARGEMENTS.

Carbon tissue of the required size may be used for enlargements taken in the solar camera, or by printing under an enlarged negative. The development and subsequent manipulations do not differ from those described in the Chapter on Carbon Printing.

Mr. Wm. H. Sherman gives in the "British Journal Photographic Annual" for 1887, the following description of a method of working which may be new to some: "Gelatine, refined lamp-black, bichromate of potassium, and water, are mixed in suitable proportions" (any of the pigments given in the Chapter on Carbon Printing can be employed). "The vessel containing these ingredients is placed in a water bath, and heated until complete admixture and the requisite degree of fluidity are obtained. It is then applied to the drawing paper upon which the picture is to be finished, in the form of fine spray by means of an air blast from a cylinder charged with compressed air." (For experimental work an ordinary spray bottle of large size will answer very well). "On this mode of applying the pigment the success of the whole operation depends. The coating thus applied is granular in form, which permits the light to penetrate it to such an extent that the middle tints are saved from being washed away in the development, thereby evading the necessity of a double transfer.

"The pigment dries rapidly, when it is ready to be exposed to the image of the solar camera, and the requisite exposure is only about one-tenth to one-fifth of that required for silver paper.

"The picture is developed by washing off the soluble portions of the pigment in hot water. For this purpose the print is wetted and placed in an upright position on a stretcher covered with muslin; the water, under considerable pressure, is showered upon it through a rose connected by a short hose to a double faucet supplying it with hot and cold water. Finally the print is washed to remove the little remaining chromium salt from the paper, and the print, when dry, is ready to be mounted."

ENLARGEMENTS BY THE COLLODION TRANSFER PROCESS.

This is the method by which most of the cheap enlargements are produced. The following description is condensed from that given in the ninth edition of Hardwich.

THE EXPOSING APPARATUS.

This consists of a base made of two parallel pine boards rigidly fastened together; a frame having a square opening and fitted with kits to take negatives of varying sizes, fixed at one end of the base boards; a solid slab of wood of a size corresponding to the dimensions of the largest enlargement likely to be made, rigidly fastened near the other end of the base, and provided near its bottom with two projecting pins to support the plate during exposure, and a lens board sliding on the base between the two end pieces. Coarse adjustment is effected by sliding the lens board back and forth on the base, the final focusing being done by the rack and pinion on the lens.

The apparatus is placed with the board carrying the negative pointing upwards through a window towards a part of the sky free from obstructions, care being taken to exclude all white light save that which passes through the lens. A plate of glass of the same size as the proposed enlargement is covered with white paper and placed in position on the end board to serve as a focusing screen. All the adjustments effected, the focusing screen is removed, the collodionized plate put in its place and the exposure made.

THE COLLODION.

To twenty-five ounces of plain collodion containing about seven or eight grains of pyroxyline to the ounce. the following bromo-iodizer is added:

Iodide of cadmium,	65 grains.
" ammonium,	25 grains.
Bromide of cadmium,	19 grains.
" ammonium,	11 grains.
Alcohol,	5 ounces.

To which has been added enough of an alcoholic solution of iodine to impart a deep sherry color.

The silver bath must not exceed twenty grains to the ounce.

THE DEVELOPER.

Pyrogallic acid,	100 grains.
Citric acid,	60 grains.
Acetic acid,	2 ounces.
Water,	20 ounces.

The development must not be carried too far or a heavy smudgy picture will result.

Fix in a saturated solution of hyposulpnite of soda.

THE TRANSFER.

The transfer paper may be made by sponging plain white paper with a warm solution of gelatine and water, 1 to 5, to which, after the gelatine has been soaked for half an hour and dissolved, four grains of chrome alum dissolved in a little water, have been added.

To make the transfer, a sheet of the gelatinized paper is soaked in water until it feels slimy, and then laid down upon the wet collodion, contact being secured by lightly squeegeeing. The glass and paper are then set aside to dry, when the collodion film can be stript from the glass. The picture can then be finished in oil if desired.

THE PHOTO-CRAYON PROCESS.

This process, while similar to that just described, is simpler, and gives more artistic results. The photo-crayon remains upon the glass, which to insure adherence of the film, should be sponged over with dilute albumen, the white of one egg to a quart of water, before collodionizing.

The operations of exposing, developing, and fixing are the same as described in the last process. The picture must, however, be vignetted by inserting a piece of card-board, having a suitable opening, between the lens and the sensitive plate.

To improve the tone it is well to flow over the surface of the developed image a weak solution of chloride of gold or chloride of platinum.

A sheet of drawing paper is placed behind the enlarged transparency in close contact with the film side. The picture now has the appearance of having been drawn on the paper. This effect is heightened by sketching upon the drawing paper a few sketchy, crayon-like line, surrounding and merging into the vignetting of the bust.

CHAPTER XII.

TRANSPARENCIES AND LANTERN SLIDES.

THERE can be no doubt about the superiority of a transparency from a negative over a positive on paper of the same subject. The transparency possesses greater apparent solidity, truer perspective, and greater perfection of detail. Then, too, there can be no doubt about the greater permanency of prints on glass. The glass positive is also more easily and quickly produced than the print on paper.

The favorite processes for this class of work are the following: The carbon process, albumen, collodio-chloride, wet collodion, gelatino-bromide.

The order of this classification is given by Mr. Ellerslie Wallace as representing the comparative values of these processes for the manufacture of lantern slides.

For the production of window transparencies, however, the gelatino-bromide process will with care yield results which will satisfy the most critical. Full details for making the different emulsions mentioned above will be given later.

The following instructions for the production of transparencies for the window, taken from Mr. W. I. Lincoln Adams' article on that subject in the "American Annual of Photography for 1887," will be found complete and satisfactory, being from the pen of an expert:

"In my own practice, I use the slowest obtainable emulsion of a well-known brand of dry plates, and select as my negatives for this purpose, those possessing the greatest technical merit, other things being equal, and of slightly denser films perhaps, than are required for making good silver prints. The printing may be done by any actinic light that is not too powerful in its action. Diffused sunlight, gas or petroleum light are most generally employed for this purpose, but to avoid confusion, it is well to use always the same light, and of the same intensity.

"When taking up a new negative, whose printing qualities are unknown, I first determine the correct time for exposure by printing a portion of it upon a smaller plate. I can then proceed with certainty, and make any number of positives, all of which will possess the same amount of density and detail, and be uniform in all their other qualities. If the small plate be under or over-exposed, little more is lost than the time used in developing it, and this slight loss is more than compensated for by the knowledge gained.

"Printing a negative upon a plate large enough to leave a liberal margin gives effect to the finished transparency, when it is framed with a ground glass having a fancy etched border. When printing upon plates of the same size as the negative, it is always best to employ a mat of black needle paper, or some other thin, non-actinic substance, in order to obtain straight margins on the finished glass positive. Use a deep printing frame, and in it, a plain clean glass as a support. First place in the frame the glass, and upon it the mat; then, facing upwards, the negative, carefully adjusted upon the mat, and upon this, film side down, the sensitive plate. It is always well to place on the back of the plate a dark pad which not only holds the plates well together, but also prevents any reflection that might otherwise occur.

"Before developing, immerse the plate in pure water for a few moments, and brush its film carefully with a camel's-hair brush to rid it of any air bubbles that may be adhering to its surface. He who makes transparencies must be more than usually careful in all the details of manipulation. He must have his trays and utensils perfectly clean, and his hands free from the slightest trace of hyposulphite of soda or other chemicals. With the neutral oxalate of potash and iron developer, the merest hint of the presence of hypo will cause a disagreeable black stain which is not easily removed. A hyposulphite of soda solution in the proportion of one part hypo to 5,000 parts water is used as an accelerator in oxalate development, so it is not difficult to see how a drop of a strong solution of hypo from the finger or tray, coming into contact with the film, suddenly develops the place where it touches into a dense black spot. Defects of different kinds in a negative can often be overcome in printing, but a blemish on a glass positive is one on the finished product. Let the beginner therefore bear this in mind when making transparencies, and be, accordingly, extremely careful in every respect.

"There are several developers published, more or less highly recommended for transparencies, any one of which, carefully followed, will undoubtedly produce fine results, but my own is a very simple one, and easy to manage. I make saturated solutions of neutral oxalate of potash and protosulphate of iron, and acidify the former solution with citric acid, and the latter with sulphuric acid. The oxalate dissolves at the usual temperature of water in a dark room (about 70 deg. Fahr.), in the proportion of one part oxalate to three parts water, and, being neutral, requires but a few grains of the citric acid to slowly turn blue litmus paper red. Six parts of protosulphate of iron will dissolve in ten parts water, and the whole may be rendered acid by several drops of strong sulphuric acid.

"To start development, I use a solution composed of six parts of the oxalate solution to one part of the iron, and afterward, if necessary, I add a few drops of a ten per cent. solution of bromide of potassium. It is best to develop slowly.

"The fixing must be thorough. The rule often given to beginners for determining when a plate is fixed is by no means a safe one. The plate must remain in the hyposulphite of soda some time after all the milky-white appearance has gone from the back. After the visible bromide of silver has been reduced, there yet remains a double salt, which, though invisible, is sensitive to light, and, if left in the film, will discolor it. This double salt is soluble in hyposulphite of soda; so, if the plate be left long enough in the fixing bath, it will dissolve out of the film. A very excellent way to accomplish the thorough fixing of a plate is to employ two hypo baths. Immerse in the first solution until all the visible bromide of silver has been reduced, and then put the plate into the second and fresh hypo bath to dissolve the invisible double salt. Ten minutes will ordinarily suffice to accomplish this.

"A good strength for the hypo solution is

Hyposulphite of soda,	4 ounces.
Water,	20 ounces.

"After the fixing is completed, the plate must be washed for a few minutes, in running water, if possible, before immersing in the clearing bath. I use the formula given by Mr. Carbutt for this purpose, and allow the plate to remain in the solution about one minute.

"The formula is as follows:

Water,	20 ounces.
Pulverized alum,	1¼ ounce.
Sulphuric acid,	¼ ounce.

"The plate is now ready for its final washing. If running water is not to be had, by means of two bent wires a support

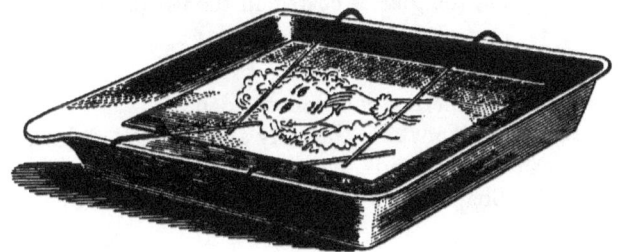

can be made in a tray, as shown in the cut, which will allow of the plates being washed, film side down.

"But if this is done, the water must be changed every ten or fifteen minutes until the washing is complete, which will require about one hour. Before setting in a rack to dry, it is well to go over the surface of the transparency with a soft camel's-hair brush while the water is flowing over it. This removes any little specks or particles that might otherwise dry on the film. When dry, the back of the plate can be easily and effectively cleaned by a tuft of cotton moistened with weak ammonia.

"There are several ways for mounting transparencies, but undoubtedly the finest effect is obtained by framing them with etched ground glass in the neat nickel frames provided by the dealers. The ground glass is placed against the transparency, rough side to the film, and the two plates secured in the frame."

Plain white glass coated with the following emulsion will

produce a ground glass effect with finer grain than can be found in most ground glass.

1.—Water,   100 parts.
   Gelatine,   5 parts.
   Chloride of barium,   6 parts.
2.—Water,   100 parts.
   Sulphate of soda,   15 parts.
   Gelatine,   5 parts.

When these solutions are mixed, a white emulsion of sulphate of baryta is formed. When set, the emulsion is broken up and washed for some time in running water, to remove the bye-product, chloride of sodium. The emulsion is then melted and filtered, and the glasses coated in the usual way.

The Carbon Process.

The following method is recommended :

The formula for making the jelly and a detailed description of the sensitizing mixture, exposure and development will be found in the Chapter on Carbon Printing, and need not be repeated here.

Any color of tissue may be used, but preference is to be given to black or purple. For black tissue nothing is better than the following :

Jelly,   8 ounces.
Indian ink,   50 grains.

The paper is coated with this mixture, dried, and sensitized by immersion for three minutes in a 1 to 20 bichromate of potash bath. It is then placed on a piece of clean glass, and the superfluous moisture swept off with a squeegee, and hung up to dry in a room heated if necessary, to about 60 deg. Fahr.

As soon as dry, cut the tissue down to the required size and keep in a dark place. The tissue should be exposed soon after drying. The printing is done as for carbon prints, using a safe edge. One or two tints of the actinometer will indicate sufficient exposure in most cases.

Development is the same as given in the Chapter on Carbon Printing, using for support old quarter-plate negative glasses most thoroughly cleaned.

The glass must be coated with a very weak solution of gelatine, containing one grain of chrome alum to the ounce; the coating is easily and quickly done by taking the glasses from the rinsing water when washing, and flowing over them enough of the gelatine solution to cover them well; this displaces the surface moisture and is to be followed by a second flowing. The glasses are then racked away to dry in a room free from dust.

The exposed pieces of tissue are cemented to the gelatinized glasses in the usual manner, and development proceeded with. The gelatinized glass plates form the permanent support. Any degree of intensity or change in tone may be obtained by using a weak solution of permanganate of potash or any of the aniline dyes.

As soon as dry, the transparencies are ready for mounting, and, if all the operations have been carefully and intelligently performed, they will be found to excel in clearness, delicacy, and gradation.

ALBUMEN METHOD.

To prepare the albumen, the whites of several eggs are separated from the yolks, all the germs removed, and to every ounce of albumen two grains of iodide of potassium are added. As soon as the iodide is dissolved, beat the albumen to a froth, and set aside for several hours to settle. Then decant the clear portion. If the decanted liquid is bright and clear, it is ready for use; but if any particles are seen, it must be filtered until clear, by pouring it upon a tuft of damp cotton placed in a glass funnel.

Coating the Plates.—The plates are well cleaned, levelled, and given a thin coating of the albumen, and allowed to dry.

To Sensitize the Plates.—Sensitizing is done by yellow light, by immersing the plates for 30 seconds in a dipping-bath filled with the following solution:

Nitrate of silver,	80 grains.
Glacial acetic acid,	80 drops.
Water,	1 ounce.

After sensitizing, the plates are washed to remove the free nitrate of silver, and set aside to dry. They will keep good for several days.

Exposure.—Full exposure must be given to avoid cold tones; 6 to 8 minutes in the shade under a negative of medium density; but it is well to use the actinometer described in the Chapter on Carbon Printing.

Development.—Development is effected by pouring the following solutions on the plate, placed on a levelling stand or in a glass dish.

1.—Pyrogallic acid,	2 grains.
Citric acid,	3 grains.
Water,	1 ounce.
2.—Nitrate of silver,	20 grains.
Citric acid,	60 grains.
Water,	1 ounce.

Begin development with No. 1, adding a few drops of No. 2, now and then, as required. Properly exposed and developed, detail and density will be obtained together.

Fixing and Toning.—The plate is fixed in a 1 to 5 hyposulphite of soda solution. After a most thorough washing, it is toned in a saturated solution of bichloride of mercury. The plate is left in this solution until completely whitened. It is then thoroughly washed and immersed in a solution of ammonia (ammonia, 20 drops; water, 1 ounce), until, by transmitted light, the tone is a rich sepia brown. It is then removed, thoroughly washed, and set aside to dry.

THE COLLODIO-CHLORIDE PROCESS.

The method of working this process has already been given under the title Collodio-Chloride Paper in Chapter VII.

For transparencies the same method is to be employed, substituting glass for paper, and omitting the enamel substratum. For flowing the glass, a pneumatic holder will be found a necessity.

THE GELATINO-BROMIDE PROCESS.

The formula and details given for making gelatino-bromide emulsion in Chapter VII. will be found to give the best results.

THE GELATINO-CHLORIDE PROCESS.

All necessary formulæ and directions for working this process have already been given in Chapter VII.

PHOTOGRAPHIC PRINTING METHODS.   139

A few additional developers are here given for the development methods.

No. 1.—For Warm Tones.

Citrate of potassium,	136 grains.
Oxalate of potassium,	44 grains.
Hot water,	1 ounce.

No. 2.—For Cold Tones.

Citric acid,	120 grains.
Carbonate of ammonia,	88 grains.
Cold water,	1 ounce.

To three parts of either of these add one part of the following at the time of using:

Sulphate of iron,	140 grains.
Sulphuric acid,	1 drop.
Water,	1 ounce.

Levy's Collodion Emulsion.

Before the advent of bromo-gelatine plates, Levy's emulsion was considered by many the best, both for negative and positive work. Although in great measure superseded by the more rapid gelatine process, its many good qualities should preserve it from oblivion. For lantern slides it is particularly valuable, as there is no deposit in the high lights, the details in the shadows are perfect, and the tone of the slide is all that can be desired.

The detailed description is as follows :
For 54 ounces of emulsion,

1.—Bromide of cadmium,	648 grains.
Alcohol (absolute),	18 ounces.
Iodide of ammonium,	162 grains.
Cotton (cream),	486 grains.
Ether,	27 ounces.
2.—Nitrate of silver,	900 grains.
Distilled water,	360 drops.
Alcohol,	9 ounces.
Nitric acid,	270 drops.

Pour No. 1 into No. 2 and leave exactly ten hours, then add 99 grains of green chloride of copper.

Method of Making the Emulsion.—Place the bromide of cadmium in a porcelain capsule and dry by gentle heat. It will first soften and boil, and care must be taken that the bubbles in breaking do not throw out any of the salt. Stir gently with a glass rod to prevent the bromide from adhering to the sides of the capsule. Continue the boiling until the bromide assumes the form of a fine powder. This is to be most carefully scraped out of the capsule, and dissolved in one-half of the given quantity of alcohol, shaking the bottle until solution is complete. The iodide of ammonium, which should be of a light yellow color, is now added and dissolved. Then add the cotton and shake well; lastly, add the ether and shake again.

Now put the nitrate of silver into a second bottle and add the water by actual drops, not measuring it. To effect solution put the bottle into a warm water bath until the crystals are dissolved; then add the remaining $13\frac{1}{2}$ ounces of alcohol and the acid. The alcohol may precipitate the silver, but this does not affect the quality of the emulsion.

All the above operations may be performed in full daylight; the remaining manipulations must, however, be carried out by yellow light.

The silver solution, after vigorous shaking, is added to the collodion, half an ounce at a time, shaking well after each addition. When all the silver solution is added, place the bath in a dark room for exactly ten hours, shaking it occasionally. Then add the chloride of copper, which must have been dried in a porcelain capsule by gentle heat until it assumes a brownish color; the chloride must be weighed after it is dried to insure accuracy in the weight. The bottle is well shaken after the addition of the chloride, and the emulsion after filtration through cotton is finished.

Coating the Plates.—Put the plate on a pneumatic holder held in the left hand, pour the emulsion on the plate with the right. Rock gently a few times and drain off the surplus into the bottle. When the film has well set, rinse in cold distilled water until the repellant action due to the alcohol and ether disappears.

The plate is then well drained, placed on the pneumatic holder and a sufficient quantity of the following preservative flowed over it for a minute:

Tincture nux vomica,	100 drams.
Tincture scilla,	42 drams.
Tincture cochineal,	120 drams.
Honey,	20 ounces.
Acetic acid,	20 drams.

The plates are now dried, exposed under the negatives and developed with the following developer:

Carbonate of soda,	1 ounce.
Bromide of ammonium,	80 grains.
Honey,	1 dram.
Pyro,	20 grains.
Water,	16 ounces.

Development is best effected by pouring the developer on and off the plate.

For over-exposure, dilute the developer with water. For under-exposure, double the strength of the developer.

LANTERN SLIDES ON WET PLATES.

Mr. E. P. Griswold recommends the following method:

The Silver Bath.—Forty grains of silver nitrate to the ounce of water, acidified with nitric acid.

The Collodion.—Any good make well ripened, with the addition of one drop of glacial acetic acid to each ounce.

The Developer.

Water,	64 ounces.
Double sulphate of iron and ammonia,	4 ounces.
Acetic acid No. 8,	4 ounces.
Rock candy,	1 ounce.

The Toning Bath.

Saturated solution of bichloride of mercury,	16 ounces.
Bichloride of palladium (liq.),	15 grains.

To Collodionize the Plate.—Take the pneumatic holder, with the glass attached, in the left hand; with the right hand pour on sufficient of the collodion to cover two-thirds of the glass; rock gently and allow the surplus to drain back into the bottle from the right-hand lower corner of the plate. As soon as the film has become tacky, put the plate on the dipper (an instrument used for lowering the plate into the sensitizing bath), keeping it in a horizontal position in order that the film may dry evenly before it is immersed in the bath.

Sensitizing.—The sensitizing solution is kept in the vertical glass dipping bath. Into this the plate is slowly lowered without any stoppage, and allowed to remain until the film appears smooth and free from greasiness. It is then ready for exposure.

Development.—The above developer is reduced with pure water about one-third and is then poured completely over the film. The plate is gently rocked to prevent the developer from collecting in pools, and the development continued until the details are just defined. Then wash well and tone to the required density. Again wash and fix in hypo. After fixing, the plate is allowed to soak in a saturated solution of chloride of barium until the next plate is ready for the same bath. This process gives very brilliant transparencies and slides. The following very complete description of the production of glass positives on "gelatino-albumen plates" is by Mr. John Carbutt, and, therefore, possesses exceptional value:

TRANSPARENCIES AND HOW TO MAKE THEM.

There are various methods and processes for making transparencies, many of which have passed into history.

At the present time two processes are in common use in America, viz., the old wet collodion process, and the new gelatine dry plates; the first is limited in use by those making lantern slides mainly for advertising purposes, while the new gelatine dry plate, of the special kind made for producing transparencies, known as Carbutt's Gelatino-albumen Plate, is universally used by amateurs and the professional portrait and landscape photographer; and it is in the use of these plates we now proceed to describe how to produce from your negative what is conceded the finest positive obtainable.

The requisites for contact printing are a deep printing framé, a size larger than the negative to be used, with a flat glass bottom free from scratches; crystal plate is best; some thin red enamelled label paper for masks, a Carbutt "Multum in Parvo" Lantern, or other artificial light, and transparency plates of suitable size. Those for lantern slides are made on thin crystal glass of the now accepted standard size, 3¼x4 inches. For the larger size transparencies they are now made on fine ground glass, which has the advantage over the clear glass since the image is rendered in its right position, when made by contact with the negative, just as a silver print would be, the obscured side of the glass being back of the image, it only remains to cover it with a clear cover-glass and mount in a suitable sized metal frame sold for that purpose. The transparency need not be confined to the size of the negative; the image can be enlarged or reduced to suit taste and circumstances; nor is it absolutely necessary, for the purpose of enlarging or reducing the image, that a camera for that purpose be provided, if the use of a small room can be commanded, and the light shut out all but one light in the lower sash. Over this light must be placed, and covering the entire surface, a light of fine ground glass which will give an even diffused light, passing through the negative; beneath this a support for the negative should be placed. The same camera and lens, used for making the negative, can be used for making the transparency, providing the image is to be *reduced* in size, and the negative can be held upright in one of the plate-holders, removing the septum and dark-slides and placing the holder with the negative on the support before the light passing through the ground glass. The camera itself may be supported on a board, raised to such a height that the lens will center with the center of the negative, care being taken in adjusting it that the side of the camera and the face of the plate-holder, holding the negative, forms a perfect right angle. If it is desirable to make an enlarged transparency, say from a 4x5 or 5x8 negative to an 8x10 plate, the same camera and lens may be used, but the ground glass of the camera must be removed, allowing the magnified image to pass *through* the camera onto the sensitive plate, supported in an upright position at the distance found to be correct. To ascertain this, the camera with its lens should slide easily between two strips, for unless your camera is provided with a front rack movement, you will have to move the camera, and with it the lens to obtain a focus, using a light of glass on which is stretched a piece of white paper to obtain a focus, and placed against a support on the board carrying the camera, and at right angles with the base of it. This is supposing you are working in a room in which *all* light, except that passing through the negative, is excluded. Before placing the negative in the holder or support, if it is desirable to have a margin on the transparency, cut out a mask from the thin red enamelled paper or tin-foil, and place on the face of the negative, being careful to see that the margin shows equally around the large plate or focusing screen.

Now, while the above description will enable any one to produce enlarged or reduced transparencies from their negatives, it is but a makeshift, and will be found to entail great loss of time and uncertainty in working, all of which can be avoided by using a properly constructed camera, such as that made by the Scovill Manufacturing Co.* The writer of this article has had one in use for years. The end holding the negative has adjustments for centering the image, and the extended range of adjustment of the lens enables a lantern transparency to be made from an 8x10 negative, or vice versa, an 8x10 transparency from a $3\tfrac{1}{4}$x$4\tfrac{1}{4}$, or other intermediate size negatives.

Having explained the tools required, we will now proceed with describing the chemicals required and the making of the transparencies.

Of chemicals the following will be required:

Neutral oxalate of potash,	1 pound.
Sulphate of iron,	1 pound.
Hyposulphite of soda,	5 pounds.
Alum,	1 pound.
Citric acid,	$\tfrac{1}{4}$ pound.
Liquor ammonia,	4 ounces.
Plain collodion varnish,	8 ounces.

Too much stress cannot be laid on procuring chemicals of the greatest purity, and known to be made for use in photography; especially is it necessary that the first two articles named should be pure. Many have been disappointed in their efforts at transparency making by applying to the country druggist for oxalate of potash, and have been supplied with bin-oxalate of potash. Be careful, therefore, to procure the chemicals from a reliable dealer in photographic materials. In compounding the solutions, first prepare, by a thorough cleansing, suitable sized bottles. For the bulky solutions, nothing is

---

* Described in the Chapter on Enlargements.

better than the ordinary glass preserve jar, and for labels, a safe plan is to cut from the circular accompanying the plates you are to use, the formulas, and paste them on the glass jar to contain the solution it describes. Next in importance is the water, clear soft river or spring water, melted ice or distilled, as most convenient, but not hard water containing lime in solution.

We will now describe a very excellent plan we have used for years in dissolving large crystals that does away with the use of a pestal and mortar. For the A solution of the following formulas, choose a half gallon glass preserve jar, and for the B solution a quart jar. Measure into each one the quantity of water required, except that in the B solution a few ounces of the water may be reserved until after solution of the iron salt and then added. To dissolve the salts so as to need no after-filtering, take a common domestic salt bag, wash it to free from salt; in this place the crystals and suspend it in the water so that the bulk of the salt is just covered by the water. Immediately a stream of denser liquid will be seen falling to the bottom of the jar, much in appearance as when pouring glycerine into water; this will continue until the whole of the salts are dissolved and a clear solution is obtained. Remove the bag, give the bottle a shake, and the solution is ready. The same method is to be employed in dissolving the iron and hyposulphite of soda, using a separate bag for each one, and completing one before commencing the another. Having everything ready, carefully weigh out by avoirdupois weight the chemicals, and make solutions as per following formula:

CARBUTT'S IMPROVED DEVELOPER FOR TRANSPARENCIES.

A.—Oxalate of potash, - - - - 8 ounces.
    Water, - - - - - 30 ounces.
    Citric acid, - - - - - 60 grains.
    Citrate of ammonia solution, - - 2 ounces.
B.—Sulphate of iron, - - - - 4 ounces.
    Water, - - - - - 32 ounces.
    Sulphuric acid, - - - - 8 drops.

C.—*Citrate of Ammonia Solution.*—Dissolve 1 ounce citric acid in 5 ounces distilled water, add liquor ammonia until a slip of litmus paper just loses the red color, then add water to make the whole measure 8 ounces.

Developer.—Add 1 ounce of B to 2 ounces of A, and half an ounce of water, and 3 to 6 drops bromide solution.

In the making of transparencies, the first requisite is a good negative, and every effort and care should be taken when producing it, to insure perfect freedom from imperfections. The second requisite is a suitable artificial light for use when making exposures by contact. The third requisite is suitable sized developing dishes; these should be of porcelain or enamelled iron ware, and cannot be used with the pyro· developer without risk of staining the transparencies, as we use for them the ferrous-oxalate developer only. Having now provided ourselves with the necessary requisites for the work, we will proceed with the making of transparencies, beginning with the popular lantern slide. We now place our negative glass in contact with the glass in a deep printing frame; a suitable size is $6\frac{1}{2}\times8\frac{1}{2}$, then it answers for 5x8 and under. Over this place one of Carbutt's thin crystal transparency plates, so as to cover the portion of the negative desired. Lay a piece of dark felt or other soft material over it, close down the back, and expose from ten to fifteen seconds to the light of a two-inch wick oil lamp. Remove the plate from the frame and cover with the developer. If correctly timed, the image should appear slowly, taking two or three minutes to complete. Allow the development to continue until the blacks look quite strong, and detail plainly shows in the high-lights to allow for reduction of intensity in the fixing bath. Wash off the developer, and immerse in a fresh solution of the hyposulphite of soda (pyro developed negatives should not be fixed in same solution) made by dissolving eight ounces of the salt in forty ounces of water, in the same manner as directed for dissolving the iron salt. Let the transparency remain in the fixing bath three to five minutes. After the white bromide seems cleared from the plate, wash for half an hour in running water, then immerse for five minutes in the

HARDENING SOLUTION.

Water,	36 ounces.
Pulverized alum,	3 ounces.
Citric acid,	¼ ounce.

Afterwards wash for twenty minutes to half an hour, then carefully go over the surface with a tuft of absorbent cotton, while water is running over it; give a final rinse, and place in drying rack to dry spontaneously, then varnish with plain collodion.

COLLODION VARNISH.

Alcohol,	4 ounces.
Pyroxyline,	30 to 40 grains.
Sulphuric ether,	4 ounces.

When, after shaking, the cotton is dissolved, filter and flow the plain collodion over the dry transparency, the same as when using varnish; then dry, cover with mat and a crystal cover-glass, and bind with binding strip.

Transparencies for window and door decoration should be made on plates somewhat larger than the negative, so that a suitable margin may surround the image. To do this, cut a mask with rectangular or other opening out of thin red enamelled paper. For an 8x10 transparency from a $6\frac{1}{2}$x$8\frac{1}{2}$ negative, take a piece of the mask paper 9x11 with two sides cut to right angles; make a line with a pencil and ruler $1\frac{1}{4}$ inches from two sides; from the side line measure $5\frac{1}{4}$ inches, and from the cross line measure $7\frac{1}{4}$ inches; cut on these lines with a sharp knife through the paper laid on glass or zinc, and remove the blank; make a X mark on left upper corner, to denote register corner; place this mask in a 10x12 deep printing frame, let it register close to the left-hand upper corner; lay the negative film side up and under the mask; adjust the negative so as to show in proper position through the opening; over this place a Carbutt A transparency plate 8x10, letting it register in the same corner as the mask; lay over a pad of black canton flannel, close the printing frame; expose to the lamp or gaslight ten to fifteen seconds or more, according to density of negative. Develop as directed for lantern slides, and in every other respect proceed the same.

The tone, both of lantern and large transparencies, can be varied from a warm brown to a velvety black. Increased exposure and weaker developer (adding water) with more bromide gives warm brown tones. Short exposure and stronger (undiluted) developer gives dark tones.

Coloring Lantern Slides.

In order to give greater value and completeness to this chapter, directions for coloring lantern slides are given below. The method is that given by Mr. A. W. Scott in the "British Journal of Photography," and the description is substantially the same as given in Nos. 297 to 300 of the "Photographic Times and American Photographer," a few minor changes having been made in the phraseology to adapt the description to its insertion here.

Mr. Scott advises learners never to do their work after dusk, since it rarely occurs that portraits and landscapes which are colored by the yellow light of an oil lamp, or gas jet, look quite natural when viewed by the whiter light of day. The limelight, which is used in all the best optical lanterns, produces an illumination very similar to ordinary daylight, and slides which have been colored in the day time may be safely relied upon to look equally well upon the screen, provided that the proper colors and varnishes have been used. Slides painted after dusk usually have the warm colors greatly in excess; in fact, the colors when seen by the light of the lamp seem totally different when compared with their aspect in daylight.

However, there are subjects to which the slight errors in tint produced by painting in artificial light will not prove detrimental. These are chromotropes and color patterns generally, also comic slips and other subjects whose exaggeration of color and form are permissible. If hand paintings were being attempted, there can be no objection to preparing outlines, and all similar work in black and white, including blocking out views of statuary, etc., by gas or lamp-light.

The ordinary retouching easel will answer well to hold the plate to be colored firmly and comfortably for the artist; and the light, be it artificial or daylight, may be regulated as the retoucher regulates his. As all colors have to be viewed by transmitted light, before applying them to the plate, a piece of white opal glass does well for a palette; while for brushes, the round-flat sable kind, of about an inch in length, is preferred. Most suitable are those known as water color sables; oil color sables being too stiff for transparency work; and, as the oil colors used are made more fluid than is usual for canvas work, softer brushes are preferable.

The colors may be either water colors or oil paints; but as the latter are better adapted for the work we give them first consideration. The list of oil colors for canvas work, sold by artist color men, is a long one. Most of these colors, however, are useless for slides, owing to their opacity; if used, they will not allow light to pass through them, and hence instead of color, black darkness would be the effect upon the screen.

Oil paints specially prepared for slides are sold in the shops, but do not in reality offer any difference or improvement when compared with the ordinary colors, which are sold in small collapsible tubes for the use of the artist.

Blue pigments
- Prusian D
- French ultramarine
- Indigo D
- Antwerp blue

Green pigments   Verdigris

Yellow pigments
- Italian pink D
- Yellow lake D
- Gamboge

Brown pigments
- Burnt sienna D
- Burnt umber D
- Caledonian brown
- Asphaltum D

Red pigments
- Crimson lake D
- Madder lake
- Rose maddder

Black pigments
- Ivory-black D
- Lamp-black D
- Blue-black D

D signifies that these colors, being of good body, can be *dabbed;* the others are useful for brush work only.

Prussian blue is of great depth of color. It is invaluable for skies and flat tints generally.

French ultramarine is a purer blue than Prussian blue, which has a tendency towards a greenish tint. A good effect is obtained by the union of this color with some of the crimson. For greens, made by mixing blue and yellow, Prussian blue is best.

Verdigris is a very useful color for brush work. It is bright and transparent, and when a little Italian pink is added, forms a brighter green for tinting foliage than the one obtained by mixing yellow lake with Prusian blue. As green shrubbery and foliage usually appear very dark in photographs, it is necessary in such cases to use the brightest tints available in order to produce any effect of color on the screen.

Italian pink is the most useful yellow, is very transparent, and forms a good green with Prusian blue, and a good scarlet with crimson lake. It is very slow in drying, and should, therefore, be mixed with a quick drying varnish.

Yellow lake not being perfectly transparent, appears darker on the screen than the above, producing more of a brownish effect; but is quicker in drying.

Gamboge is perfectly transparent, but so thin as to be nearly useless for slides. When laid on thick it produces an orange tint, and is useful for giving the effect of gold. It dries but slowly.

Burnt sienna is a brown pigment; it is of good body, and dabs easily. With Prussian blue it forms a sober olive-green; and supplies, with crimson, a good color for tiles or brick work. Not being perfectly transparent, it appears darker on the screen, for which allowance must be made.

Burnt umber has a more sober hue; but it has a good intensity, dabs well, and dries quickly. It is not perfectly transparent.

Caledonian brown is more yellow in tone than the two preceding, dries quickly, but being of less intensity is used only to a limited extent.

Crimson lake is the most useful red tint. It possesses but moderate intensity, so that pale tints can be produced by dabbing. It is not perfectly transparent, and always appears darker on the screen than on the slide. Frequently a very transparent crimson for brush work may be obtained by diluting the pigment with turpentine, so as to be of a creamy consistency, and then allowing it to stand quietly for a little while. Usually a part of the color settles to the bottom first, and when this occurs the upper part should be carefully poured off. The color that has settled will be found to be nearly opaque, while the other portion is clear and transparent. If left for hours to settle, nearly all the color will be precipitated, leaving the turpentine nearly colorless; some of the latter can be removed, a little mastic varnish may be added, and it will then be ready for use. If a little Italian pink is mixed with it, a bright scarlet is obtained.

Madder lake and rose madder being nearly identical in character, may be classed together. They are perfectly transparent, and appear as bright pinks and crimsons on the screen. Possessing but little intensity, they are useless for dabbing, and require piling up on the slide to approach deep tints. Gamboge and Italian pink are sometimes added to enrich their color. Being very slow dryers, they should always be mixed with a quick drying varnish.

Ivory-black, lamp-black and blue-black have characteristics in common; they are all capable of being dabbed, and dry quickly. When diluted with varnish, they form good grays, and when mixed with the other pigments previously mentioned, a great variety of sober tints can be obtained.

The brilliancy of the colors depends largely upon the mediums employed. The oils (nut, linseed and poppy) should be avoided, as they tend to lower the transparency of the colors. The three mediums recommended by Mr. Scott are mastic varnish, japanner's gold size, and the well-known Robinson's medium, sold in large collapsible tubes. The turpentine used to thin the colors, should be of the best quality, but for the cleansing of brushes, etc., the common turpentine will answer. No oil color will answer without the addition of one or other of the three mediums mentioned; a very little is, however, sufficient to insure transparency in the colors. For dabbing purposes it is not necessary to render the paint fluid with turpentine, but for brush work the color should always be thinned to a creamy consistency, so that the tint may be swum on to the glass. This fluidity of the color will allow the streaks produced by the hairs of the brush to quickly subside to a level surface, so as to give an even layer of paint. Japanner's gold size, being of a yellow tint, should only be used for warm tints. It is used for laying the larger washes of paint in brush work, and for mixing with pigments which of themselves are naturally slow in drying. Mastic varnish and gold size are quick in drying, and hence should be used for the first washes of color, which have to be worked upon afterwards with extra touches.

When Prussian blue is used to produce smooth tints, such as skies, etc., a little of Robinson's medium should be mixed with it, which will materially assist the dabbing process. The same addition may be made to burnt sienna and burnt umber for flat tints. If these mixtures are thinned with turpentine to a creamy consistence, they are fit for brush work, which can also be dabbed when required, after the turpentine has evaporated from the paint.

When crimson lake, yellow lake, or Italian pink are used to produce flat tints by dabbing, a very little mastic varnish should be added, the quick drying property of which takes away the oiliness of the color, and hence renders it easier to produce an even tint.

Dabbing.—The greatest difficulty the beginner experiences is the laying of even tints of color, free from brush marks, spots, or other irregularities. The remarkable magnifying power possessed by the optical lantern renders it necessary for a sky tint, for instance, to be as smooth on the slide as to compare with stained glass. This evenness is produced by a special operation known as dabbing, of which frequent mention has been made in the preceding paragraphs.

The dabbing process can be applied only to colors which possess considerable intensity, so that an extremely thin layer of the paint will suffice. The color has to be of a certain consistency, about that of a stiff paste. This condition may be produced by adding a little of Robinson's medium to colors which have great intensity of tint, and a very little mastic varnish to the weaker colors, which have more oil in their composition. The pigment, having been mixed with a suitable medium, a little of it is put on the slide, and is then spread about and rendered even by the action of the dabber. There are several kinds of dabbers; one method requires a large, round camel's-hair brush, with the hair cut off in the middle of their length, so that they terminate in a flat surface instead of a point. The brush is then used to stipple the paint with, not by stroking, but with an up and down action.

Another dabber, and a better one, consists of a short stick, the end of which is formed into a miniature cushion by a thin, smooth piece of leather, or part of an old kid glove, being tied on, with a little cotton-wool within. A very small dabber of this description is handy to use for working the tint close up to an outline. But the cleanest and most useful dabber is one supplied to most persons by nature, one that is not likely to wear out or get mislaid, namely, the finger-end. Nothing can exceed the evenness of tint which a practiced hand can produce by lightly tapping the paint on the glass he is working on, which gradually renders the color even and smooth.

The finger to be selected is that which has the smoothest skin; generally, the third finger of the right hand is the best. The skin has always a kind of furrowed surface, and some artists, hence, rub the end of the finger lightly on a piece of smooth sand-paper, by which some of the roughness is removed. This cure of the furrows is very temporary; nature, in a day or two, indignant at this treatment of the cuticle, will retort by growing a skin thicker and rougher than at first, so it is better for beginners to use their dabbers as they find them.

The marks caused by the furrows can easily be obliterated by going over the paint again with an extremely light and gentle tapping action of the finger, the position of the hand being altered from time to time, so that one set of furrow-marks shall cross another. In this process, practice is the best teacher.

The condition of the surface which is to be dabbed upon should be observed when mixing up the tint. If the clear unvarnished glass is being worked upon, the paint should not be very stiff, otherwise it will be apt to leave bare spaces in the tint, caused by the color not adhering properly to the glass. In such a case, a little of Robinson's medium should be added to soften the color. If the glass is varnished, as most photographic slides are, the paint may be stiffer, as it holds better to the varnish, and it is then usually easier to make the tint smooth; hence, it is best to varnish all glasses before the dabbing process is commenced. A film of negative varnish is generally easy to work upon; however, there are some varnishes, containing Canada balsam and resin, which become soft and sticky when oil-colors are applied on the film; such a sample should be rejected for this purpose, as it will be impossible to produce a good, even tint, by dabbing.

When the photograph to be colored is made by the gelatino-bromide or chloride process, it is not necessary to varnish when oil colors are used. The gelatine forms an excellent surface to work upon free from scratches. If there are any abrasions of the film, it is then advisable to apply a coat of negative varnish, which will fill up these depressions and give a smooth, even surface. In the case of water colors, on these plates it is, of course, absolutely necessary to varnish.

Painting Skies.—In tinting a landscape, the first thing to do, according to Mr. Scott, is to tint the sky. Prussian blue is always used for the blue skies; when applied to the glass it is rendered smooth and even by dabbing. Crimson lake and Italian blue are used for sunsets, the different colors being gradually merged into one another by the finger alone. Having by this means produced a uniform or graduated tint it is usual to introduce clouds. The white cumulus clouds are the easiest. A stick, the size of a penholder, is cut to a tapering wedge-shape at one end; over this wedge-point is stretched a piece of soft, clean wash-leather, about four or six inches square, the loose ends of the leather being gathered together and held by the fingers. With this single stump the paint can be wiped off where required, leaving a sharp, clean edge for the upper part of the cloud; the lower portion of the cumulus is softened into the sky tint by dabbing. When the stump becomes charged with paint at the end, the leather is moved so as to bring a clean portion of it to the wedge-point.

The fleecy cirrus clouds may be made by the stump, with clean leather over it, being used as a dabber, so as to slightly disturb and remove the sky tint in some places. Long, thin streaks of white cloud are produced by the wedge-stump without any leather covering, being gently tapped over the sky tint, so as to displace the color and leave irregular white lines, which may be softened slightly by dabbing it afterwards with a corner of the leather. In making the sky, it is usual to carry the color temporarily over objects in the foreground—hence the wedge-stump is again required to remove the surplus paint from church steeples, roofs, etc., and the horizon generally. Clouds, which are darker than the sky itself, are usually put on with the brush after the dabbed tint has become dry; this is a difficult operation, as it is very easy to ruin a sky in this way, so beginners are recommended to attempt only the lighter clouds in their first essays.

Moonlight scenes are produced in a similar manner—the blue tint is made darker by the addition of lamp-black or burnt umber; a trace of gold size should be mixed with the colors to assist in dabbing deep tints. The moon is made by scraping away the paint with a wedge-pointed stick of boxwood; sometimes a sharp knife is used, in which case it is usual to cut through both the paint and the underlying varnish.

Water Colors.—There are some dissolving-view artists of good repute who use only water colors in their pictures. This method is more difficult for a beginner to learn, especially in the case of the sky tints. The list of colors available is nearly the same as the list of oil paints; thus Prussian blue, indigo, gallstone, gamboge, brown pink, Italian pink, burnt sienna, burnt umber, sepia, bistre, crimson lake, carmine, and lamp-black, is a fair list of the most transparent water colors, which should be of the "moist" variety, sold in small porcelain cups.

The mediums used to mix these colors with are pure water, ox-gall, and occasionally gum arabic and glycerine. The method of dabbing water colors is similar to that of oil paints; if the color (which is sometimes easier to work with by the addition of a trace of ox-gall and glycerine) becomes too dry, it may be softened by breathing gently on it. In order to allow the tints to take nicely to the glass, it is usual to rub the surface over with a little ox-gall, to remove all greasiness.

Water colors are not so safe to use as the oils, so far as permanence is concerned. In some instances the colors have been found to have run together when slides were exposed to the great heat of a powerful lantern, after having been stored in a damp place; in other cases the heat has caused the color to contract and shell off the glass in places. With regard to the dust which after a time is often found to have settled on the colors, it is usually a risky matter to remove it with a linen cloth in the case of a slide tinted with water colors; an operation of this kind may spoil the picture, as the cloth is liable to produce streaks and lines of an undesirable character in the view.

The crimson lake and carmine water colors, as they are sold, are not very transparent; the beginner, therefore, is often at a loss when he desires a brilliant crimson or scarlet color, as the addition of ox-gall or gum arabic does not increase the transparency much.

The moist color is taken from the porcelain cup and mixed with a few drops of glycerine; a little ox-gall is also added, and the whole intimately mingled together into a pasty mass with the aid of heat and a few drops of water. The mixture is then put into the metal dish or saucer and gradually heated. The water will soon be expelled by the heat, and when steam ceases to rise the heat should be increased, care, however, being taken not to burn the pigment. The color of the pigment, viewed by reflected light as it lies in bulk in the dish, is a brick red up to this point; but at a certain heat this color will suddenly change to black. This blackness is due to the crimson becoming transparent, on the same principle that a stained ruby glass looks black when placed on a dark surface. The color may then be allowed to cool, and will be found quite bright and transparent. The color may be thinned with water, and if it shows any tendency to return to its original semi-opaque condition when on the slide, it is only necessary to make the glass pretty hot after the painting is finished, so as to restore the transparency of the crimson, which may be rendered quite permanent by a little touch of mastic varnish, to prevent the color again attracting moisture. The ox-gall is added in order to stiffen the pigment; if it were not used the glycerine, which is the real agent in rendering the carmine transparent, would keep it in a pasty condition, owing to its peculiar non-evaporating nature.

The addition of a trace of glycerine to other colors will tend to prevent cracking and shelling off of the pigment when on the glass. The tints may be made of a better consistency for brush work by being mixed with ox-gall and a solution of gum arabic. The ox-gall sold by the artists' material dealers is rather expensive if used in quantity; it is supplied in little white pots in a stiff pasty condition, but is easily softened by warmth. A cheaper plan is to get some liquid ox-gall from the butchers' and boil it down to a proper consistency, but it is not a very pleasant operation, owing to its messiness and odorousness.

If gum arabic is used to mix the colors with, a little lump sugar should be added to the solution, as it will then be less liable to chip off the glass when dry.

Aniline Colors.—The thought has doubtless occurred to many persons who have observed the brilliant tints of stuffs dyed with aniline crystals, whether these could not be employed for coloring transparencies. There are many difficulties in the way, but it is quite possible to use these colors and produce effective and artistic slides with them.

There is a remarkable property which is possessed by some of the aniline colors, namely, that of changing tint according to the acidity or alkalinity of the mixture. Thus the addition of a drop of ammonia may change a deep scarlet or crimson to a pale yellow, or *vice versa.* Supposing a picture colored with aniline tints was exposed successively to the fumes of ammonia and nitric acid, a great change would probably be perceived in some of the colors. This is one of the drawbacks of the process.

The brilliancy of aniline colors exceeds that of most oil and water colors. The former can be made perfectly transparent, which is not usually the case with the two latter; hence, for chromatropes and other subjects where brilliancy of tint is of importance, they are well adapted. Flat tints produced by dabbing can be made with them as easily as with oil colors; the warmer aniline colors especially compare favorably for such work with the corresponding tints in oils.

Ordinary water colors can be easily used in conjunction with the aniline tints—for instance, a Prussian blue sky tint may be merged by dabbing into an aniline orange color near the horizon. Oil colors can also be used after the aniline tints are laid on. This method is likely to preserve the aniline colors in their original condition by protecting them from the atmosphere and moisture. A sky may be commenced with aniline colors, and when dry another layer of colors in oil may be dabbed on without much fear of disturbing the underlying tints. This method is occasionally useful for producing cloud and sunset effects.

Let us take one of the packets of aniline dyes labelled "blue"; we find that it contains a powder which will easily dissolve in cold water, and possesses considerable intensity of tint. A little ox-gall or gum arabic added will make it a very useful color for slide work; it is used just as Prussian blue is in water color. It has complete transparency, and the tone inclines slightly to purple.

Another packet labelled "scarlet," contains a powder also soluble in water. It is an expensive dye, and the penny packet contains a very small quantity, which is, however, sufficient for several slides. It may be treated in the same way as the aniline blue. This color being one of those liable to change according to its acidity, or otherwise, it is advisable to varnish the tint, after drying it thoroughly by warmth, with mastic varnish, to secure it from atmospheric influences. This remark applies to nearly all the aniline tints. The scarlet is a very bright and transparent color, and can be dabbed for sunset effects, etc.

The packet labelled "yellow" is of a warm yellow tint, and can be treated as the above, being a water color. These aniline water colors are preferable to the spirit colors in that they are less liable to change. The above will not lose their transparency, but may possibly change color if unvarnished.

Spirit colors embrace most of the other dyes not previously mentioned, and are more difficult to manage. They quickly dissolve in methylated spirits, but are insoluble in cold water. If a little of the tincture is put on the glass it is remarkably transparent and vivid in tint so long as the color is liquid, but as soon as the spirit evaporates, which it does of course very quickly, the tint becomes opaque and turns to a kind of bronze powder; the tincture besides spreads in all directions, and is unmanageable for that reason alone, even if it retained its transparency. Hence something is needed to give consistency to the solution to prevent the spreading of the color. Gum arabic, being insoluble in spirit, cannot be used. Canada balsam is also non-effective, as the color becomes opaque on drying. The same may be said of shellac, sandarac, and other resins, which require heat to enable them to dry in a transparent condition. It is possible to get transparent tints with collodion, but for slide work it is unsuitable, as it dries on the brush before it can be put on the glass. However, for certain work, collodion tinted with aniline colors may be applied by pouring it on the glass, so as to cover the whole surface, and returning the excess fluid to the bottle as is customary with wet-plate photography; it is useless for local treatment with the brush or for dabbing. The only substance that Mr. Scott was able to use with success was ox-gall, used in considerable quantity, so as to make the aniline tincture of a workable consistency. Ox-gall is freely soluble in spirits as well as water, and is suitable both for dabbing and brush work. Ox-gall only overcomes the difficulty of the spreading of the tincture; it does not prevent the color becoming opaque on drying.

As the tincture is transparent only so long as there is any spirit present, it would seem that fluidity is a necessary condition to maintain transparency. The addition of water, however, to the tincture, produced a precipitate, and the color becomes opaque. Glycerine, like ox-gall, dissolves easily in spirits of wine, and these two substances used together proved capable of transforming the aniline tincture into a suitable color for tinting slides, which could be thinned with spirit and was also capable of being dabbed. There are a number of dyes, which Mr. Scott calls spirit colors, that may be treated in this way, which are of great brilliancy and intensity. The spirit colors are generally warm in tint. There are magenta, crimson, orange, and yellow, for instance, in spirit colors; cardinal, rose, and purple are also obtainable.

If faint tints are desired of the above, more ox-gall is added; glycerine should be sparingly employed, as if too much is used in proportion to the ox-gall, the color remains pasty, and refuses to harden.

The tints of aniline dyes are too bright and vivid for many subjects, and are not readily mixed together to produce secondary colors. Aniline dyes, therefore, seem more useful as an occasional accessory than as a complete system for the painting of slides; but they are useful in cases where local tints of special brilliance are required.

CHAPTER XIII.

OPAL AND PORCELAIN PRINTING.

ANY of the emulsions given in Chapter VII. can be used for coating the glass and the directions thus given for exposure and development, or toning, apply to the opal process. The emulsion given below is a very good one, and it can be prepared in a weak white light. For coating, however, it is better to work by yellow light. This emulsion is for printing-out, not development.

Hard gelatine,	120 grains.
Chloride of ammonium,	20 grains.
Citrate of potash,	40 grains.
Water,	5 ounces.
Nitrate of silver,	120 grains.

Place all the ingredients, except the silver, in a bottle capable of holding ten ounces. Allow them to soak until the gelatine is thoroughly softened. Then shake well, and add the silver in crystals. Shake again until the silver is dissolved. Place in a water bath at a temperature of 100 deg. Fahr., and digest for an hour at that temperature. Then cool down to 75 deg. Fahr., and add twelve ounces of alcohol. The emulsion will be precipitated in a pasty mass. Let it stand for a couple of hours in the dark. Then pour off the fluid as closely as possible. Add three ounces more of alcohol and shake well. The alcohol is now poured off, five ounces of water are added, and, after half an hour's soaking, the emulsion is melted and filtered; after which the plates, previously well cleaned, are coated. Opal glass is easily and cheaply had of any large dealer in glass.

Before coating, the plates should be slightly warmed. For opals coat as thinly as possible. The coated plates are placed on a levelled slab to set, and when set racked away to dry in a well-ventilated room free from light and dust.

Positives are printed on these plates exactly as they are on sensitized paper, but they print more rapidly.

In order to be able to judge of the progress of the printing one edge of the negative and the plate should be bound with gummed paper. This will permit the plate to be turned back for inspection and insure its registering accurately when again laid down on the negative.

The printing must be deep, as the prints lose much in depth in the later manipulations. When sufficiently printed, the plates are well washed, and then toned in any good bath. The sulpho-cyanide of ammonium bath, given on page 45, will be found to give good results. Fix and wash as usual. For opals, by development, either Wellington's or Eder's methods given in Chapter VII., can be confidently recommended.

If the opal plates are purchased ready-made, the directions inclosed with each box should be implicitly followed.

Opals by the Powder Process.

Coat the glass with the following solution:

Dextrine,	4 drams.
White sugar,	4 drams.
Bichromate of potash,	4 drams.
Glycerine,	2 drops.
Water,	12 ounces.

The coated plate is dried with gentle heat and exposed under a positive reversed as regards right and left. A few moments' exposure to sunlight will suffice.

The plate is then developed by dusting over it with a fine camel's-hair brush finely powdered ivory-black, to which has been added a little Indian red if a warm tone is desired. The action of light having made those parts of the plate acted upon by light, hygroscopic, the powder will adhere to them in proportion to the moisture which they hold. If any of the details are slow in coming up, gently breathe upon them and repeat the dusting.

When the details are all out the plate is cleaned of all superfluous powder, and the image fixed by pouring over it a saturated solution of boracic acid and alcohol. The plate is then dried by gentle heat, and exposed to light for a brief period, again dried, and placed in warm water to dissolve out all the unchanged bichromate.

After two changes of water a few drops of sulphuric acid

are added to harden the film; after this acid treatment the plate is washed in two changes of water and allowed to dry.

The treatment with boracic acid may be omitted, and the bichromate dissolved out in warm water immediately after development.

If ordinary unreversed positions are used for printing, the image must be printed and developed on a glass plate previously coated with the sensitive bath. After development and drying, the image is coated with plain collodion and transferred to the opal glass as described in the Chapter on Carbon Prints.

Printing on Porcelain.

Collodion.

1.—Gun Cotton (negative),	60 grains.
Alcohol,	2 ounces.
Ether,	3 ounces.

Powder finely 120 grains of silver nitrate and add it to 3 ounces of alcohol. Place the bottle in a water bath and bring the water to the boiling point; continue the boiling until the silver is entirely dissolved; when solution is complete pour it hot into the collodion with constant stirring.

2.—Chloride of Strontium,	32 grains.
Citric Acid,	24 ounces.

Reduce to a fine powder and dissolve in four ounces of alcohol, add:

Ether	4 ounces.
Gun Cotton,	60 grains.

These two collodions will keep indefinitely, and are to be mixed in equal quantities when wanted for use.

Preparation of the Plate.—Coat the porcelain with albumen from fresh eggs and water, using equal quantities of each. Dry without heat, then warm the plate and when cool coat with the mixed collodion. Dry over a spirit lamp.

The Exposure.—Bind one edge of the negative to the corresponding edge of the porcelain plate and expose in a printing frame; or, place the negative in the proper position on the porcelain, protect the back of the latter with yellow paper, and secure contact by using plenty of spring clips.

Toning.—The plates are first washed in plain water, then in water containing a little salt, and toned in the following bath:

Water, - - - - - -	8 ounces.
Gold solution (1 grain to 1 ounce), - -	1 dram.

When sufficiently toned, wash and fix in a 1 to 10 hyposulphite of soda solution. The prints are then thoroughly washed.

RED PRINTS.

Red prints have two uses, one æsthetic, the other practical. Æsthetic, when it is sought by means of them to reproduce the tone seen in some old-time engravings. Practical when they are used as a base for the relief plates or zinc etchings, so largely employed at present for illustrating newspapers, trade journals, price lists, etc.

Several methods are in use to obtain the tone desired.

The simplest and most common is to fix a print in silver without toning it. The print is transferred from the printing frame to a dish of clean water, and after a brief soaking it is placed in a dilute solution of acetic acid, after which it is treated with a solution of carbonate of soda to remove all traces of acid. After this treatment the print is fixed and washed as usual. A second method of producing red prints is by the carbon process, using red chalk or some similar pigment, instead of lamp-black or carbon.

A third method is to float plain paper on a sixty grain solution of nitrate of uranium. After ten to twenty minutes' exposure under the negative the print is developed by floating on a forty-five grain solution of red prussiate of potash. The print is well washed and finally immersed in a very dilute solution of nitric acid to clear the lights. The print is then fixed in a solution of alum. When wanted for the draughtsman red prints are best made by the first method. The outlines needed for the work in hand are sketched in India ink and the rest of the photograph bleached out in a strong solution of bichloride of mercury which dissolves the silver, but leaves the India ink unharmed.

The sketch thus made is used for the production in the camera of a negative of sufficient intensity to produce a relief or etched plate. If the original print was an enlargement of the subject to be reproduced, and the negative was reduced to the desired size, extreme sharpness and delicacy of line will be obtained.

Ordinary Rives paper sized with gelatine, is salted on a bath containing twenty grains of chloride of ammonium or barium, and the same amount of citric acid to the ounce of water. It is then dried and sensitized as usual.

CHAPTER XIV.

PHOTO-CERAMICS.

ONE of the most beautiful and permanent applications of photography is that of photo-ceramics, which is comparatively little known or practiced in this country.

The author believes that careful study and intelligent following out of the methods now to be described, will enable any skillful photographer to produce enamels of a high grade of excellence. The methods given are those now in use by the most skillful Continental producers of ceramic work, and may be relied on as trustworthy.

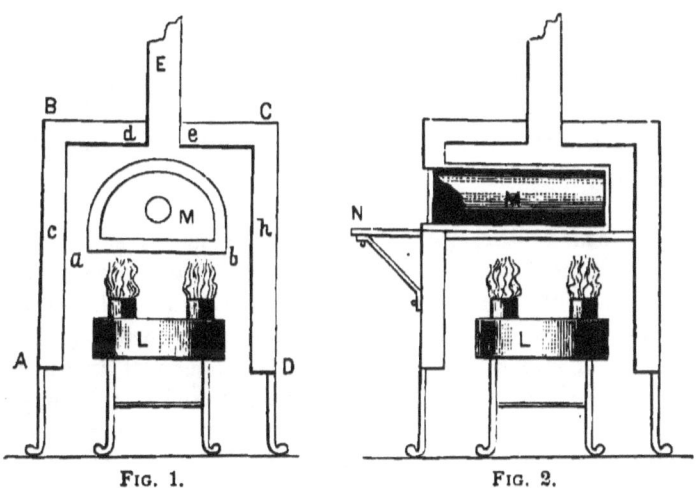

FIG. 1.   FIG. 2.

THE APPARATUS.

The Muffle Furnace.—A muffle furnace of some description is necessary for firing the enamels. They can be had in portable form of any large dealer in such materials, burning either coal or gas.

When enamels of small size only are attempted, the form here illustrated and described will do good work. Its construction is so simple that any good metal worker can construct it.

Fig. 1 is the front elevation, and Fig. 2 the side elevation. The muffle, M, is made of moderately thick sheet brass, permanently closed at one end, with a hinged or sliding door, provided with a peep-hole in front. The muffle slides into the furnace on two iron bars let into the walls. One of these bars is seen in Fig. 2.

The furnace walls, A, B, C, D, Fig. 1, are of thick iron plate and doubled, the space between being filled with ashes or some other non-conductor of heat. The furnace is supported by four iron legs attached to the outer wall by screws, in order to be easily removed for convenience of transportation. A chimney, E, also detachable, fits into a hole in the middle of the furnace top. Heat is generated by a Berzelius or Liebig spirit lamp, having two or more wicks, which stands on an iron tripod.

The opening in the walls by which the muffle is introduced into the furnace must be of such a size and shape as to be completely closed when the muffle is in place. A shelf, N, of thick iron plate, is fastened by brackets just underneath this opening.

It is impossible to give any specific dimensions, as they are determined by the size of the muffle, which must be large enough to hold the largest piece of enamel likely to be fired.

The height of the muffle need not be more than three inches, nor its other dimensions more than seven by nine inches. A muffle four by five, by two-and-one-half inches, is, perhaps, as large as can be advantageously used in this simple form of furnace. The furnace proper should be about seven inches high, and the legs about the same. The chimney is a piece of iron pipe two inches in diameter, and about fifteen inches in height. The hot-air space surrounding the muffle may be one or two inches larger each way. The lamp must not be brought too near the bottom of the muffle, or it will not burn well.

The Drying Box.—Much of the success of the various methods given for enamels depends upon the way in which the drying is done. The form of drying box here illustrated,

Fig. 3, taken from "Schwier's Manual on Photo-Enamels," is recommended.

The box is made of strong sheet iron, and may be made ten to twelve inches square, and five to six inches high. The legs are of sufficient height to allow of the introduction underneath of the source of heat. These legs stand upon a wooden framework provided with stout thumb-screws, to secure a perfectly horizontal position of the slab on which the plates are dried. Upon the bottom of the box is placed a slate or marble slab, two or three inches thick, smoothly and squarely polished.

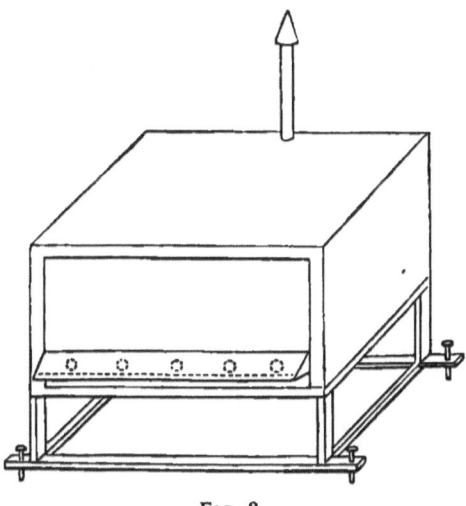

FIG. 3.

The top of the box is provided with a ventilating shaft opening into the interior. In the door are openings for the ingress of air, covered with a roof to shut out light.

If desired, a thermometer may be attached in such a way as to have its bulb within the box.

The slab is warmed to 100 deg. Fahr. by any convenient means, precautions being taken to insure this temperature being maintained.

THE NEGATIVES.

To secure the best results in the various ceramic processes the old wet collodion process should be employed in preference to the gelatino-bromide process. Gelatino-bromide plates may, however, be used if one is content with results a trifle inferior to those obtainable on wet collodion plates.

The two formulas given below for the preparation of the collodion will serve for all the processes described later.

1.—For the Reproduction of Line Drawings.

Alcohol,	12⅞ ounces.
Ether,	19¼ ounces.
Azotic cotton,	185 grains.
Iodide of cadmium,	62 grains.
Iodide of ammonium,	77½ grains.
Iodine,	7.7 grains.

2.—For the Reproduction of Drawings, Engravings, Aquarells, etc., in Half-Tones.

Alcohol,	12⅞ ounces.
Ether,	19¼ ounces.
Azotic cotton,	185 grains.
Iodide of cadmium,	62 grains.
Iodide of ammonium,	62 grains.
Bromide of cadmium,	13 grains.
Iodine,	3.8 grains.

Sensitizing Bath for Nos. 1 and 2.

Distilled water,	34 ounces.
Nitrate of silver,	1,234½ grains.
Acetic acid,	13½ drams.

Developer.

Water,	34 ounces.
Sulphate of iron,	776½ grains.
Acetic acid,	13½ drams.
Alcohol,	13½ drams.

Intensifier.

A. To be used after development and before fixing.

1.—Water,	16 ounces.
Pyrogallic acid,	77 grains.
Citric acid,	154 grains.
2.—Distilled water,	16 ounces.
Nitrate of silver,	77 grains.
Acetic acid.	2½ drams.

To use, mix equal parts of Nos. 1 and 2, and immerse the negative until proper density in gained. Wash well before fixing.

The ordinary bichloride of mercury intensifier with ammonia or sulphite of soda can also be used.

Fixing.—Either a saturated solution of hyposulphite of soda, or a one to fifty solution of cyanide of potassium.

The glass used must be plate or patent plate. The following method of cleaning the glasses previous to coating is recommended.

Soak the glasses for an hour or two in a solution of bichromate of potassium to which has been added about one-third of its bulk of ordinary nitric acid. The glasses are then washed, wiped off with a piece of fine linen, and immersed for a few moments in a bath of iodized alcohol, and finally wiped perfectly dry with a clean piece of chamois skin.

The operations of coating and sensitizing are the same as customarily employed in the wet collodion process.

Stripping Films.—The negative or positive when perfectly dry is covered with a thin film of the following solution:

Pure gutta-percha,	1 part.
Chloroform,	30 parts.

The image is covered with this solution by flowing, and the rubber film is allowed to dry. When dry a second coating is given to the negative of the following:

Ether,	$18\frac{1}{4}$ ounces.
Alcohol,	$12\frac{7}{8}$ ounces.
Azotic cotton,	154 grains.
Castor oil,	15 drops.

After the application of this solution the negative is allowed to dry in the open air. When dry the film is to be cut through to the glass with the point of a sharp penknife, at a slight distance from the edges of the negative, or from that portion of it containing the picture to be used.

The plate is then soaked in water with a piece of Japanese paper, which, after soaking until limp, is brought in contact with the prepared surface. After a brief interval one corner of both paper and film is separated from the glass with the point of a penknife, the paper and film are then taken between the thumb and index finger, and the film pulled from the glass with its paper support. It is then dried between blotters, and when dry is ready for use. The use of Eastman's American films will greatly simplify this operation for those who are content to employ gelatine in place of collodion. They should, however, be developed with the ferrous oxalate developer.

Positives.—For positives, by contact, any of the dry plate methods given in Chapter VII. may be employed, preference being given to the albumen method or Levy's collodion process.

M. Roux, in his work on Decorative Photography ("Traité Pratique de Photographie Décorative," etc.), recommends the following tannin process:

"Well cleaned and polished patent plate glass is coated with the collodion given at the beginning of this chapter, sensitized as usual in the bath there given, and after immersion in distilled water until all traces of greasiness have disappeared, the plate is washed under the tap for five or six minutes, and finally immersed for three minutes in the following bath:

Water,	34 ounces.
Tannin,	463 grains.
Acetic acid,	13 drams.

"The plate is then dried in the drying-box.

"These plates, kept in a dry place, will retain their good qualities for a fortnight, and will be found to yield very fine results."

The time of exposure to diffused light is about five seconds for negatives of medium density. Before development the plates are well washed in running water and developed by flowing one of the following solutions over the collodionized surface:

DEVELOPER FOR POSITIVES FROM NEGATIVES OF LINE DRAWINGS.

Equal parts of the following:

1.—Water,	16 ounces.
Pyrogallic acid,	77 grains.
Citric acid,	154 grains.
2.—Distilled water,	16 ounces.
Nitrate of silver,	77 grains.
Acetic acid,	2½ drams.

Developer for Positives containing Half Tones.

1.—Distilled water, - - - - 32 ounces.
    Bromide of potassium, - - - 617 grains.
2.—Distilled water, - - - 32 ounces.
    Pyrogallic acid, - - - - 154 grains.
3.—Distilled water, - - - - 6¼ ounces.
    Strong ammonia, - - - - 5 drams.

For the developer mix the above solutions in the following proportions:

No. 1, - - - - - - 2½ drams.
No. 2, - - - - - - 7¾ drams.
No. 3, - - - - - - 46 drops.

Fixation must be thoroughly done in a saturated solution of hyposulphite of soda.

If the positives are to be used only on flat surfaces, it is only necessary to varnish them with any good negative varnish. If, however, they are intended to be used for printing on curved surfaces, they must be stript from the glass as described above for stripping negatives.

The Firing or Burning-in.

This operation is performed as with enamels painted by hand. The enamel plate is placed on a piece of fire-clay and gradually introduced to the full heat of the furnace, avoiding overheating, the muffle door being left open until the plate is well heated. The door is then closed and the plate allowed to remain in the muffle until the enamel glaze just melts. The plate should be turned occasionally, to insure equal firing, using for this purpose a wire set in a wooden handle with an inch or so of the other end bent to a right angle.

The burning is a most delicate operation, and requires skill and attention to secure the best results; given these, however, with a little experience, enamels can be fired with almost absolute certainty.

For further details for firing, the reader is referred to the section describing Mr. Watson's substitution method, at the end of this chapter.

Even with the utmost care, the pictures, after firing, will sometimes have a dull or mat surface. They must, in this case, receive a coating of flux, and be fired again.

The following fluxes are recommended by the best authorities.

1.—*For Colors Containing Iron.*

Crystallized borax, red lead, pounded glass, equal parts of each.

Mix and fuse for one hour in a crucible. Pour out into water, then dry and powder fine upon a marble slab, with a glass muller.

2.—*For Colors Containing Gold.*

Silica (powdered),	1 part.
Glass of borax,	1¼ part.
Red lead,	⅝ part.

3.—*For Colors Containing Silver.*

Sand,	1 part.
Litharge,	2 parts.
Glass of borax,	1 part.

4.—*For General Use.*

Red lead,	4 parts.
Silica (powdered),	1 part.

Powdered silica is obtained by calcining the purest flints three or four times in a crucible, washing each time; it is then powdered in a porcelain mortar and sifted through a lawn sieve.

RETOUCHING.

Retouching is often necessary to fill up white spots, to clear up portions which are veiled or too dense, or to apply a different tint to various parts of the picture. This retouching is always to be done after the first firing, the enamel being again fired after retouching.

Bare spots are filled in with a fine brush dipped in a solution formed by dissolving a small portion of the enamel powder, used to form the image, in a little spirits of lavender. The high lights are cleared up, if necessary, with a brush dipped in a 1 to 10 solution of fluorhydric acid and water.

Touching up isolated spots in different tints is effected with enamel powders of the proper tints dissolved in essence of lavender, enamelled by subjecting them to the action of the heat.

As a rule, the colors are easily procured of the trade, those made by La Croix, of Paris, being thoroughly reliable. It is as well to sift the dry colors through a fine lawn sieve to remove all coarse particles.

Most operators will prefer to purchase the enamel mixtures ready made, but for the benefit of those who may wish to prepare them for themselves, a few formulas are given below. All the ingredients given in these formulas must be very pure, ground or pulverized very finely, and perfectly mixed together.

Stock Mixtures.

These serve as a base in some of the formulas given, and may be made up in quantities to suit the needs of the artist.

Stock No. 1.

Red lead,	3 parts.
White sand,	1 part.

Stock No. 2.

Stock No. 1,	8 parts.
Calcined borax,	1 part.

Stock No. 3.

Calcined borax,	5 parts.
Silica,	3 parts.
Red lead,	1 part.

Gray.

Manganese,	2 parts.
Stock No. 1,	3 parts.
Borax,	1 part.
Oxide of cobalt,	$\frac{1}{10}$ part.

Indigo Blue.

Oxide of cobalt,	1 part.
Stock No. 3,	2 parts.

Turquoise Blue.

Oxide of cobalt,	1 part.
Oxide of zinc,	4 parts.
Stock No. 2,	6 parts.

Azure Blue.

Oxide of cobalt,	1 part.
Oxide of zinc,	2 parts.
Stock No. 2,	5 parts.

Emerald Green.

Oxide of copper,	1 part.
Antimoniac acid,	10 parts.
Stock No. 1,	30 parts.

Blue Green.

Oxide of chromium,	1 part.
Oxide of cobalt,	2 parts.
Stock No. 3,	9 parts.

Jonquil Yellow for Flowers.

Litharge,	18 parts.
Silica,	4 parts.
Oxide of antimony,	2 parts.
Sienna clay,	2 parts.
Sub-sulphate of iron,	$\frac{1}{10}$ part.

Red.

Red oxide of iron,	1 part.
Stock No. 2,	3 parts.

Carmine.

Cassius's purple,	2 parts.
Chloride of silver,	10 parts.
Stock No. 3,	10 parts.

Purple.

Cassius's purple,	2 parts.
Stock No. 3,	10 parts.

Violet.

Peroxide of iron (calcined),	1 part.
Stock No. 3,	2 parts.

Black Pigment.

Oxide of copper,	2 parts.
Oxide of cobalt,	1½ parts.
Oxide of manganese,	2 parts.
Flint glass,	12 parts.

Melt in a crucible and add of—

Oxide of copper,	1½ parts.
Oxide of manganese,	2 parts.

The melted mixture is poured into water and then finely pulverized.

White Pigment.

(The white enamel glaze of commerce.)

Gold or Cassius's Purple.
(Precipitate a solution of chloride of gold with salt of tin, and wash the precipitate.)

PRACTICAL MANIPULATIONS.

Four methods are in common use for producing photo-enamels, viz.: the Dusting-on Process; the Pigment Process; the Collotype Process; and the Substitution Process.

As the limits of this book will not admit of a detailed description of all these methods, I have selected the Pigment and the Substitution Methods for detailed treatment, adding a brief *résumé* of the Dusting-on Method, taken from the (British) "Photo. News Almanac" for 1887.

PAVLOWSKY'S METHOD WITH PIGMENT PAPER.

The following solution is made up:

Best gum arabic,	385 grains.
Water,	26 drams.

When the gum is dissolved the solution is filtered through flannel, and the following mixture added:

Enamel mixture,	248-308 grains.
Honey,	10 grains.

The mixed solution is poured out upon a marble or glass slab and thoroughly incorporated together.

An addition of a solution of 6 grains bichromate of potash in a small quantity of hot water is then made, and the resulting mixture filtered through flannel. This solution must be kept in darkness for one week before using.

A well-cleaned piece of plate glass is coated with the solution and dried in the drying box at a temperature of about 110 deg. Fahr.

The exposure to light is made as usual, the time required being about one-fourth of that required for silver paper. The exposed plate is then coated with plain collodion, and, as soon as the film is set, washed in cold water; a sheet of unsized paper is then laid down upon the film, perfect contact secured with the squeegee, when the paper bearing the collodionized tissue is easily stripped from the glass by first raising one corner.

The development is the same as described in Chapter for Carbon Tissue.

The developed tissue is first washed in diluted alcohol, and finally in absolute alcohol, and the picture transferred in the usual way to the object to be enamelled. When dry it is ready for firing.

This method is well adapted to the production of enamels on curved and irregular substances.

Husnik's Method.

Husnik coats paper with the following mixture:

Gum arabic,	3 parts.
Water,	30 parts.

Filter well and add:

White sugar,	1 part.
Bichromate of potash,	2 parts.
Glycerine,	5 drops.

Black enamel is thoroughly incorporated with this solution in sufficient quantity to give a non-transparent film.

The remaining operations are the same as in Pavlowsky's method.

Liesegang's Dusting-on Method.

The six stages are as follows: 1. A glass plate is coated with the sensitive mixture of organic matter and bichromate. 2. The plate is, after drying, exposed under a positive. 3. After the shaded parts of the plate have absorbed sufficient moisture, it is dusted with a vitrifiable pigment in fine powder. The united action of the bichromate and light so modify the deliquescent organic matter that it loses its property of absorbing moisture from the air, and the exposed parts of the plate consequently refuse to hold the vitrifiable pigment. 4. The powder picture is coated with collodion, and then soaked in a slightly alkaline solution, in order to remove all traces of soluble materials. 5. The collodion film bearing the image is next floated off and laid on a tile or other suitable surface. 6. The image is vitrified or burned in.

The composition of the sensitive mixture may be varied considerably without any very material influence on the result, but the following composition gives very excellent results in ordinary cases:

Water,	100 parts.
Moist sugar,	10 parts.
Gum-arabic,	10 parts.
Bichromate of ammonium,	4 parts.

This solution should be used within one or two days of its preparation, and ought to be filtered with the most scrupulous care, as any particle of dust or fibre is likely to cause a white spot on the finished work. The solution is poured on the glass plate after the manner of collodion, and after the plate has been held in a tolerably horizontal position for a few seconds, the excess of solution is quickly poured off, and the plate is set to dry on a kind of desk formed of a piece of sheet iron mounted at an angle of about 15 deg. with the horizon, and kept warm by a spirit lamp placed underneath; but it is advisable to distribute the heat by means of a few layers of blotting paper placed under the glass, and the heat should not rise above a temperature which the hand can easily bear. It is best to use patent plate glass, and the greatest care must be exercised in cleaning it thoroughly. It is necessary that the positive under which the exposure is made should be quite dry, or even slightly warm, and in ordinary cases an exposure of one minute in sunshine, or ten minutes in diffused daylight, will suffice; but an actinometer should be used as in carbon printing. As soon as the exposure is finished, the plate is taken into the dark-room, placed on a white surface, and some of the enamel color is sprinkled on and worked round and about with a long-haired camel's-hair pencil, both the powder and the brush being perfectly dry. The image now gradually develops, and it is often necessary to shake the powder from off the plate and allow the moisture of the air to act on the film for a short period, after which the treatment with the enamel pigment is resumed. Should the picture appear hard, only the extreme dark shades appearing, the exposure has been too long; but if the image is flat, and all the high-lights are veiled, under-exposure is indicated. Just as in ordinary silver printing, the image should appear a few shades over dark at this stage, as the enamel colors lose a little intensity when fired; but if there should be any difficulty experienced in attaining the required vigor, it is advisable to very gently breathe on the plate—previously freed from all loosely-adhering powder—and then to proceed with the development. When the development is finished, all non-adherent powder should be removed by means of the brush, and any required retouching can be performed either by breathing on the plate and cautiously applying the pigment on the part requiring it, or by removing the pigment by friction with a tuft of cotton wool or a stump. The plate is next coated with a collodion containing from $1\frac{1}{2}$ to 2 per cent. of pyroxyline, and about $\frac{1}{8}$ per cent. of castor oil; and after the film has set it is cleared away from the edges of the plate, so as to leave a clear border of about $\frac{1}{8}$ of an inch. The collodionized plate is next soaked in a 2 per cent. solution of caustic potash, until all traces of soluble chromium salts are removed from the film, and after a thorough rinsing in clean water, the plate is immersed in water containing enough nitric acid to make it taste about as sour as weak vinegar, where it should remain some hours. By now placing the glass bearing the film in a large vessel containing clean water, and gently manipulating the pellicle with the fingers, it becomes easy to detach the collodion film, which is then caught, collodion side downwards, on the enamel tablet or tile. Should it be necessary to vitrify the picture with the collodion side upwards, the final transfer must be made in a solution of sugar containing one-fifth of its weight of this material, as otherwise the collodion film would be liable to scale off. In this latter case, the collodion must be dissolved away before firing; but when the collodion film is mounted downwards on the enamel plate or tile, this proceeding is not necessary. The most convenient method of dissolving away the collodion film is by soaking the dried plate for a whole day in the following mixture:

Alcohol,	50 volumes.
Ether,	50 volumes.
Oil of lavender,	100 volumes.
Oil of turpentine,	3 volumes.

The plate having been again retouched, if necessary, all is ready for the final operation, or the burning-in of the image.

WATSON'S SUBSTITUTION METHOD.

No better form of the substitution process exists than that of Mr. Watson, of Hull, which with some modifications made by Mr. N. K. Cherrill, was published by the latter gentleman.

The following is Mr. Cherrill's description of the process given in the "Photographic News Almanac" for 1886:

A piece of glass is cleaned with nitric acid, well washed, dried, polished, and coated three times with collodion.

This stage reached, plunge the plate in the bath without letting the collodion get too much set; if the setting be prolonged, the result is not so good. A nitrate bath with me means a solution of thirty grains of pure nitrate of silver in one ounce of pure water, sunned all the while it is not in actual use, and, when used, rendered acid, in the proportion of two drops of pure nitric acid to a half gallon of solution. The plate remains in this solution till the greasy marks disappear; it is then taken out at once, and placed in a funnel to drain; it is allowed to drain not less than five minutes, and is then ready for the slide.

I arrange the copying camera in the studio so that the light which passes through the negative to be copied comes only through one of the side lights, and I have no reflectors of any kind. Behind the negative, however, I place a piece of finely-ground glass, which renders the light perfectly even. For this beautiful adaptation I am indebted to the late Mr. Baden Pritchard, who showed me the plan at Woolwich. The lens I use is a Dallmeyer No. 2B. With this, with the arrangement I describe, the exposure is from five to twenty seconds. If the enamel to be taken is of small size, I prefer to have a mask on the negative, and to block out all light except that actually needed, as this enables me to take four or five images side by side, by simply pushing the camera dark slide a little way each time.

The exposure and development of the image is a matter requiring the greatest care and attention, as on the complete success of the transparency the whole process turns. The developing solution is made as follows:

Pyrogallic acid,	12 grains.
Glacial acetic,	4 drams.
Alcohol,	4 drams.
Water to fill a 12-ounce bottle.	

In warm weather this may be more dilute—say, as far as giving 20 ounces of water to the same quantity of pyro. Then, of course, more alcohol will be needed.

This should be made three days before it is used, as it is too vigorous in its action at first. On the other hand, it must not be kept too long, as then it deteriorates in the other direction. These are the characteristics in development which, according to my experience, *must* be obtained in order to secure a good result. The image must develop very slowly. The image must attain the exact density required at the same moment that it attains the right amount of detail in the high-lights. The image, when examined by reflected light, must not be "filling up" (if I may use the term) in the dark parts, or at least the "filling up" must only extend to a very few tones, and above the very darkest. The image, when examined by reflected light, should show, in fact, nearly all the drawing and shading of the subject; while, of course, when seen by transmitted light, it should show up with extreme perfection. Every detail must be there, with a fair amount of density; but heavy blacks are to be avoided.

In actual practice I find it best to place the plate on a level stand during the last stage of development, right under the tap; a full stream can thus be turned on at the exact instant at which it is required to stop the action of the developer.

The plate must be well washed at this stage, and the fixing must be done with cyanide of potassium. I prefer a weak solution, and carefully avoid pouring it upon the face or other delicate parts of the picture. The washing should be copious, and it should follow as quickly as possible on the completion of the fixation.

When the washing is complete, break off a small piece of the film at one corner of the plate, and direct a thin stream of water from the tap on this corner, making it strike on the bare glass. The use of a camel's-hair brush here will facilitate raising the edge of the collodion, so that a large jet of water can be got under the film; this being directed in the proper manner, by tilting the plate, will effectually loosen the film from the glass. As soon as this is done, restore the plate to the horizontal position, and, with a pointed stick, like a penholder, break away from around the picture as much film as can well be spared. Clear off the broken pieces with the finger, and give a slight extra rinse under the tap. This must be gently done, as our film is all loose now, and may slip off if we are not very careful. Get about two or three ounces of water on the plate, holding it quite level, then, bringing the whole over a large dish filled a couple of inches deep with water, lower one end gently into the water, when the film will slip off into the dish without the slightest injury. If protected from dust, the film may be left at this stage quite twenty-four hours without any injury or deterioration.

The next stage is the toning. To make up the toning bath just right is an important feature in the process. My procedure is as follows: Get a sixteen-ounce bottle, half fill it with water, put it into a saucepan, also half full of water, and set the whole arrangement on the fire, or over the gas, till the water in the saucepan comes to the boil. If the glass bottle does not crack under this trial, it may be used with safety. Place in the bottle a quarter of an ounce of potassio-chloride of iridium, fill it up with cold water, and set it in the saucepan again; this time, however, do not boil the water in the saucepan, but place it where it will keep very hot. Shake the bottle occasionally. After about half an hour, remove the bottle from the hot water, and place it aside to settle and cool. When quite cold it will be fit for use. This solution will remain good any length of time. I have a suspicion that it improves by keeping, but I am not sure on this point. To make up the toning bath, proceed as follows: Place 12 ounces of pure water in a bottle, add to this 14 drams of the iridium solution. Shake it up well. Now add a few drops at a time, and shaking well between each addition, 7 drams of a solution of chloride of gold (strength, 1 grain to 1 dram). The bath is then ready for immediate use, but is better after keeping. It keeps indefinitely. It is particular to note in this place that the solution in the iridium bottle will have a nearly black sediment. This is simply undissolved chloride. When all the clear solution has been used up, more water may be added, and this remainder used in the same manner as the first lot, but care must be taken that too much water is not added, as a quarter of an ounce of the chloride will not make two sixteen-ounce bottles full of the saturated solution, but only about one and one-third, or one and a-half.

To use the enamel toning bath proceed as follows: Pour some out into a clean dish to the depth of about half an inch. Stand near to this a large dish filled to the depth of one inch with clean water, and also a small dish with pieces of glass in it under water. The glasses may be about quarter-plate size, or such as will be found most convenient. Now take up one of these glasses, and slip it under the film containing a transparency to be toned, gently raise the glass to the surface (at the same time manipulating the film with a camel's-hair brush held in the right hand) in such a manner that when the glass and film on it are lifted out of the water, there will be an edge of film (say) a quarter of a inch wide lapping over one edge of the glass. The action of the water, as the plate is taken out, will wash this piece or edge of film round to the back of the plate, and, by so doing, will fix the transparency on the glass in a very satisfactory manner. If care be taken that the edge where the film laps over is kept uppermost, or highest, a very considerable stream of water may be poured on the film without any danger of it slipping. Having got the film on the glass, it should be rinsed under the tap in the manner just suggested, and the film may then immediately be transferred to the toning bath. To do this, turn the glass over so that the body of the film is underneath, lower it gently under the surface of the solution, and, with a brush, disengage the lap of film where it had turned the edge of the plate, now, of course, uppermost. As soon as this is done, the film will move off into the solution free of glass, which can then be removed. When the film has floated free for about a minute, turn it over with the brush, and note carefully if the deepest shadows are toned through, so as to give one uniform tint to the whole film. Turn the film over and over, and move it about till this is effected, and, as soon as it is so, remove it from the bath by the same piece of glass, used in the same manner, *i.e.*, securing the film by making a little piece of it lap over to the back along one edge of the glass. Let the film drain a few moments, and then transfer it to the large dish of clean water. As soon as it is free of the glass in this dish, gently agitate the water with a brush, so as to wash away the toning solution still adherent to the film.

I strongly object at this stage to washing the film under a tap—dish washing is far preferable, and as little of that as possible should be employed. As each print is toned in succession it is placed in the same large dish of water. I use one that will take a half-sheet of paper. When all are finished so far, change them one by one into another dish of water, taking up each film with the glass as before described. This is all the washing they are to have. Now proceed to mount them on the tablets. First of all, pour back the toning bath and put away the dish it was used in, then set before you on the table two dishes, one filled about half an inch deep with ammonia solution, and the other about the same depth with clean water.

Ammonia solution at 880 deg., - - 6 drams.
Water, - - - - - - 12 ounces.

This must be kept well corked.

Half an ounce of this mixture diluted with one pint of water makes the bath, into which the films are to be plunged.

Get a chair and sit down to the work, as it is far easier to manipulate the films if both arms can rest on the table. Take off your watch and place it before you, so that you can see it as you work. Now place in the dish of clean water a clean glass, and on that an enamel tablet, carefully washed previously. Now take another clean glass, and with it remove one of the toned films from the dish in which it was washed, and plunge the same into the ammonia bath. As the film enters the solution, take the time by the seconds' hand of the watch, and withdraw the film when it has been in twenty seconds; plunge it as rapidly as possible into the water where the tablet is, disengage the glass, and slightly agitate the water in the dish to give the film a sort of wash. Now take up, with the left hand, the piece of glass on which the tablet rests, and raise it about half way to the surface; then, manipulating with the brush, held in the right hand, bring the film to its proper position over the tablet. By raising the latter very gradually the film can be laid in its place in this way with the utmost certainty. As soon as the glass is fairly out of the water, place it with one edge raised a little, so as to drain. If the glass is placed at too steep an angle there is danger that the tablet will slip out, or, at any rate, get disarranged.

It is proper to note, in this place, that the tablets being curved, the films will not lie flat without the exercise of a little care on the part of the operator. Care must be taken to avoid the formation of one ridge or two around the edges of the tablet, but the spare film should be made to lie as nearly as possible equally in all directions. If this is done with care, no puckers or laps will be found in the film when it is completed in the next stage of the proceedings. When the films have got almost surface-dry, the tablets are to be removed from the glass plates in which they were lifted from the water. To do this, place the plate level, and, with a sharp-pointed stick, tear away the useless film around the edges of the tablet, slip a thin knife under the tablet, and lift it off the glass on to a sheet of blotting paper, and at once cover it with a large bell jar, or other glass vessel, to protect it from dust and accident.

The picture is now ready for burning, and it should at this stage look like a finished enamel, and be as perfect in every respect, in the matter of light and shade and tone, etc., only it will be of a bluer shade of color than the finished result; but it ought to have the same relative shade of color now as it is to have in the completed result. The tablet may be burned at once, or left many days, or even weeks, without change.

I much prefer a gas muffle furnace for burning the enamels in, to one heated by coke; whichever is used, it should be ready and at the full heat, a clear cherry red inclining to white, but by no means a full white heat; too much heat is a mistake, as it renders the process unmanageable, and produces no good result to make up for the extra difficulty of work.

The burning is a most delicate operation, and all the care and attention of the artist are required to secure the result at its very best point; still, with care, I do not hesitate to say that nine out of ten enamels can be burned to a successful issue.

Take up one of the tablets and place it upon a piece of fire-clay in front of the muffle, but not too near, say at a distance of about six or eight inches. The fire-clay should be supported in such a manner as to tip the enamel towards the heat, so that the rays may fall upon it, as near as may be equally all over it. When it has been roasted in this manner a little while, move it a little nearer, and then a little nearer, examining it each time. As soon as the action of the heat has turned the color of the film brown in the least degree, it may be dealt with fearlessly; the fire-clay, with the enamel on it, may then be placed level, just in the mouth of the muffle, where in a few moments the film will take all the shades of brown till it gets quite dark all over; now push it into the heat. (A wire set in a wooden handle, and with about half-an-inch at the other end bent to a right angle, is a most useful tool in manipulating the fire-clay plates when in the muffle.) As soon as the plate is in the heat, watch it with great care; it will seem to get perfectly black all over, and then almost on a sudden the whites of the picture will be seen coming out quite clear; the moment this takes place, draw the tablet towards the mouth of the muffle, and remove it to the outside to cool a little gradually, and then take the tablet right away and place on wood to get cold. All beauty will by this time have disappeared from the enamel, the whites will stand out, and the few tones next to them will have some clearness, but all the other tones will be a dark and confused mass—hardly distinguishable the one from the other. This is the true characteristic of a good enamel at this stage. It is now ready to glaze.

The enamel glaze as prepared for photographic work can be had of most dealers in artists' materials. About a thimbleful of the glaze (which is a fine powder like flour) is placed in a small, narrow bottle—say, a two-ounce medicine bottle—and the bottle filled up about three parts with alcohol. This is marked "Glaze in alcohol." To make up the glazing mixture, take a two-ounce medicine bottle, and put in it half an ounce of uniodized collodion, such as would be used for negatives; add to this a quarter of an ounce of methylated ether, and half an ounce of alcohol; now add as much water as it will take without throwing the gun-cotton down. To do this, set the tap to drip very slowly, and get one drop into the bottle; shake violently, and then get another drop in, and repeat the shaking; so go on till six or eight drops are added, which will be about enough. Shake up the bottle of "Glaze in alcohol," and let it rest about two minutes for the coarser particles to subside, then carefully add some of the upper part of the mixture to the diluted collodion—enough to make it rather opaque and milky-looking will do. This is the glaze ready for use; it must be well shaken up each time it is used.

When the enamel is quite cold, balance it on the top of one finger if small, or near the edge of a piece of flat wood if large, and pour the glaze mixture over it; then immediately tilt the enamel up to the vertical position, letting the glaze run off on to soft blotting paper, rocking the tablet in the meantime to prevent the formation of lines. When the collodion is set, place the tablet in a muffle on a piece of fire-clay, and gradually introduce it to the full heat; keep a careful watch now to see that the burning does not proceed too far. The glaze should only just melt. As soon as this is the case—which will be seen by looking at the reflection of the bent wire held just above the tablet—pull the enamel out, and, when a little cool, remove to a block of wood to get cold again.

The image is now indelibly fixed, and it may be treated roughly with impunity. The picture is not, however, at its full beauty as yet, as, if all the baths etc., have been in good order, one glazing will not be sufficient. The whites will be glazed, or have a polished appearance, but the darks will be still of a mat surface, and not transparent in effect, as they should be. This is overcome by repeated glazings. No enamel is perfect that has not been glazed at least five times. The number of separate burnings (say, five or six) as here recommended give a totally different effect to what would be obtained by one great burn, with the glaze applied thicker. Those who wish to save themselves trouble will work in this way; but anyone who wants to get the best results will not mind the trouble of five or six, or even a dozen glazes.

When the glazing comes nearly to an end, there will be

found some little points where improvement is needed in the way of retouching. This point is very easily gained; collect all the trimmings of films after they have been through the toning and ammonia baths, and all waste or torn films as well; place them a few moments in the muffle on a piece of fire-clay; they will instantly burn, and the ash is to be carefully collected and kept in a small bottle. A little of this may be put out on a palette, with a minute atom of the glaze powder, and one drop of some essential oil, and then well rubbed down with a muller. The paint so obtained may be used with fine brushes, dipped in turpentine, and, the work being burned into the enamel, will take the same color and surface as the rest of the picture.

Ceramic colors may be applied to enamels, and burnt in with considerable success; but I have found much difficulty hitherto in getting the red shades wanted about the lips and cheeks right. I have used the colors made by La Croix, of Paris.

When an enamel has failed, it may be put on one side, and when there is a sufficient collection of them, the images may be dissolved off with fluoric acid, applied with a rag at the end of a stick; and then, after washing, the tablet may be fired in the muffle till it melts to a good bright surface. If this be carefully done, the tablet so renewed will be as good as a new one. In this firing after cleaning, the image will often appear again when in the heat. If this be the case, the heat should be continued till a full glaze has been obtained, when the tablet, after cooling, may be again treated with the acid, and again fired.

Failures in enamels are of four distinct classes, which may be thus enumerated:—Class I. Failures in development. Class II. Failures in the direction of getting poor, slaty, bluish colors, which glaze all at once when put in the muffle. Class III. Failures in the direction of excessive blackness, just the opposite to the last. And—Class IV. Failures in the glazing operation itself.

With regard to the first class of failures, I would suggest that it is imperative that the development proceed slowly; this seems to me the only condition of success. The photographer's knowledge of his business will enable him so to manage the light, lens, exposure, etc., of the film as to secure this necessary condition. I do not think the developer I have given is by any means the only one that will do, though, as in my hands it succeeds the best, I never use any other.

The second class of failures arises from there being too much gold in the toning bath, or rather, perhaps, too much in proportion.

The third class arises from there being too much iridium, or too much in proportion. Both these may be avoided by a strict adherence to the formula I have given.

The fourth class of failure—the only one to be really feared—is the most difficult to deal with. It is much more difficult to describe than to show. The chief thing to avoid in glazing is the getting an unequal layer of glaze on the tablet *the first time*. *Until the first glaze is burned in, the picture will rub very easily*, therefore a badly-laid glaze will be its ruin, as it cannot be removed. After the first glaze is burned, the enamel is safe, and any further error in the matter of pouring on the glaze, etc., can be rectified by simply washing it off again under the tap. Then, again, there is a possibility that, when too much glaze is used, the enamel will spoil by what I have, till recently, looked at as "burning out," but which I have since found out to be simply a sinking in of the image. The best remedies for all errors in glazing are to use plenty of alcohol in the collodion, and plenty of water; and, at the same time, the smallest workable quantity of glaze, making more burns of it, but doing less work at each burn.

Enamelled Intaglios.

A very beautiful application of photographic ceramics is the production of enamelled intaglios in copper, bronze, gold, silver, etc.

The process is a combination of photo-chemigraphic and photo-enamel methods. The metal plate is first covered with one of the sensitive mixtures as described in the Chapter on Photo-chemigraphy. It is then dried, exposed under an ordinary intense positive, developed and etched. The lines of the plate are then filled with an enamel powder, which is burned in as in enamelling.

For all the details relating to the production of the engraved plate the reader is referred to the Chapter on Photo-mechanical printing methods.

For a black enamel the following mixture is recommended :

Silver (powdered),	38 parts.
Copper,	72 parts.
Lead,	50 parts.
Borax,	36 parts.
Sulphur,	384 parts.

The sulphur is fused alone, the silver and copper together, adding the lead when fusion is complete. The mixture is then placed in the retort containing the fused sulphur, closing the mouth of the retort tightly to avoid all danger of the mixture taking fire. As soon as the substances are well incorporated together, the borax is added, and the whole turned out into an iron mortar and finely pulverized. The enamel is then washed in water containing a little sal ammoniac, finishing up with water in which a little gum has been dissolved. The powder is applied with a wooden spatula to the well-cleaned plate. Great care is to be taken to have the filling-in lines well filled with the enamel. When all the lines are filled, all excess of powder is removed, and the plate placed in the muffle and fired as usual. When the fusion is finished the plate is removed from the muffle, cooled gradually, and polished with any good metal polisher.

As the beauty of these enamelled intaglios depends upon harmonious contrast between the enamelled lines and the surface of the plate, enamel powders of different colors must be employed to secure the best results, using for this purpose any of the powders given in the Chapter on Photo-ceramics. This process is capable of producing beautiful results, and being simpler than the process of producing surface enamels, the beginner is advised to commence with this simpler process before passing on to the more complex operations of enamelling.

CHAPTER XV.

PHOTO-MECHANICAL PRINTING METHODS.

THE term Photo-chemigraphic is used to designate a large class of methods in which photography is used to assist in the production of engraved or relief plates for printing from. All these processes may be described in general terms as consisting in the coating of a wood block or metal plate with a solution of asphalt or bichromatised gelatine, exposing the plate so prepared under a positive or negative; developing the image by immersion in hot water to dissolve all the unaltered asphalt or gelatine, and finally etching with some acid to produce the relief or intaglio.

Detailed description of some of the best of the methods in common use is given below.

THE METAL PLATES.

The metals most commonly employed in the various photo-chemigraphic or photo-mechanical processes are steel, lead, copper and zinc: the first three being most in use for the production of engraved plates, while zinc is used indifferently for both engraved and typographic plates.

As it would be impossible in a general treatise like the present to discuss in detail all the manifold applications of photography to the production of heliographic or typographic plates, the author has selected two or three typical processes of each type for detailed treatment.

The principle underlying the production of relief blocks or engraved plates is the same in either case, viz.: the insolubility of gelatine when treated with a bichromate and exposed to light. In the case of a relief block the parts to be etched, or bitten in, are the parts between the lines; hence those parts must be protected from the action of light, as otherwise the gelatine film covering them could not be dissolved in hot water, and etching would therefore be impossible. For photo-reliefs therefore, an ordinary negative is employed. For photo-intaglios, however, a reversed positive is required, since in this case it is the lines that are to be etched; they must therefore retain their solubility in order that the etching process may be possible.

The Positives and Negatives.

As it is imperative that these should be of extreme opaqueness in those parts which are to protect the sensitive film from the action of light, and as the customary process of development rarely confers this quality, a method is given by which "black and white" negatives or positives, as these intense printing subjects are technically called, can be obtained. The method is the modified ferrous-oxalate development as recommended by J. O. Moerch in his valuable work on photo-chemigraphy, and is applicable only to gelatine plates.

Herr Moerch adds to every eight ounces of the ordinary ferrous-oxalate developer fifty drops of a solution of one part of iodine and of iodide of potassium in 150 parts of water. With this developer and proper exposure, gelatine plates of a low degree of sensitiveness can be given all the opacity needed, if a few drops of bromide be added as soon as the image appears.

Intensifying.

This should be resorted to only as a last resort. It would be far better to make another negative more correctly exposed. If, however, this is impracticable, Mr. John Carbutt's formula is undoubtedly the best; as follows:

1.—Bichloride of mercury, - - - - 4 drams.
    Chloride of ammonium, - - - - 4 drams.
    Water, - - - - - - 20 ounces.
2.—Chloride of ammonium, - - - - 1 ounce.
    Water, - - - - - - 20 ounces.
3.—(a) Cyanide of potassium, - - - - 2 drams.
    Water, - - - - - 16 ounces.
    (b) Nitrate of silver, - - - 100 grains.
    Water, - - - - - 4 ounces.

Add (b) to (a) until a small amount of the precipitate remains undissolved.

The plate, after fixing, is most thoroughly washed and immersed in No. 1 until it is perfectly white; it is then well washed and immersed in No. 2 for a few minutes; after washing well, the plate is flooded with No. 3, when it turns intensely black. The plate is to be thoroughly washed after this treatment. By the above method it is easily possible to make negatives or positives suitable for line or stipple work on slow gelatine plates.

If, however, the operator prefers collodion plates, the formulas given in the Chapter on Photo-enamels will give the best plates.

The Metal Plate.

For the sake of brevity and conciseness, zinc has been selected as the metal to be treated of in the following pages. The operations are the same for copper, steel, bronze or lead, differing only in the acids used for etching.

The plates are carefully planished and polished with pumice stone. They are then ready for coating with the sensitive substance, but better results will be obtained if they are first given a coating of resin, as recommended by Mr. Roux in his book on heliographic methods (Traité Pratique de Gravure Heliographique), as follows: A box is constructed of a size proportioned to the size of the plates to be treated; its height should not be less than twenty inches. At the top and bottom of one side hinged doors are cut about four inches from each end. Screws are then placed on the inside of each end to hold the plate. The box is mounted on tressels in such a manner as to allow it to be easily rotated.

Half a pound of finely powdered resin is placed in the bottom of the box, the door closed, and the apparatus given two or three rotations. After two or three minutes' rest the zinc plate is placed on the the screw-heads. In a short time it will be covered with an even deposit of the resin; it is then taken from the box, placed on a wire toasting iron, and heated until the resin assumes the appearance of amber. It is then removed and dried. The heating must not be carried too far, lest the resin be converted into a varnish which would make etching impossible.

When dry the plate is ready for coating.

Sensitizing Mixtures.

The following solutions may be taken as types of the various mixtures in common use:

1.—Dry albumen from eggs, - - - 15 to 20 parts.
　　Water, - - - - - 100 parts.
　　Bicarbonate of ammonia, - - - 2½ parts.

The solution is allowed to settle, and then filtered and a few drops of ammonia added.

2.—Albumen of one egg.
　　Bichromate of potassium, - - - 30 grains.
　　Water, - - - - - 6 ounces.

The bichromate is to be finely powdered and then dissolved in the water, and the solution added to the albumen beaten to a froth. After settling, the solution is filtered.

3.—Gelatine (hard), - - - - 231 grains.
　　Gelatine (soft), - - - - 231 grains.
　　Bichromate of potassium, - - 462 grains.
　　Bichromate of ammonium, - - - 308 grains.
　　Water, - - - - - 9½ ounces.

The gelatine is first swelled in a portion of the water, and then dissolved by gentle heat in the remainder of the water containing the salts. Filter.

Coating the Plate.

The plate is levelled, the mixture poured on and evenly distributed by means of a triangular piece of soft paper. When evenly coated, the surplus is drained off into a reserve bottle to be filtered before using again. The coated plate is dried at 120 deg. Fahr. in the drying-box described in the chapter on Enamels.

If the operator is in possession of a turning table having a pneumatic holder in the center, the plate may be dried very quickly by placing it on the table, previously moistening the rubber ring of the holder, inverting the table, and rotating it rapidly. Another way of coating and drying is to immerse the polished plate in water and flow the solution over it while wet, draining off the surplus, and drying the plate by holding it at an angle over a lamp, avoiding over-heating.

All these operations should be performed in a subdued light.

The Exposure.

The exposure varies in length according to the density of the printing medium and the intensity of the light. Generally from three to five minutes in full sunlight and from fifteen to twenty in diffused light will be sufficient. Experience is the only guide.

Development.

This is effected in water to which has been added sufficient of some aniline dye to give it a decided tinge. This enables the progress of the development to be more readily observed. As soon as the details are well out, the plate is dried spontaneously, or with gentle heat. It is then ready for etching.

Clausnitzer's Method of Developing.

The exposed plate, coated with solution No. 2, is inked up with a fine-grained lithographic roller, using thick transfer ink. It is then placed in a tray of cold water and the ink washed away from the non-exposed parts with a well-wet dabber of cotton. This is to be done with a gentle circular motion, beginning at one corner of the plate and working towards the center; care must be taken to avoid washing away fine lines and marks. If the plate was over-exposed, the ink will stick; if under exposed, the finer portions of the work will be washed away. When all the superfluous ink is removed, the plate is washed in water, and dried with gentle heat. When it has cooled down, finely-powdered resin is dusted over it and well rubbed in, all excess being removed. The plate is then warmed until the resin begins to melt; it is then etched, dried, rolled up, washed, resinized, and again etched. These operations are repeated until the necessary relief has been obtained. This process gives a lithographic block.

The Etching.

The biting-in is done by means of a dilute solution of an acid. The following are recommended:

1.—*For Zinc Plates.*

Perchloride of iron (well dried), - - 50 grains.
Alcohol (Atwood's), - - - - 100 grains.

2.—Perchloride of iron,   1 dram.
Water,   40 drams.
Hydrochloric acid,   30 drops.
3.—Nitric acid,   ½ ounce.
Water,   10 ounces.

4.—*For Copper, Bronze, and Steel.*

Perchloride of iron,   1 dram.
Water,   35 drams.
Hydrochloric acid,   20 drops.

5.—*For Aluminium.*

Hydrochloric acid,   1 ounce.
Water,   5 to 10 ounces.

6.—*For Gold and Platinum.*

Aqua regia.

7.—*For Silver.*

Nitric acid,   1 ounce.
Water,   10 to 30 ounces.

8.—*For Stone and Marble.*

Hydrochloric acid more or less diluted with water.

9.—*Glass.*

Fluorhydric acid (liquid) for transparent lines on a mat surface, and fluorhydric acid gas for mat lines on a transparent surface.

In all these formulas the proportions of the acid may be increased or diminished at will, but a weak solution will usually be found to give the best results.

Before etching, the edges and backs of the plates should be covered with a varnish of bitumen of Judæa to protect it from the action of the etching fluid.

The duration of the etching depends entirely on the depth desired. For engraved work the etching need not be very deep. From one-quarter to one-half an hour will be sufficient. When the etching is completed the plate is well washed, rubbed with a cloth to remove all traces of albumen or gelatine, and polished with pumice stone. It is then ready for the press, unless it is desired to harden it in the galvanic battery, as will be presently described.

During the etching it is always well to keep the solution in constant motion in order to renew the portion which touches the plate. This may be done by rocking the tray.

The process of etching reliefs is more difficult than with engraved plates. In the former case the biting-in must be deeper, and to avoid the undermining of the relief lines by the acid it is necessary now and then to remove the plate, rinse, and dry it with heat, apply resin, and again warm to melt the resin that it may flow down the sides of the relief lines, and continue the etching. This process is to be repeated till sufficient depth is obtained.

Hardening the Plate.

When a large number of impressions are to be taken from the plate, it is necessary to protect it from wear by giving it a coating of some more resisting metal, such as iron or steel.

M. Roux recommends the following method: The well-cleaned plate is attached to the negative pole of a Bunsen pile of five or six elements, and placed in a copper dish containing the following solution:—

Chloride of ammonium,	8 ounces.
Water,	40 ounces.

Two plates of sheet iron of equal size are then attached to the two wires of a pile, which enter the solution. Several days are required to complete the operation. The plate, when well coated, is rinsed in water, polished with rouge, and wiped dry with a wad of fine linen slightly oiled.

All the above methods can be employed for the production of engraved or relief plates, as reversed positives or ordinary negatives are used to give the impression.

The process of printing from these blocks lies outside the province of this book to describe.

Collotype.

This name is given to a process of mechanical printing from glass plates coated with a thin film of bichromated gelatine. Full working details of the process as practiced in one of the largest establishments in Vienna are here given. The glass for the machine press should be patent plate one half an inch thick; for the hand press, it need be no thicker than ordinary glass.

Preliminary Coating.—The glass is thoroughly cleaned and coated with the following:

Soluble glass,	3 parts.
Albumen,	7 parts.
Water,	9 to 10 parts.

The soluble glass must be free from caustic potash. The mixture is to be carefully filtered and used fresh. Apply an even coat, drain off the superfluous liquid, and dry. When dried, rinse the plate in water and dry again. It is now ready for the next stage of the process.

The Sensitive Film.

Bichromate of potash,	1 part.
Gelatine,	3 parts.
Water,	18 parts.

The plate is warmed slightly on a slate slab, placed in contact with the surface of a water bath, and flooded with the above solution, leaving just enough to make a very thin film. As soon as coated, the plate is placed on the levelled shelf of a drying box and dried at a temperature of 122 deg. Fahr. The time of drying must not exceed three hours.

Exposure.—The time required for exposure is short, and can only be measured by the actinometer. Experience is the only guide.

When the printing is done the plate is washed in cold water for an hour to remove the soluble bichromate. If upon removal from the washing water the plate has a decided yellow tinge it will take up too much ink when rolled, and fail to give clear impressions. When washed and dried the plate should have the appearance of ground and polished glass, the highlights being almost transparent and the shadows opalescent.

Etching the Plate.—This is only necessary when the printing is done on the steam press. The following is the etching fluid:

Glycerine,	500 parts.
Chloride of sodium,	15 parts.
Water,	500 parts.

The plate is immersed in this fluid for half an hour, during which time the image gains in relief. It is then dried without washing and is ready for printing from. Inking and printing can be learned only from practice, and this cannot be taught in books. It is best learned at the press.

When the printing is done on the small hand lithographic press, the plate requires no etching; merely moistening with glycerine and water is all that is needed to prepare the image for the ink.

Inking.—The best results are obtained by rolling once with thick ink, followed by an application of a thin ink. The plate is laid upon a bed of plate-glass; a moist sponge is passed over the surface; it is then rolled two or three times with a soft roller, covered with wash-leather; then a roller of glue, charged with lithographic ink is applied, and then another charged with thin ink. The paper to be printed is laid down on the plate and the impression taken off.

Mr. Riley's Method for Amateurs.

The Substratum.

Ale,	1 ounce.
Silicate of soda,	8 drops.

Place in a bottle and shake well; allow the mixture to settle for twenty minutes, then filter. The plate, thoroughly clean, is given a coating of this substratum and stood on end to dry. When dry another coating is applied in the same manner, and the plate stood on the opposite end to dry.

The Sensitive Film.—Soak 44 grains of soft gelatine one quarter of an hour in sufficient water to cover; then dissolve in a water bath. Then pour upon it the following solution, hot, but not boiling:

Water,	4 drams.
Bichromate of ammonia,	6 grains.

Mix well and filter.

Flow the prepared plate with this mixture, using one-half an ounce for a 5 x 8 plate, and place on a levelled slab in the drying-box. It should dry in two hours.

Expose under an ordinary negative for an hour, then wash

PHOTOGRAPHIC PRINTING METHODS. 199

in cold water for one and a half hour, and dry in the open air. When dry, damp with a weak solution of glycerine and water, ink as described above, and take off impression at once.

Drying-Box.—The box is 20 inches high and 12 inches square. Two ledges carrying two thumb-screws each are placed about six inches from the top. A glass slab covered with two or three sheets of blotting paper rests on the ends of the screws, and is to be carefully levelled before the plate is put in. A piece of iron 6 x 4 x 3 inches, heated in the fire, rests on angle irons about 6 inches below the glass slab. Ventilation holes are bored at the top and bottom of the box. The heat should not exceed 120 deg. Fahr., and should be kept as near that point as possible.

METHODS OF GRAINING TYPOGRAPHIC PLATES.

The word "grain" is technically used to express the ink-holding power of the printing block or plate. In the case of a subject in line it is only necessary to produce incised lines or grooves below the surface of the metal. But this method will be found insufficient where there are shadows or half-shadows. The ink will be wiped away from these unless means are taken to prevent it. The lines must be broken up into dots or dashes in order to give a block which can be printed from.

Many ingenious methods of producing this result have been devised. Of these, three of the most valuable have been selected for description.

The Ives' Method.—This consists in obtaining a positive on a bichromated gelatine film, which is swelled until the light parts of the picture stand out in bold relief. A plaster mould or cast is made from this. The cast is then inked in the following manner: The elastic composition of glue and molasses used in inking-rollers, is made in flat sheets, furrowed by V-shaped depressions, crossed by others not quite so deep. This gives an inking surface made up of a series of tiny pyramids, standing close together, and the ink is applied in such a way as to ink both the tops and sides of the pyramids and the intervening depressions or ditches. The inking surface so prepared is pressed upon the white plaster cast, and when it is removed, a reproduction of the original picture is seen, only in little blocks instead of in continuous tone. This is photographed, and from the picture in line or point thus produced a relief plate is produced by any of the usual methods.

The Meisenbach Method.—In this process the original picture is photographed through a grating made by coating glass with an opaque film, through which transparent lines are closely cut and crossing each other. This grating is placed a short distance in front of the picture, and it produces the curious effect of transforming the darker portions of the picture into thicker lines. The relief plate is made from this line effect.

The Photo-lithographic and Photo-gravure Methods.—In photo-lithographic work the grain is produced by transferring the image in ink as described above to a grained lithographic stone.

In the photo-gravure process the grain is produced by sprinkling emery powder on the mould which gives the granulated surface seen in all photo-gravures.

The same effect is sometimes produced by dusting the negative before printing with emery or gelatine powder.

THE ART OF MAKING PHOTO-GRAVURES.

At a recent meeting of the Photographic Section of the American Institute, Mr. Ernest Edwards, President of the Photo-gravure Company, read a highly interesting paper on "The Art of making Photo-gravures," which was listened to with the closest attention by all present. To illustrate the grain and line work of the different photo-mechanical printing processes, he projected them upon the screen with the sciopticon. At the conclusion of his lecture, Mr. Edwards' head printer, Mr. Solman, who was in attendance with his presses, made some prints from various plates, and Mr. Edwards presented each of his auditors with a souvenir illustrative of this important branch of photography. The following are extracts from Mr. Edwards's article as published in the *Photographic Times:*

"If I may venture the prediction, I think the history of photography for the next decade will be the history of orthochromatic work. Surely, next to the production of the colors themselves, there is nothing to be desired so much as the rendering of the true values of these colors. I place the orthochromatic or isochromatic negative as the highest point yet attained in negative-making, and as constituting the outcome to-day of that germ that was brought into being nearly a hundred years ago.

*　　*　　*　　*　　*　　*

"Now let us consider for the moment what are the conditions necessary to be secured in a metal plate made by photography and suitable for plate-printing. In the case of a subject in line only, an incised line or groove must be made below the surface of the surrounding metal. The ink is dabbed or rolled into such lines, and the surface of the plate cleaned with cloths and the ball of the hand, leaving the ink only in the incised lines. This ink is transferred to paper by pressure, and becomes the impression. This is all well enough in the case of lines, but it is clear it will not be sufficient where there are masses of shadow or half-shadow. The cloth, or the hand, will wipe away the ink from these masses of shadow, unless something is done to prevent it. Of course, in line-engraving a series of lines may be made which forms a shadow, each of which series has an ink-holding capacity, and, out of which, the ink cannot be wiped. The closer these lines are together and the deeper they are, the stronger is the shadow produced, because the smaller is the amount of surface to be wiped clean. Again, to go a step further, a series of lines may be incised or engraved on a plate, and at right angles to these a similar series. In this way, assuming that the incised lines are V-shaped, nothing will be left of the surface of the plate but a series of points, each of which is the apex of a pyramid and each of which prevents the cloth or the hand from wiping the ink out of that portion of the plate surrounding it. This is the essential cardinal feature of a plate for plate-printing, and this is the essential cardinal feature which must be obtained in any photographically-produced plate of a similar kind. Whether formed in the way I have described, or whether the plate, is honeycombed with a series of cells, of which the walls reach to the surface of the plate, there must be an ink-holding capacity to the plate, which must not, therefore, simply be a a plate in relief and depression. If that only were needed, it would be easy enough to make, by means of gelatine and bichromate, a picture or matrix in relief and depression from any photographic negative, and deposit copper on it till thick enough to print from. But such a plate could have no value, as it would have no ink-holding capacity, and, therefore, all the ink would be wiped out of it in the process of cleaning. Some device must be obtained by which this ink-holding capacity, or grain, as it is commonly called, shall be given to the plate. The solution of this problem has been sought by an army of experimentalists, and numberless ingenious devices have been utilized in order to solve it. It may be broadly stated that the production of a grain which shall be effective for the purpose and yet shall not be apparent in the finished picture, is the keystone of all methods or processes for making successful photo-gravure plates.

* * * * * * *

"You see we have here the aquatint device for graining, the keystone of success for his process, though possibly not understood to be so by him. Mr. Talbot then goes on to describe minutely the methods and the preparation of the chemicals used for etching, and I can say that his description, given nearly forty years ago, will serve as a text-book for the etcher of to-day. Altogether his process is marvellously close to the method of producing photo-gravure plates by etching as now practiced.

"But of all these processes, with all the ingenious devices invented in connection with them, two only remain in general use to-day. One is the deposit, the other is the etching process. I venture to predict that finally the etching process will be master of the situation. Letting alone the greater facility and economy of production it offers, the results produced by it are equally good in the case of reproductions, and better in the case of photographic work directly from nature or life. I have stated that the etching process is the one used by our company, and the results are before you. I am bold enough to say that photo-gravure work in America to-day equals any in the world in the matter of reproductions, and excels any in the world in the matter of pure photographic work. I shall ask your patience a moment longer whilst I describe broadly our method of producing a photo-gravure plate.

* * * * * * *

"But I would like to say a word as to the advantages of photo-gravure as a method of photo-mechanical printing. It is not a cheap process. It cannot be printed with type. But just as a steel or copper-plate print has qualities which are not possessed by a wood-cut, a photo-gravure has qualities—qualities which go without saying, not possessed by any method of typographic photo-engraving. What is known as the photo-gelatine process also produces results superior to the type method. But, although photo-gelatine work has a quality of its own, and is in some respects unexcelled, photo-gravure, in other respects, has advantages over it. A photo-gravure can be improved and altered as much as may be desired after the plate is made till just the result needed is obtained, and when obtained the printing ceases to be a source of anxiety, as the edition printed should always be uniform. The plate is good for subsequent editions—which are exactly like the first— whenever desired, and they are made without the further action of light. There is a strength and robustness, and the blacks are more nearly velvet in a good photo-gravure plate than in any other photographic method. And there is room for far greater artistic development in photo-gravure than in any other photographic method. I cannot forbear in this connection from adverting to an unfortunate tendency that exists among some manufacturers and some publishers to call photo-gelatine work by the name of photo-gravure. What is the sense of this? Nothing in the world can beat the special qualities of gelatine printing—qualities which photo-gravures do not possess. And nothing in the world can beat the special qualities of photo-gravures—qualities which photo-gelatine prints do not possess. To my mind it is as much an outrage on photo-gelatine as on photo-gravure work to reverse the names. Yet the tendency is to do just this thing—a serious mistake that will become, if not checked, a serious misfortune. Would there be any sense in calling a lithograph a steel-engraving? It would be just about the same as calling a photo-gelatine print a photo-gravure, and, though the result might benefit the producer for the moment, it would be otherwise when the deception was discovered.

"In going through all the ancient, yet modern, history of the development of photo-gravure, one can but ask that old, old question, 'What is there new under the sun?'

"With the story before us of Fox-Talbot's process and the process of Pretch, of Woodbury's process, and of aquatint engraving, of steel-facing, and all the other tricks and turns, what is there new in what we are doing to-day? Nothing, absolutely nothing. These men played the same play that we are playing, knew the words and the cues just as well as we do, only in one respect, one grand respect, is the situation changed. They played to empty benches. We have an audience—largely in this vast new world—an audience ready to applaud and to support all those results and efforts which tend to raise photography into art."

CHAPTER XVI.

VARIOUS METHODS FOR PUTTING PICTURES ON BLOCKS AND METAL PLATES FOR THE USE OF THE ENGRAVER.

ALTHOUGH photo-mechanical methods have made great advances within the last few years, the results obtained by them remain still vastly inferior to those obtained by the older method of hand engraving. No photo-chemigraphic method has yet been made public which will give a good rendering to subjects in half-tone. There are several secret processes which give good results, but doubtless much of their excellence is due to skillful touching up of the plate with the graver.

A plate produced by any of the photo-mechanical methods is necessarily lacking in that subtle interpretation of nature in various moods, which gives charm and value to a good impression from a hand-made block.

While photo-engraving methods will probably always be deficient in this all-important quality, photography itself can render great assistance in transferring to the block or metal plate accurately reduced or enlarged copies of any subject, leaving the artist free to interpret the subject in his own fashion.

The methods given below are those which have been approved by practical operators; they may, therefore, be employed with perfect confidence. They all belong to that class of methods to which the name autographic has been given.

Good Rives paper sized with gelatine is floated for three minutes on the following solution, taking great care to remove all air bubbles, as these will produce white spots in the developed print:

Water,	34 ounces.
Gelatine,	4½ ounces.
Isinglass,	1 ounce.
Bichromate of potassium,	231 grains.

After floating, the paper is carefully removed from the bath and dried on a slightly inclined piece of wood or glass. The floating and drying must be done by yellow light.

As soon as the paper is dry it is exposed under a negative or a positive, the former for proofs in black on a white ground; the latter for prints in white on a black ground.

The time of exposure varies from two to ten minutes, according to the density of the negative and the strength of the light.

After exposure the print is soaked in cold water until all yellowness has disappeared; it is then placed on a piece of glass, and inked with a soft roller charged with lithographic transfer ink.

When all the details are well out, the image is copied on wood, glass, or metal, in a lithographic press, the paper bearing the image having been previously placed face down on the block. After the impression is made on the block it is lightly washed with a sponge dipped in acidulated water, and when dry it is ready for the engraver.

The Asphaltum Method.

The block or plate to be engraved is coated evenly with the following solution:

Benzine,	17 ounces.
Asphaltum (oriental),	308 grains.

When the block is dry it is exposed under a negative or positive twenty minutes in full sunlight, or one hour in diffused light. The image is developed in turpentine, and when fully developed the plate is washed under a tap and allowed to dry spontaneously. It is then ready for engraving.

Copying Maps, Plans, Etc., Without a Camera.

When tracings, maps, etc., are to be copied on the same scale, the method introduced by M. Vidal in 1883 can be used to advantage. The engraving or other object to be copied is immersed for twenty minutes in the following bath:

Distilled water,	34 ounces.
Caustic potash (pure),	154 grains.
Alcohol,	13 drams.
Acitate of soda,	771 grains.

After immersion the paper is carefully withdrawn from the bath and placed on a piece of glass covered with a coating of plaster-paris about one-eighth of an inch in thickness. As soon as the surface moisture has evaporated, turpentine in sufficient quantity to form a thin layer is rapidly poured over the paper and allowed to dry partially. The picture is then inked with a velvet roller charged with lithographic ink. The inking is to be continued until all the lines appear black by reflected light. The print is then allowed to dry for fifteen minutes, when it is ready for the impression on the block in the press as described above. The impressed block can be engraved as usual.

A very easy method of preparing metal plates for the engraver is to flow iodized collodion over them and expose them in the camera in the ordinary wet plate holder.

The Collodion.

Alcohol	16 ounces.
Ether,	16 ounces.
Iodide of ammonium,	62 grains,
Iodide of cadmium,	46 grains.
Bromide of cadmium,	15 grains.
Azotic cotton,	123 grains.

The cotton, the iodides, and the bromide are first dissolved in the alcohol and the ether added when solution is complete. The collodion must be at least one day old before it is used, and should be decanted just before the plates are flowed.

Preparing the Metal Plates.

Before collodionizing, the plates should be varnished with a black engraving varnish, such as the following:

Virgin wax,	15½ drams.
Amber,	15½ drams.
Mastic,	15½ drams.
Resin,	7¾ drams.
Black pitch,	7¾ drams.
Turpentine,	8⅞ drams.

When the varnish is dry the collodion is flowed over the metal plate just as a glass plate is flowed. Exposure in the camera follows, and development is effected by pouring over the surface of the plate a sufficient quantity of the following solution:

Water, - - - - - - 34 ounces.
Sulphate of iron, - - - - 617 grains.
Acetic acid, - - - - - $7\tfrac{7}{10}$ drams.
Alcohol, - - - - - - $7\tfrac{7}{10}$ drams.
Sulphuric acid, - - - - - $1\tfrac{1}{10}$ drams.

The developer is allowed to act until all the details are well out. The plate is then washed and fixed by flowing over it sufficient of the following bath:

Water, - - - - - - 34 ounces.
Cyanide of potassium, - - - 462 grains.

The plate is ready for the engraver as soon as it is washed and dried.

The author finds that the gelatine emulsion given in a previous chapter for bromide of silver paper is well adapted for this process, applying a very thin film to the plate.

PHOTOGRAPHING ON WOOD.—FREWING'S METHOD.

Preliminary Preparation of the Block.

The block is first coated with the following:—

Gelatine, - - - - - - 2 drams.
White soap, - - - - - 2 drams.
Water, - - - - - - 16 ounces.

The gelatine is to be soaked for some hours, and then dissolved in a water bath. The soap is added in thin shavings, and the mixture well stirred with a glass rod; after which powdered alum is added until the frothiness disappears. The solution is then strained through muslin. Coat the face of the block with this mixture and a little zinc white, giving it a very thin coating. Rub it in well and evenly, and set aside to dry.

When dry the block is again coated with the following mixture, using a wide camel's-hair brush, and applying the solution with one sweep of the brush from end to end:—

Albumen, - - - - - - 1 ounce.
Water, - - - - - - 5 drams.
Sal ammoniac, - - - - - 18 grains.
Citric acid, - - - - - 5 grains.

Beat the albumen to a froth, and allow it to settle; use only the clear part. Then add the sal ammoniac, stirring well with a glass rod, and finally the citric acid. Coat the block, and when dry sensitize with the following solution :—

Nitrate of silver, - - - - - 50 grains.
Water, distilled, - - - - 1 ounce.

Pour a small quantity on the block, and spread it evenly with a glass rod, any surplus being preserved for use again after filtering. When dry, print under a reversed negative.

Over-printing is not necessary, as the print does not lose in finishing. After printing, hold the block, face down, in a strong chloride of sodium solution for three minutes. The picture will fade slightly in this bath, but as the fixing-bath will bring back all the detail, this is of no consequence.

Wash the block well under a spray of water, and fix by holding face down in a saturated solution of hypo for five minutes. Then wash for ten minutes under a spray, and set on end to dry. The block is then ready for the engraver. The image may be toned by any of the usual methods.

Ives' Method.

Whiten the block by putting on two or three drops of thick salted albumen; then sprinkling on a little pure white lead, and spreading and mixing them with the ball of the hand until the coating is thin, smooth, and even. Set the block on end to dry. Then polish with a brush, and sensitize by covering the surface for two minutes with a sixty-grain solution of silver nitrate. Rub off with a blotter, and again set on end to dry. Then fume twenty minutes with ammonia, and expose under a reversed negative. When sufficiently printed, wash thirty seconds in running water, and tone and fix in a 1 to 6 hyposulphite of soda solution, to which has been added a pinch of carbonate of soda and a little chloride of gold. The block should be kept face down in this solution for twenty minutes, and then well washed and set on end to dry. It is then ready for the engraver.

There seems to be little choice between these two methods, both being equally simple, and both leaving the block in good condition for the graver's tool.

CHAPTER XVII.

RECOVERY OF SILVER FROM PHOTOGRAPHIC WASTES, PREPARATION OF SILVER NITRATE, Etc.

THE photographic practitioner will do well to save his wastes for treatment for the recovery of the silver and gold contained in them. Only an exceedingly small portion of the silver and gold used in the various operations appears in the finished negative or print. The remainder is dissolved out in the fixing bath, washing water, etc. These should therefore be placed in a convenient vessel and treated with zinc to precipitate the silver.

No process of recovery is simpler or more effective than Dr. Stolze's method with hypo and zinc.

The following description of the process is taken from the *Photographic Times:*

"Chloride, iodide, and bromide of silver are the salts we find in photographic wastes, either when in a pure state or mixed with others, frequently soluble salts. One of the best methods to reduce them metallically is to dissolve them first in a saturated solution of hyposulphite of soda, diluted with one or two volumes of water, and subject the solution to the following process:

"Silver haloids in substance require simply to be dissolved, but when in emulsions, like residues in bottles, or failures in preparing them, the emulsion should first be reduced to shreds or nodules, and then thrown into the fixing bath till they have become semi-transparent, when the solution is squeezed from them, and the residue again subjected to the hypo bath. Very old emulsion, the viscosity of which has been partly or totally destroyed, must be solidified by slightly warming, and mixing with it a sufficient quantity of a five per cent. solution of chrome alum.

"When all the silver has been dissolved, narrow strips of sheet zinc, previously cleaned with muriatic acid and well washed with water, are placed in the solution. There is no absolute necessity of cleaning the zinc, still its pure metallic surface, freed from cuticles of oxide, accelerates the reduction of silver very considerably. When a number of zinc strips are suspended on different parts of the vessel holding the solution, a thorough reduction of the silver is effected in about forty-eight hours, but sometimes it will take longer time. The contents of the vessel should be stirred up frequently. A coarse black deposit settles upon the bottom of the vessel and the strips of zinc, from which it must be brushed occasionally, to allow more of it to precipitate. The precipitate consists of metallic silver, zinc, and some sulphide of silver, and before it is subjected to further operations it must be well washed in water—an easy matter on account of its coarseness and gravity.

"Old fixing baths, accumulating in the photographer's laboratory, may be utilized for the dissolving of emulsion remnants or haloids in substance, as long as they possess the power to do so. When perfectly well saturated, a little fresh hyposulphite solution may be added.

"The clear liquid, from which the precipitate has been removed, still contains traces of silver, which will be separated by heating. This amount of silver is insignificant if the operation has been conducted with care; and if the zinc has remained in contact with the solution for about two days, it it so small that it can scarcely be detected by reagents.

"The washed precipitate can then be dissolved in nitric acid, diluted with half its volume of water. The substance is not dissolved totally, and a black residue remains, consisting partly of impurities of the zinc, of chloride of silver (the consequence of impure nitric acid), or of gold, and should, therefore, be treated separately with aqua regia for its recovery.

"The filtered solution of impure and acid nitrate of silver is then precipitated with a strong solution of common washing soda, as long as carbonate of silver is forming. An excess of soda is not important.

"By repeated decantation and changes of distilled water, the precipitate is washed to perfection and then dissolved in chemically pure nitric acid. To avoid an excess of acid in the solution, great care must be observed; some of the carbonate of silver remaining undissolved is a guard against undue acidity. A more convenient plan would be to divide the precipitate, acid being added to four-fifths of it, till all effervescence has ceased. A decidedly acid solution will be the result, which may be neutralized by adding gradually small portions of the fifth part of the precipitate of carbonate of silver. By carefully adding diluted nitric acid, when necessary, and carbonate again, an absolutely neutral solution can be obtained, which consists of chemically pure nitrate of silver.

"By reducing the product to about ten per cent. and a slight acidulation, it can be used as a negative bath, or as a positive printing solution, by giving it alkalinity with carbonate of soda.

"To evaporate the result to crystallization, or to fuse the nitrate of silver obtained, is useless; neither of the operations can improve it, and would incur only a waste of time and labor.

"A great part of the silver waste, not soluble in hyposulphite of soda, comes from paper. Unfixed prints when not toned, had better be fixed, and the remnant be refused. The exceedingly small quantity of reduced silver, contained in them pays neither the cost of incineration nor refining. It is different with toned pictures, where gold and silver combined may still give returns sufficient to exceed the cost of labor and time.

"The main condition in doing this is to incinerate the paper, which is quite a difficult piece of work. If the draft of the furnace is not strong enough, the combustion of the paper is not thorough, and large masses of carbon remain, which make the reduction of the metal a difficult operation; and if too strong, a great part of the paper will go up the chimney. A better method is to soak all the paper in a concentrated solution of saltpeter at a temperature of 100 deg. Fahr. The well-impregnated paper burns well, after being dried; it needs no draft, and it can be consumed in an open vessel, where it burns without flame, glimmering away into ashes. Macerating the ashes in a five per cent. solution of sulphuric acid will dissolve the greatest part of foreign salts, leaving a residue of pure metallic silver, soluble in nitric acid. The presence of gold will be indicated by a black powder, remaining after dissolution, which can be worked up with nitro-muriatic acid. The acid silver solution when treated with carbonate of soda, as described above, will give the same results.

"The method given is evidently cheaper and more reliable than the one generally resorted to by photographers, that is, by refining the ashes. If they contain much ashes a large quantity of saltpeter must be added with the flux, and no matter how high the temperature of melting will be, some silver remains unreduced. Another part of it remains suspended in the flux, and sinks into the mass of the crucible. In large refineries, flux and crucibles are crushed, roasted and worked over again. To the photographer the other method is without doubt more profitable, as with it but a trifling loss of the precious metal can occur.

"To regain silver from the washings of albumen prints, most photographers use salt as a precipitant. This is quite correct so long as an excess of salt is avoided. Chloride of silver being soluble in chloride of sodium it happens invariably with careless operators that a part of the valuable and redissolved silver precipitate is thrown away. Hydrochloric acid is preferable, for with it the danger of too much salt is out of the question. Still better is the precipitation with carbonate of soda, and a repetition of the process as described.

"When the photographic papers have been salted with chloride of ammonium instead of with chloride of sodium, the nitrate of ammonia formed during the silvering of the paper partly prevents the formation of carbonate of silver. In such cases the supernatant clear liquid should be again tested for silver, and eventually be reprecipitated.

"Remnants of emulsions can be liquified by hydrochloric or sulphuric acid, from which, after proper dilution, the silver bromide will precipitate, in which state it may be dissolved in hypo at once.

"With all these methods, time and attention must be given to the work; precipitations must be perfect, the clear waters being removed carefully, and the deposits washed thoroughly. In comparison with the older modes of working, those which

I have here described will be found to be far more reliable and economical."

Platinum Residues.

Old developing solutions and acid baths containing platinum are placed in any convenient receptacle. Strips of sheet zinc are then suspended in the liquid. After three or four days a black precipitate containing platinum will deposit on the bottom of the vessel. When a sufficient quantity of the precipitate has deposited, the liquid is poured off, the precipitate dried and sent to the refiner.

Preparation of Silver Nitrate.

Dissolve an old-fashioned silver dollar in nitric acid with gentle heat, and evaporate until crystals are formed. Wash the crystals on filter paper with dilute nitric acid, redissolve in water, and again evaporate to dryness. The resulting crystals may be used for the sensitizing bath. If adulteration with copper be suspected, the aqueous solution must be treated with silver oxide before evaporation.

The silver oxide is added in small quantities, until the blue or greenish color, due to the presence of copper, disappears. The copper will precipitate as a black powder, carrying with it all excess of silver oxide. To test the completeness of the substitution of silver for copper, place two or three drops of the solution in a glass measure, add a dram of water, and then add ammonia drop by drop until the resulting precipitate is redissolved. If no blue color is apparent the substitution is complete; if not, more silver oxide must be added.

When the substitution of silver for copper is completed, the solution is decanted and filtered. It is then tested with the hydrometer and distilled water added, if necessary, to give the proper strength.

Preparation of Gold Chloride.

Bend a quarter-eagle gold piece, and place it in a wide-mouthed bottle; then mix one dram of nitric acid with five drams of hydrochloric acid, and add about three drams of this mixture to the gold in the flask. Place the flask in the sun until the gold is nearly all dissolved, occasionally shaking it. Then pour the clear liquid into a fifteen-ounce bottle, add a little more of the mixed acids to the gold, and when the latter is dissolved, pour the clear liquid into the fifteen-ounce bottle, adding to the liquid remaining in the flask eight or ten ounces of water. Shake well, and allow the white deposit, chloride of gold, to settle.

While this is taking place, add gradually to the contents of the fifteen-ounce bottle small lumps of common whiting, until effervescence ceases, an indication that all the acid has been neutralized. Now add the water in the flask, and make up to fifteen ounces. This will give a slightly acid solution which will keep indefinitely if kept in darkness.

The solution contains one grain of gold to each dram of water.

ENCAUSTIC PASTE.—(*Dr. Eder's.*)

White wax,	28 drams.
Gum dammar varnish,	1 dram.
Rectified essence of turpentine,	28 drams.

This paste is to be kept in a well-stoppered bottle and thinned with turpentine whenever it thickens.

To use, apply it to the mounted print with a flannel and polish with a dry flannel. The paste gives a fine gloss and adds very much to the brilliancy of the prints.

ENAMELLING ALBUMEN PRINTS.

Patent plates of the required size are thoroughly cleaned, polished with finely powdered French chalk, and coated with plain collodion containing 1 to 1½ per cent. of azotic gun cotton and a little castor oil.

The following formula will answer:

Azotic gun cotton,	120 grains.
Methylated alcohol,	10 ounces.
Methylated ether sulph.,	10 ounces.
Castor oil,	20 drops.

These plates will keep indefinitely, and may be made in quantity, and stored in dust-proof boxes in a dry place.

When ready to enamel the prints, a sufficient number of plates are washed in water until all greasiness disappears. One of the washed plates is placed collodion-side uppermost, in a dish filled with cold water. The print, previously soaked in cold water is placed face down upon the plate, the print and plate are then raised from the water, raising one end first. They are then placed between blotters, and all excess of moisture removed with the squeegee. Print and glass are now set aside to dry. When dry the print will leave the glass.

APPENDIX.

THE REV. W. H. BURBANK.

The author of "Photographic Printing Methods," "The Photographic Negative," and other valuable contributions to photographic literature, was born in the city of Lowell, Mass., October 18th, 1853.

In 1858 his parents removed to Vermont, and he, of course, went with them. Here the family resided until 1865, when they all made another move, and this time westward. Young Burbank lived successively in Indiana, Ohio and Kansas for the next four years, in 1869 returning eastward with his parents to Cambridge, Mass.

Here he prepared himself for college at the Boston Latin and the Cambridge High Schools, entering Harvard University in 1872, and graduating in 1876. During the last two years of his University course much time was devoted to the study of fine arts under Prof. Charles Eliot Norton, and the year succeeding graduation was spent mostly in private study with Prof. Norton. Then followed three years of study at the Episcopal Theological School at Cambridge.

Mr. Burbank's first ministerial work was in a mission in a New Hampshire hamlet, under the shadow of the White Mountains; and here it was that he became interested in photography, his first camera being "a Walker box." With this instrument he scoured the entire country-side for miles surrounding his home, in search of the many picturesque views that abound in this region, and soon became an expert photographer.

About 1882 he removed to the banks of the Hudson, and, with a larger camera, spent much time in field work. At Newburgh-on-the-Hudson, Mr. Burbank commenced the close study of photographic literature, which he has continued ever since, and the result of which and the experimental work it involved, was the production of the two contributions to the literature of photography, which are now so well and widely read.

"Photographic Printing Methods" appeared first in July of 1887, because its need was the most apparent, there being no work on that subject then in the American market. Its companion, "The Photographic Negative," appeared later, in February of '88, and proved itself scarcely less popular than its predecessor. A second edition of the former work has been in demand for many months, more than five hundred copies of the book being sold within the first month after publication. This was an unprecedented sale for a photographic book.

About this time Mr. Burbank began to write for the *Photographic Times*, contributing monthly since then, his review of "Pictures of the Month," and "Chips from an Amateur's Workshop," besides frequent reviews of French and other foreign photographic publications, as the result of his wide and careful reading, and for which his knowledge of the foreign languages so well fits him. He has also conducted a department devoted to amateur photography in *The Art Amateur*, since January 1st, 1889. And all this in addition to his regular parish duties!

In the summer of 1887 he carried a Scovill Detective Camera across the Atlantic, and did some photographic work on British soil. On returning to America again, he began the study of photo-engraving and photo-mechanical printing processes, becoming familiar with their practical manipulations, and since then writing considerably on this important department of photographic work.

In the spring of 1888 he removed to Brunswick, Maine, where he found a wide field for his camera. Mr. Burbank is a devoted admirer of photography, and a close student of its literature. "In ten years," he says, "I hope to know something about the subject;" and he continues his study and work as if he intended to know *all* about the subject.

Mr. Burbank has done considerable in the making of emulsion; bromide, chloride, and other papers; and in "The

Photographic Times Annual for 1888," described a new camera and tripod head, of which numbers have since been made. He has also made a detective camera which is ingenious and useful.

The portrait which embellishes this volume, as a frontispiece, is an excellent one, made by A. O. Reed, of Brunswick, Maine; and was reproduced from the negative, in Meisenbach, by William Kurtz, of New York.

W. I. LINCOLN ADAMS.

INDEX.

ACTION of Light on Sensitive Compounds.................. 12
Ammonia-Nitrate of Silver Bath, The, 28
Floating the Paper on........... 28
Time of Floating............... 28
Asphaltum Method of Printing on Blocks or Metals................. 207
Autographic Methods.............. 205
Sensitizing...................... 205
Exposure....................... 205
Inking 205
Printing 206

BLUE PRINTS................... 22
Collachi's Methods for Making. 22
Pizzeghilli's Method " ... 22
Poitivin's " " ... 23
Bromide Enlargements, Finishing on, 119
Crayon Finishing............... 120
Pastel " 121
Water Color and Indian Ink Finishing 121
Bromide of Silver Emulsion, Printing with 66
Coating....................... 67
Other Methods of Coating 69
How to Use the Apparatus for Coating 71
Exposure..................... 73
Development.................. 73
Eastman's Developer 73
" Clearing Solution..... 73
" Fixing Bath......... 74
The Use of Bromide as a Restrainer...................... 74
Enamelling.................... 75

Another Method of Enamelling, 75
Flexible Prints................. 76
Straightening Unmounted Prints. 76
How to get Black Tones like Platinum..................... 76
Sepia Tones 76
Ferrous-Citro Oxalate Developer 77
Preserving the Ferrous Oxalate Developer..................... 77
Hints.......................... 77
Treating the Prints with Platinum........................ 78
Bromide Prints for Photo-Mechanical Engraving...................... 79

CARBON PRINTING.,. 96
Negatives Suitable for......... 96
Reversed negatives for.......... 97
Drying the Sensitized Tissue.... 97
Developing Trays 98
Formulas for Single and Double Transfers.................... 98
Pigment Solutions.............. 99
Printing....................... 100
Development................... 100
Single Transfers 100
Double " 101
Printing from ordinary negatives without transfers................ 102
Continuing Action of Light in... 103
Failures in.... 103
Collodio-Chloride Process, The...... 86
Coating the Paper.............. 87
Toning......................... 88
Collotype, The 196
Preliminary Coating............ 197

INDEX.

The Sensitive Film 197
Exposure 197
Etching the Plate...~........... 197
Inking 197
Copying Cameras................ 119
Copying Maps, Plans, etc., Without a Camera........................ 206

DEFECTS IN SILVER PRINTS,
  How to Overcome............ 39
  Marbled and Streaking......... 39
  Clear on the Surface, but Streaky when examined by transmitted light 39
  Cold and Faded Appearance..... 40
  Spots on surface............... 40
  High-Lights, Yellow............ 40
  Intense Bronzing of Shadows during Printing................. 40
  Yellow Spots on Surface or Back 40
  Mealiness.................... 40
  Refusing to Tone............... 40

ENLARGING..................... 109
  Negatives for 109
  The Light for.................. 109
  The Apparatus for............. 109
  An Ordinary Camera for........ 109
  An Improvised Apparatus for.... 111
  The Eastman Apparatus for. ... 112
  An easily constructed Apparatus for........................... 114
  Apparatus for Electric Light.... 115
  With the Oil Lantern........... 116
Enlargments, Table for............. 118
  On Opal Glass................. 121
  On Canvas.................... 122
  By the Powder Process......... 122
  On Canvas in the Solar Camera. 123
  In the Solar Camera by Development.... 124
  Platinum in the Solar Camera... 125
  From Enlarged Negatives....... 128
  Carbon....................... 128
  By the Collodion Transfer Process 129

By the Photo-Crayon Process.... 130
Enamelling Albumen Prints......... 215
Enamelled Intaglios, the Process for Making. 188

FABRICS, Printing on, by the Carbon Process................... 108
Ferric Oxalate, Preparation of....... 56
Fixing Bath, The................ 47
  Its Purpose 47
  Its Composition............... 48
  How Long to Fix.............. 48
  Maxims for Fixing............. 48
Fuming.......................... 33
  Time of 33

GELATINO-BROMIDE EMULsion, Printing with........... 65
  Apparatus.................... 65
Gelatino-Chloride Paper, Printing on 82
  The Emulsion................. 82
  Development.................. 82
  Wellington's Method with Citric Acid......................... 83
  Eder's Method....'............ 84
  Ferrous Nitrate Developer for... 85
Gelatino-Chloride Printing-out Paper 85
  J. Barker's Method for Printing on........................... 86
  Printing, Toning and Fixing on.. 86
Gelatinized Paper, Printing on....... 53
Gold Chloride, Preparation of....... 214

IRON COMPOUNDS, Printing with....................... 17
  The Law of................... 17
  Two Methods of.............. 17
  Method for Obtaining Blue Prints 17
  "   "   "   Purple Image 18
  Methods "   " Other Tones 18
  Points to be attended to in...... 18
  Various Formulas............. 18
  To Sensitize Paper for Blue Prints 20

INDEX. 223

	PAGE
To Deepen the Color of Blue...	20
To Give Blue Prints a Green Tone	20
To Give Blue Prints a Brownish Tone...	21
To Give Blue Prints Sepia Tones	21
To Give Blue Prints Lilac Tones	21
To Make Black Lines on a White Ground...	23

LANTERN SLIDES............. 142
  On Wet Plates............... 142
  Coloring...................... 148
Leatherized Paper, Printing on...... 53
Linen, Printing on................ 105
  Sizing Solution............... 105
  Salting Solution.............. 105

MECHANICAL PRINTING ... 190
  The Metal Plates for......... 190
  The Positives and Negatives for.. 191
  Intensifying................... 191
  The Metal Plate............... 192
  Sensitizing Mixtures........... 193
  Coating the Plate.............. 193
  The Exposure.................. 194
  Development................... 194
  Clausintzer's Method of Developing..... 194
  The Etching................... 194
  Hardening the Plate............ 196
  Mr. Riley's Method for Amateurs 198
  Ives' Method of Graining Typographic Plates for............. 199
  The Meisenbach Method........ 200
  The Photo-lithographic and Photo-gravure Methods........... 200
Mounting........................ 90
  The Card Mount for........... 90
  Placing the Print in Position.... 90
  Treatment of the Prints before... 91
  Medium for.................... 91
  W. J. Stillman's Mountant...... 92
  In Optical Contact with Glass... 92
  On Plate Paper................. 94
  Enlargements on Cloth......... 117

OPAL PRINTING............... 160
  The Emulsion................ 160
  Coating....................... 160
  Printing...................... 161
  By the Powder Process.......... 161

PASTE, Encaustic................ 215
Photo-ceramics................... 165
  The Apparatus................. 165
  The Negatives................. 167
  Formulas for the Collodion...... 168
  Sensitizing Bath............... 168
  Developer..................... 168
  Intensifier.................... 168
  Fixing........................ 167
  Stripping the Films............ 169
  The Firing or Burning-in....... 171
  Retouching.................... 172
  Stock Mixtures for............. 173
  Practical Manipulation......... 175
  Pavlowsky's Method with Pigment Paper.................. 175
  Husnick's Methods............. 176
  Liesegang's Dusting-in Method.. 176
  Watson's Substitution Method... 179
Photo-gravures.................... 200
  The Process for Making......... 201
  Graining...................... 202
  Etching....................... 202
  Advantages of................. 203
Photographing on Wood by Frewing's Method................... 208
Photographing on Wood by Ives' Method...................... 209
Plain Paper, Printing on.......... 51
Platinotype, The................. 55
  Sizing........................ 55
  Stock Solutions............... 56
  Chlorate of Iron Solution...... 57
  Sensitizing Solution........... 57
  Keeping Apparatus Dry........ 58
  Sensitizing the Paper.......... 58
  Drying the Sensitized Paper.... 59
  Preserving the Paper.......... 59
  Printing...................... 60
  Developer..................... 61

INDEX.

	PAGE
Development...	61
Washing the Prints........	62
Porcelain Printing.................	162
Collodion.....	162
Preparation of the Plate.........	162
The Exposure....	162
Toning........................	163
Potassic Ferric Oxalate, Preparation of....	56
Preparing Metal Plates for the Engraver...........................	207
The Collodion..................	207
Preparing the Plates............	207
Developing....................	207
Fixing........................	207
Printing.	34
The Frame.................... .	34
Printing Maxims..................	35
Printing Rules for Cold Weather....	50
Preserving Sensitized Paper.	39

READY-SENSITIZED PAPER,	
Printing on....................	36
Toning Bath......	37
Fixing Bath....................	37
Recovery of Silver from Photographic Wastes........................	210
Recovery of Platinum from Residues...........................	214
Red Prints.......................	163
Methods for Making............	163
On Silvered Paper......	163
By the Carbon Process..........	163
By the Nitrate of Uranium Process........................	163
Resinized Paper, Printing on.......	51
Bertrand's Method......	51
Henry Cooper's Method.........	52
Résumé of Printing Processes	14

SILVER BATH, The...............	25
To Determine the Strength of Salting of any Paper........	25
Preparation of the Bath.........	26
Formula for Sensitizing Baths for Strong Negatives.............	27

	PAGE
Formula for Sensitizing Baths for Thin Negatives....	27
The Author's Favorite Bath.....	27
C. W. Hearn's Formula	27
Management of....	30
Methods of Removing Impurities from........................	30
Points in Sensitizing............	32
Silk, Printing on....................	105
Platinum Process for.	105
The Carbon Process for.........	108
Silver Nitrate, Preparation of........	214

THEORY OF LIGHT, The......	11
Toning................................	41
Stock Solution for...............	41
For Brown Tones...............	41
For Black, Velvety Tones.......	41
For Purple and Black Tones....	42
For Rich Purple Tones.........	42
For Sepia and Black Tones.....	42
For Sepia Tones................	44
With Platinum Bath............	42
With Borax....................	42
Charles W. Hearn's Toning Bath	43
The PHOTOGRAPHIC TIMES Toning Bath.......................	43
The Chautauqua Toning Bath...	44
Spaulding's Toning Bath........	44
The Price Formula	44
Formula for Resinized, Gelatinized, Leatherized and Plain Paper........................	45
Sulphocyanide of Ammonia.....	45
General Directions..............	45
Remarks on General Composition for Toning Baths.........	46
Maxims of Toning.........	48
Rules for Toning in Cold Weather	50
Transparencies....................	132
Best Plate for...................	132
Exposure of...................	133
Printing	133
Developing	133
Fixing........................	134
Clearing..................... .	135
Washing.......	135

INDEX.

	PAGE
Mounting	135
By the Carbon Process	136
By the Albumen Method	137
By the Collodio-chloride Process	138
By the Gelatino-bromide Process	138
By the Gelatino-chloride Process	138
By Levy's Collodion Emulsion	139
By Carbutt's Method	142

URANIUM COMPOUNDS,
   Printing with.................. 24
   Sensitizing Solution.......... 24

	PAGE
Developing Solution for Brown Tones	24
Developing Solution for Gray Tones	24

WASHING.................... 48
   With Eau de Javelle........ 49
   With the Hypochlorite of Zinc Hypo Eliminator............ 50
Willis' Permanent Paper, Printing on........................... 38

THE
Scovill & Adams Company,

423 Broome Street, New York City,

SUCCESSORS TO THE

PHOTOGRAPHIC DEPARTMENT

—OF THE—

Scovill Manufacturing Company.

Are Manufacturers, Importers of and Dealers in

AN UNEQUALED VARIETY OF

PHOTOGRAPHIC GOODS,

EMBRACING

Every Requisite of the
Practical Photographer,
Professional and Amateur.

PUBLICATION DEPARTMENT.

Publishers of "THE SCOVILL PHOTOGRAPHIC SERIES" (38 publications), the "Photographic Times Annual," etc., etc.

Latest Catalogue of Photographic Books and Albums, and a copy of "HOW TO MAKE PHOTOGRAPHS" sent free on application.

W. IRVING ADAMS,   H. LITTLEJOHN,
President & Treasurer.   *Secretary.*

A. M. COLLINS MFG. CO.,

No. 527 Arch Street,

PHILADELPHIA, PA.,

MANUFACTURERS OF

Photographers' Cards

AND

CARD BOARD.

Quality, the Best. Styles and Colors in Variety Unexcelled.

These Standard Goods are for Sale

BY ALL PHOTOGRAPHIC MERCHANTS.

BRANDS AND SENSITOMETER NUMBERS.

CARBUTT'S ⚓ DRY PLATES
TRADE MARK
and "CELLULOID" FILMS.

"ECLIPSE," Sen. 27.—Is extremely sensitive, and specially intended for quick studio exposures, concealed and detective cameras, instantaneous views, and magnesium flash-light photography.

"SPECIAL," Sen. 23 to 25.—For portraits, instantaneous views, outdoor groups, etc. *Blue Label.* This plate and our Ortho, Sen. 23 to 25, are the best plates for professionals and view work.

"ORTHOCHROMATIC" Plates, Sen. 23 to 27, give correct color values. The best plates for landscapes, interiors, **photo-micrography**, portraiture in varied-colored draperies, photographing paintings, flowers, etc.

"B" Plates, Sen. 16 to 20.—For landscape views and general photography. Admittedly the finest plate for professional and amateur all-around work.

"B" PROCESS Plates, Sen. 12.—For use by photo-lithographers, photo-engravers, and zinc-etchers in making intense and clear-line negatives.

"A" GELATINO-ALBUMEN Plates.—For lantern slides and copying.

"A" GELATINO-ALBUMEN GROUND GLASS Plates, specially prepared for window transparencies.

STRIPPING PLATES.—For photo-mechanical printers. Emulsions "B" 20 and "Special" 23 to 25, kept in stock. "Eclipse" 27 made to order.

"CELLULOID" FILMS—TRANSPARENT—Emulsion "B," Sen. 12, for producing intense negatives for photo-reproductive processes.

"CELLULOID" FILMS—MAT-SURFACE.—Emulsions "Eclipse," Sens. 26 and 27; "Orthochromatic," Sens. 23 to 27; "Special," Sens. 23 to 25; "B," Sens. 16 to 20.

Patented April 25, 1882.

PRICE
$6.00

Lantern arranged for making positives by contact.

CARBUTT'S
Multum in Parvo
LANTERN

For use in developing room filling kits, developing negatives, making positives, etc.

The Only Practical Lantern in the Market.

For Sale by all Dealers.

Send to factory for descriptive circulars and price-list.

JOHN CARBUTT, Keystone Dry Plate and Film Works, Wayne Junction, Phila.

TO PROGRESSIVE PHOTOGRAPHERS.

The New Metal Vignetter,

FOR

Producing the Black Background, or Ebony Photographs.

Hundreds of these Vignetters are now in use, GIVING UNIVERSAL SATISFACTION. They can be easily adjusted to any camera, and require no more trouble or expense than making plain photographs. Every progressive photographer should have one. Its work will attract attention in your case and increase your business. Every one guaranteed.

PRICE, each, · $8.00.

Sample Photographs made with it sent on application.

Patented May 31, 1887.

Kuhn's Sensitized Paper Stretched and Dried.

Paper dried with it lays perfectly flat, and therefore better prints can be obtained.

You can also cut your paper either lengthwise or crosswise of the sheet, as it neither stretches nor shrinks afterwards.

In addition, it is very desirable for handling Bromide Paper.

PRICE.

18 x 22 size, each.......$1 50
20 x 24 "   " 1 75

Patented April 13, 1886.

KUHN'S
Improved Vignetting Attachment

For Vignetting the Negative.

LIGHT, STRONG and DURABLE.

It is perfectly reliable and quickly adjusted to any lens by the means of a thumb-screw. It can be raised or lowered at will to any position desired by the operator, by simply pulling a cord, without leaving his position behind the camera.

Patented September 6, 1887.

PRICE, each, - $3.50.

These articles can be procured through your dealer, or

H. A. HYATT, Sole Agent,

AND DEALER IN

PHOTOGRAPHIC SUPPLIES OF EVERY DESCRIPTION.

N. E. Cor. Eighth and Locust Streets, St. Louis, Mo.

MAX LEVY.
Late M'g'r Levytype Co., Phila.

Perfected Engraved Gratings or Screens

— FOR THE —

HALF-TONE PROCESS.

THESE screens are each separately and accurately ruled, the lines being engraved deeply into the glass and filled with opaque enamel. The black lines are sharp, clear, and absolutely opaque, and the white spaces are clear glass, and each screen is protected by a cover glass thoroughly cemented to the ruled side.

Negatives made with these screens develop perfectly clear in the finest dots or stipples. An operator in one of the leading establishments, after working with these screens, says:

"*Making* HALF-TONE NEGATIVES with your screens is *as simple and easy* AS LINE WORK."

By reason of the perfect opacity of the lines and transparency of the shadows, these screens are incomparably superior to any made by photographic means, the results obtained with them are better, and are obtained with far greater facility and certainty.

In ruling large screens, local imperfections frequently occur, and they are cut to the most available sizes that will avoid all defects, yielding irregular sized plates of great perfection. These plates, especially the larger sizes of them, are very useful for experimenters, as well as for regular work, as a plate 5 x 7 or 5 x 8 is large enough to include the greater part of the work required even in a very large establishment. These I sell as TRIAL SIZES. They are all ruled *crossed*. Single rulings to order.

$3\frac{1}{4}$ x $4\frac{1}{4}$ up to 5 x 7, $5.00 to $12.00 ; 5 x 8, $15.00.

PRICES ON APPLICATION.

Send for circular descriptive of the PRISMATIC RECTILINEAR LENS for making negatives in reverse by direct exposure in the camera.

MAX LEVY,
106 N. 6th Street, Philadelphia, Pa.

137 West 23d Street,
New York.

Illustrative and Pictorial Work
of the highest class only by the

PHOTO-GRAVURE
and
PHOTO-GELATINE
PROCESSES.

Also Publishers of

An Artistic Periodical without Letter-press.

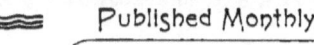
Published Monthly.

EACH ISSUE OF "SUN AND SHADE" CONSISTS OF EIGHT OR MORE PLATES OF THE HIGHEST GRADE, ON PAPER 11 X 14.

Single or sample copies are 40 cents each (except Nos. 1, 2 and 3, which are 60 cents each, and No. 4, $1.00 each).
Yearly subscription, $4.00.
Vol. I (in numbers), $5.47.
Vol. II (in numbers), $4.00.
Binding any volume in cloth, $2.50 extra.
Binding any volume in half morocco, $3.75 extra.
Binders for current numbers, $1.50; by mail, $1.80.
Back numbers are always kept in print.
Order of any newsdealer or direct from the publishers.

FOR SILVERING,
THE WATERBURY TRAYS ARE THE BEST AND CHEAPEST.

These Trays are made by the

AMERICAN
OPTICAL CO.

which of itself is a guarantee of the superiority of the wood work.

Canvas is not required for the seams, as the bottoms are seamless. The bottom rests on cross-strips—a great improvement, for steadiness, over knobs at the corners, which were liable to be broken off.

THE
Waterbury Trays

are guaranteed not to warp or crack.

PRICE LIST.

	Each.		Each.
15x19 Waterbury Trays	$3 50	22x28 Waterbury Trays	$6 50
19x24 " "	5 00	25x30 " "	9 00

For Sale by all Dealers in Photographic Requisites, and by

THE SCOVILL & ADAMS COMPANY.

Three Crown

Albumenized Paper

Is the choicest brand yet introduced.

IT DOES NOT BLISTER.

IF YOUR STOCK DEALER DOES NOT SUPPLY IT,

SEND TO

THE SCOVILL & ADAMS COMPANY, Importers,

423 Broome Street, NEW YORK,

and be sure that you get the GENUINE with the Three Crown trade-mark. Formula furnished with the paper.

Sample Sheet sent upon Application.

S. P. C.
READY SENSITIZED ALBUMEN PAPER.

This Paper was expressly manufactured for and introduced by us to give to those who have not the skill, time, inclination or appliances to sensitize photographic paper preparatory to printing, an article of the finest quality and of uniform sensitiveness.

PRICE LIST.

Size.						Per Package.
3¼ x 4¼	inches, in light-tight packages,	2 dozen	....	...	$0 30
4 x 5	"	"	"	2 "	....	45
4¼ x 6½	"	"	"	2 "	....	55
5 x 7	"	"	"	2 "	....	80
5 x 8	"	"	"	2 "	....	85
6½ x 8½	"	"	"	2 "	....	1 10
8 x10	"	"	"	2 "	....	1 65
18 x22	"	"	"	1 "	... . per doz.	3 80

To save loss, rolls are not broken.

FERRO-PRUSSIATE * PAPER,
For Making Blue and White Pictures.

Our brand is a sure index of superiority in texture, the paper is better wrapped than any other, and is noticeably free from spots streaks or flaws. This paper is extremely simple in its manipulation, and therefore very convenient for making proofs from negatives. It is also adapted for the reproduction of *Mottoes, Plans, Drawings, Manuscript, Circulars,* and to show representations of Scenery, Boats, Machinery, &c., for an engraver to copy from. The rapidity with which a print can be made with this paper is for numerous purposes, and to men in some occupations, a very great recommendation in its favor.

PRICE LIST.

Size				Per Package.
4 x 5	inches, in 2 dozen light-tight parcels..............	...$0 28
5 x 8	" 2 " " "	....	50
6½ x 8½	" 2 " " "	....	67
8 x10	" 2 " " "	....	83

To save loss, parcels are not broken.

In full rolls of 10 yards each, 30 inches wide, $3.50 per roll.

—THE—
DONALDSON STAR BROMIDE PAPER.

No. "1," **Smooth surface, thin,** for proofs, positive printing, copying drawings, etc., by contact.

No. "2," **Smooth surface, heavy,** for positive printing, enlarging, and working in ink, oil and water colors.

No. "3," **Rough surface, heavy,** for positive printing, enlarging, and working in crayon, ink, water colors and oils.

We recommend the No. "3" for enlargement, and Nos. "1" and "2" smooth surface paper for contact prints. Enlargements on our paper require no finishing when taken from good original negatives. ☞ *This paper does not blister.* ☜
Send for book of directions.

—— PRICE LIST ——
OF
STAR BROMIDE PAPERS, Nos. "1," "2," or "3."

CUT SHEETS.

Size.	Per Doz.	Size.	Per Doz.	Size.	Per Doz.
3¼x4¼	$0 25	6 x 8	$1 00	17x20	$6 40
4 x5	0 40	6½x 8½	1 10	18x22	7 50
4¼x5½	0 50	8 x10	1 50	20x24	9 00
4¼x6½	0 55	10 x12	2 25	22x28	11 25
5¾x6½	0 60	11 x14	3 00	24x30	13 00
5 x7	0 65	12 x15	3 25	25x30	14 00
5 x7½	0 70	14 x17	4 50	24x36	16 00
5 x8	0 75	16 x20	6 00	30x40	22 50

Other sizes in proportion.

If ordered in packages of less than one dozen, 25c. extra will be charged for packing.

IN ROLLS.

10 in. wide, p. yd..	$0 56	16 in. wide, p. yd..	$0 90	24 in. wide, p. yd..	$1 35
11 " "	0 62	18 " "	1 00	25 " "	1 40
12 " "	0 68	20 " "	1 12	30 " "	1 68
14 " "	0 79	22 " "	1 24	31 " "	1 75

OMEGA PAPER.

(Chloro-Bromide Emulsion.)

(MANUFACTURED BY BRADFISH & HOPKINS.)

WITH the introduction of Gelatino-Emulsion Paper a new era has been started in Photographic Printing, especially for the Amateur, who appreciates so many marked advantages in this paper over Sensitized Albumen Paper. After many and costly experiments Sensitized Emulsion Paper for direct printing out has been produced which far excels any heretofore made, and which is guaranteed to be fully reliable in every respect.

The paper is unexcelled FOR FINE RESULTS and SIMPLICITY OF OPERATION.

Its KEEPING QUALITIES are unsurpassed, it being in good condition for months after manufacture. It will give the fine effects of fresh silver paper, without the necessary separate operations attending toning, fixing, etc. The different solutions are combined in one bath, making it specially desirable to the amateur, there being only two operations, toning and washing, then mounting the same as albumen or other paper.

Any tone from a rich brown to a dark purple may be obtained, according to the time left in the toning bath.

The print is permanent, can be burnished, also glacéd by squeegeeing on a ferrotype plate.

PRICE LIST OF OMEGA PAPER.

Size	Per Doz.	Per Gr.	Size	Per Doz.	Per Gr.
3¼ x 4¼	0 20		5 x 8	0 45	$4 50
4 x 5	0 25	$2 50	6½ x 8½	0 70	
3⅞ x 5½ (cabinets trim'd)	0 30	2 25	8 x 10	0 90	
4¼ x 6½ (" untrimmed)	0 35	3 50	20 x 24	4 00 ½ dz, 2 25	
5 x 7	0 40	4 00	20 x 24	pr sheet, 0 40	

FULL AND EXPLICIT DIRECTIONS ON EACH PACKAGE.

OMEGA TONING SOLUTION.

For toning and fixing Aristotype, Omega, or Albumen Prints. Gives any tone and clear prints. 10 oz. Bottles 50 cents.

Ferro Plates for Enamelling the Prints, 10 x 14 inches, 15 cents each.

Preserve the Shadow Ere the Substance Fades!

Preserve Your Prints From Fading!

READ WHAT IS SAID ABOUT

Flandreau's S. P. C. Hypo Eliminator.

Taken from THE PHOTOGRAPHIC TIMES of June 3d, 1887.

THE NEW HYPO ELIMINATOR.

To the Editor of the PHOTOGRAPHIC TIMES.

Dear Sir: In the number of your Journal for May 6, appears an editorial article entitled "Hypo Eliminator; do they Eliminate?" in which you strongly recommend the hypochlorite of zinc for removing the last traces of hypo from silver prints.

In doing this you doubtless bring to the attention of photographers the most important improvement in print washing that has been suggested since prints were first made. There is no doubt in my mind that the worst evil pertaining to silver prints, and that for which a simple and practical remedy is most needed, is the hypo that is not eliminated from them. Now that the means for accomplishing this desirable end in an effectual and perfectly harmless manner has been pointed out, what excuse can possibly exist for its not being at once universally adopted? For one, I shall put it to use as soon as I can obtain a supply of the requisite material.

Photographers are proverbially slow in introducing changes in their practice in which the immediate advantages are not tangible or visible. But here is something decidedly tangible. By using this agent the prints may be washed in half the time, with half the water, and what is much more, so thoroughly may the work be done that not a particle of hypo or sulphur shall remain in them. Surely this is an improvement which every conscientious photographer should lose no time in putting into practice.

Not having practically tested the process I do not speak of it from actual experience, but its application is certainly theoretically correct, and it seems impossible that there can be any drawback in its use.

I trust that at the coming Convention the merits of the New Hypo Eliminator will be fully discussed. Very respectfully,

W. H. SHERMAN.

Flandreau's S. P. C. Hypo Eliminator

— IS A —

HYPOCHLORITE OF ZINC,

Of which the Letter Speaks so Favorably.

IT IS HARMLESS! IT IS EFFECTIVE!

It Saves TIME, PATIENCE, NEGATIVES and PRINTS.

Do not prove the assertion that "PHOTOGRAPHERS ARE PROVERBIALLY SLOW IN INTRODUCING CHANGES IN THEIR PRACTICE," by delaying to procure this "*most important improvement in print-washing, which has been suggested since prints were first made.*"

BUY A BOTTLE AT ONCE!

IT COSTS BUT FIFTY CENTS!

And is accompanied by a BOOK OF TEST PAPER, for detecting the slightest trace of Hypo in negative or print.

For sale by all Dealers in Photographic Requisites, and by the

The Scovill & Adams Company.

SCOVILL PRINTING FRAMES.

The Scovill Printing Frames are made of cherry, and have superior brass springs constructed on scientific principles. On the flat printing frames, these springs are secured by rivets and turn on brass washers, being held at the end by buttons made so that they cannot turn around.

PATENT APPLIED FOR.

They are so constructed that a uniform pressure is obtained, thus insuring perfect contact between the paper and the negative, and removing the danger of breaking the latter.

The back-boards are also so arranged that the progress of the printing may be watched without danger of shifting the paper, and each frame has the tally shown in the illustration.

For Plates.	Regular Flat or Two-Thirds.	Deep.	For Plates.	Regular Flat or Two-Thirds.	Deep.
3¼ x 4¼	...$0 35...	$0 75	13 x 16	...$2 25	...$2 75
4 x 5	... 38...	75	14 x 17	... 2 45	... 3 00
4¼ x 5½	... 40...	75	16 x 20	... 4 50	... 4 75
4¼ x 6½	... 42...	85	17 x 20	... 4 50	... 4 75
5 x 7	... 50...	95	18 x 22	... 5 00	... 5 25
5 x 8	... 52...	95	20 x 24	... 5 50	... 5 50
6½ x 8½	... 60...	1 25	24 x 30	....	... 9 00
8 x 10	... 75...	1 60	35 x 45	....	...16 00
10 x 12	... 1 00...	2 00	30 x 60	....	...22 00
11 x 14	... 2 00...	2 50			

SCOVILL FLAT PRINTING FRAMES. For Sale by all Dealers in Photo Goods.

The SCOVILL PRINTING FRAME PADS.

1st Quality, GRAY.

FOR					
3¼ x 4¼	Frames, in boxes, per doz.				$0 24
4 x 5	"	"	"		33
4¼ x 5½	"	"	"		36
4¼ x 6½	"	"	"		38
5 x 7	"	"	"		54
5 x 8	"	"	"		57
6½ x 8½	"	"	"		84
8 x 10	"	"	"		1 44
10 x 12	"	"	"		2 16
11 x 14	"	"	"		2 88
14 x 17	"	"	"		4 08
16 x 20	"	"	"		5 04
17 x 20	"	"	"		5 28
18 x 22	"	"	"		6 48
20 x 24	"	"	"		8 40

The above goods are very desirable, and the demand for them is increasing. They are put up in boxes containing one dozen pads each.

ADT'S PATENT PRINTING FRAME.

These Frames are now supplied (without extra charge) with Adt's Patent Support with which the frame can be stood on either end, and at four different angles, for exposure while printing. It is out of the way of the printer when introducing the paper, or examining the print, for when the frame lies or is held with back up, the support instantly drops upon its stops for rest, and is entirely out of the way of the hand of the printer, so that he may remove or open the back-board, or replace it, as if there were no support present. Being arranged close around the sides and ends of the frame, it occupies so little space as not to interfere with the packing or storage of the frames, and when the printer places his frame for exposure the support readily finds its position for supporting the frame without any special manipulation.

PRICES.

3¼ x 4¼	$0 50
4 x 5	50
4¼ x 5½	50
4¾ x 6½	60
5 x 7	65
5 x 8	65
6½ x 8½	75
8 x 10	85
10 x 12	1 15
11 x 14	2 15
13 x 16	2 40
14 x 17	2 80

When made with back to open lengthways, an additional charge of 10 per cent. will be added to the above prices.

As will be seen by a glance at the cut, the adjacent edges of the parts of the back-board are beveled outward, and the hinges placed on the sides with their axes on a line with the surface. This permits the attachment to the face of the back-board of a **Heavy, Continuous Elastic Felt Pad.** This obviates the necessity of using a separate pad, which is so easily misplaced and lost.

IRVING PRINTING FRAMES

WITH ADJUSTABLE SUPPORTS.
(PATENTED.)

IRVING PRINTING FRAME, CLOSED.
FRONT VIEW.

IRVING PRINTING FRAME, OPEN.
BACK VIEW.

The IRVING FRAMES have valuable features which cannot be copied. They are in workmanship, design, and other respects, superior to all other printing frames.

The continuous felt pads made especially to order for us, insure absolute protection and uniform pressure throughout. The Irving Patent Catches lock the back, so that when one flap is open there is not the slightest danger of the flaps, paper or negative slipping.

The springs are cut by dies of specially tempered and tested metal, and are riveted to the backs with washers underneath to protect the woodwork.

The IRVING FRAMES are made of cherry guaranteed not to warp or crack.

The tally does not depend upon any other part of the frame to lock it, for the pointer will remain in place no matter what is done to other parts of the frame.

Prices for Half or Two-thirds Opening Styles.

3¼ x 4¼	$0 45	5 x 7	$0 60
4 x 5	48	5 x 8	65
4¼ x 5½	50	6½ x 8½	70
4¼ x 6½	55	8 x 10	80

When made with backs to open lengthways, ten per cent. is added to the foregoing prices, for the respective sizes.

Fac-simile of Bronze medal awarded at the Boston Convention of the Photographers' Association of America, August, 1889, to THE SCOVILL & ADAMS CO., for improvements in Photographic Apparatus.

This was the only medal awarded by the Association for this contest in which there were twenty competitors.

www.ingramcontent.com/pod-product-compliance
Lightning Source LLC
Chambersburg PA
CBHW031738230426
43669CB00007B/391